*To Pauline, Andrew, Joseph, Amy and family and friends
who kept me going.*

Contents

Author's Note

Without Pauline's selfless support, the run wouldn't have gone further than a hundred miles and this book wouldn't have gone beyond chapter one. I owe Pauline more than I can give. To spend months amongst mountains she loves without being able to climb to their tops and to follow that by spending months sat by a word processor is more than I should ever have asked. The reality is that I never did ask. Pauline has been the drive behind the run and the story, and for that I know I am more than lucky.

Generosity and support came from many friends, family and several companies. I am particularly grateful to the headmaster and governors of Sedbergh School. By allowing me a term off from teaching, and continuing to pay me my normal salary, they gave me the opportunity to run over mountains. I am also indebted to Paul Tuson for operating the essential phone link to all the supportive runners who accompanied me en route; to Ann Parratt who answered the calls of the press and provided the main injection of fundraising energy for Intermediate Technology; to Dr Bev Holt for his medical expertise and regular support; to Yorkshire Bank for being extremely tolerant in the slow repayment of their generous interest free loan to buy the essential motor caravan; to Reebok for all the running shoes I needed and a cash grant towards the van; to Berghaus who kept me warm and dry on the mountains and to Rohan who kept us all cosy and well dressed throughout the journey.

There are scores of others who helped before, during and after the run. I am grateful to them all. In particular, I thank my father for drawing all the maps for the book. Little did he know that by taking me to the Welsh Hills at the tender age of three, he was sowing the seeds for a love of mountains. Also, little did he know that he was gradually going to get to know all 303 mountains himself as he carefully transferred them from OS maps to the pages of this book.

Foreword

By Chris Bonington

When Hugh Symonds first told me of his plan to climb all the peaks over 3000 feet in Scotland, England and Wales in 100 days, including running every step between them, as he proposed using no mechanical transport, I was amazed. I knew of his reputation as a fell runner, of course, but I wondered if even he would be able to achieve this outstanding feat or, for that matter, if his body would take such a pounding without any of the injuries which often beset long distance runners.

When I heard that he had not only accomplished it in 83 days but had felt so good that he had carried straight on from Snowdon to Holyhead to board the ferry for Ireland, had then run across Ireland to the Atlantic coast, taking in its seven 3000 foot mountains on the way, and still finishing in 97 days, I knew this was a quite exceptional performance. The fact that his back-up throughout came not from a highly sponsored, sophisticated media circus but from his wife, Pauline driving a motor caravan (accompanied by their three children), and a band of volunteer support runners, makes it the more remarkable. In addition he raised over £25 000 for Intermediate Technology.

This journey follows the highest traditions of long distance fell running and ranks among the most impressive achievements, being the first continuous traverse of the mountains of Britain and Ireland.

Hugh Symonds's account of his adventures makes not only fascinating reading but will serve as an invaluable guide either to anyone wishing to emulate him, or for the fair weather walker just wanting to pick off one Munro at a time on warm summer days.

October 1991

Chris Bonington
Caldbeck

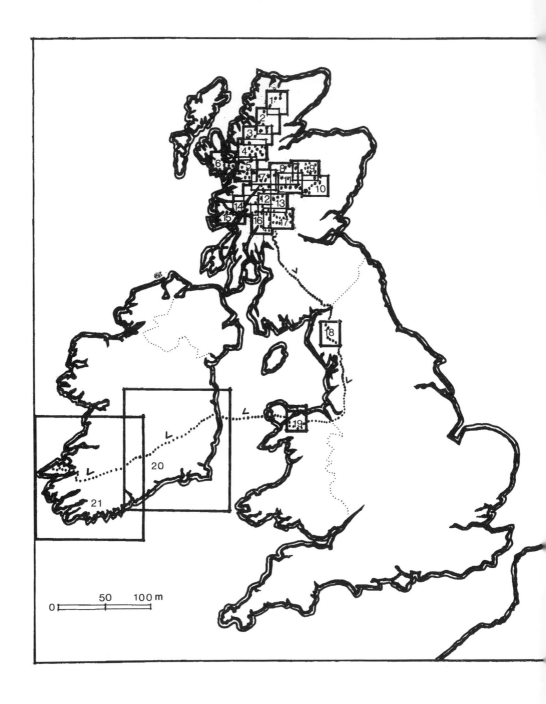

Key to Maps

▲   Mountain.
Munro Numbers refer to order of height as given by SMC tables.
e.g. Ben Nevis – Munro Number – 1. (highest Munro)
      Ben Macdui – Munro Number – 2. (second highest Munro)

●   Position at end of day.
e.g. D3 – position at end of third day.

•••••>•••••   Route and direction.

□   ▫   Towns and villages.

△   Mountain also on other map.

○   Day position also on other map.

Map Contents

Prologue

I couldn't go on. I had climbed only two of the seven mountains planned for the day. The solitude in the mountains was enjoyable and invigorating but today I was intimidated by the dark shadows echoing through the clouds as they rushed across the vicious rocky landscape. As I gained height, this darkness turned lighter as the snow cover increased. I was without crampons. The snow on the northern edge of Creag a'Mhàim had hardened to ice within 100 metres of the summit and I felt foolish kicking steps with flimsy running shoes. It was futile to dig my fingers into the steepening slope in front of my face but I scratched the surface through thin gloves and edged my way higher becoming more frightened of the increasing slope below me. I stopped to look up, down and to both sides. I thought about reversing my steps and tried two, but it felt more delicate than climbing. To ease my nerves I moved upwards faster, hoping to reach the safe ground of a flat summit. The slope eased and I looked westward to the second peak as I ran the last few safe strides to the cairn. I had already taken an unnecessary risk and I was glad that I was not being watched. The next mountain had more snow and the cornices leaning over Glen Shiel looked poised to collapse. The Cluanie ridge was supposed to be an easy run and one of the simplest collections of seven Munros in any district. This April day the ridge was in winter condition and was no place for a scantily clad runner in light shoes. I knew I had to reach Allt Mhalagain further down the glen. After studying various options with the map I descended southward on less snow towards the River Loyne. The early clouds had vanished and the view across to Gleouraich was Alpine in the rich blue sky. The beauty was stunning, and I stopped several times on the descent to watch herds of deer and the distant mountains. The mountains looked wonderful but also dangerous and certainly unrunnable. I now felt happy to be running with the security of the footpath in Glen Quoich but unhappy to be underneath mountains which I had hoped to traverse today. I was now reduced to tee shirt and shorts. The warmer clothes were packed in my small sack and I was bounding down towards the boarded house at Alltbeithe occasionally hopping to avoid squashing frogs which had been brought out in their hundreds by the warm spring sunshine. My planned return to the family was through the Bealach Duibh Leac at the Western end of the ridge. I salvaged something of the mountain plan by turning east from the Bealach to Creag nan Damh. Again I was nervous on the steep snow slopes but at least the top layer of ice had now melted and after four hours of mountain and valley I was reunited with Pauline and the children who were bathing in the burn.

We returned to our rented cottage in Glenelg and when the children were in bed we talked at length, eventually deciding to drop the idea of 'Running the Munros'. The previous day I had crossed Beinn Sgritheall from Arnisdale to Glenelg and had opted out of the final 100m to the summit because of ice.

The following day we crossed to Skye and I made a rapid ascent of Blà Bheinn stopping on the top to look at the Cuillin Ridge jutting its way above the cloud which was hanging at 3000 feet. Fear and excitement propelled me down the snow chute into Coire Uaigneich and I returned in an hour and a half secretly thinking that the run was on again. Although Pauline and I had scrapped the project the previous evening, I was permanently haunted by the idea and was addicted to it as much as I had become addicted to running over the previous twenty years. It was Easter 1987 and I returned home at the end of the week's feasibility test, tired but hungry to pursue the plan even though I knew the sensible and easy thing to do was to drop it.

Chapter 1   THE IDEA

The idea of a long run had been with me for over twenty years. As a child I had spent many days of my school holidays swimming lengths of the local pool dreaming that I was crossing the channel. I had come to learn that it was satisfying to repeat the movements of exercise. As the body grew fitter it became easier to go further. I was never going to be a sprinter. The choice of motion through running was made at the age of 15 whilst on holiday in the West Highlands. I had played golf at sixpence a round at Gairloch. The ball game didn't suit my temperament or ability, nor did it suit the other golfers who had to duck my erratic balls. Short runs of half an hour had been adventures capturing glimpses of fearsome distant mountains. Deteriorating eyesight caused me to loosen my grip on rugby and my school in Manchester encouraged me to run. Running became a natural part of each day. The training and enjoyment of covering ground became far more necessary than the competition of weekend races.

In 1981 my son Andrew was born, we moved to the Yorkshire Dales and my running took to the hills. Regular running in the Howgill Fells changed me from a Cheshire county cross-country runner to an England International fell runner; but more important than that, it increased my competence in the hills and my desire to pursue a major mountain challenge.

The main 3000 foot peaks of Scotland have become known as Munros after the late Sir Hugh Munro. Munro was born in London in 1856, the eldest of nine children. After inheriting the estate of Lindertis near Kirriemuir, he came to regard Scotland as his home and spent many years exploring and surveying the mountains. Before he produced his *Tables of Heights over 3000 feet* in 1891, it was generally believed that only about 30 hills were of that altitude. Sir Hugh died of pneumonia in 1919, having never quite completed the ascent of all the mountains he had listed. The notorious 'Inaccessible Pinnacle', the end of so many Munroists dreams, eluded him as did his local Munro – saved until last – saved a little too long! Today 277 Scottish Munros, the result of many revisions of the original list, provide a rewarding challenge for mountain lovers. It is the goal of the 'Munroist' to ascend them all.

I had sometimes wondered whether there would be sufficient time in the long summer vacation to run the Munros, and had come to the conclusion that there wouldn't be, and that July and August were too late in the summer anyway. It is harder to enjoy Scotland once the midges have hatched.

Thoughts of a real opportunity to run a major challenge came in 1986 when Roger Baxter, my headmaster at Sedbergh School, announced a change in the terms of employment to include sabbaticals. Every seven years, teachers would be able to take one term off to refuel and return to teaching with new vitality. He would consider all applications but said that reading books on a Californian beach was more likely to meet the governors' approval than simply sunbathing on the sand. Minutes after the staff meeting I was at home with Pauline talking about running the Munros. From that moment onwards, with Pauline's encouragement, we were looking at how to convert the opportunity into something positive for the whole family. We went to Glenelg in early April 1987 with a strong desire to pursue the challenge, but with strong reservations as to whether it was possible.

Pauline

I gave Hugh my support but frequently doubted my wisdom in doing so. Whilst I was eager to encourage him to fulfil his desire for challenge and adventure, I had no wish to be party to a suicidal venture. Not that I doubted Hugh's navigational ability and level-headedness in dangerous circumstances. He assured me that his sense of self-preservation was high and he would always err on the side of caution, an assurance which I have since had reason to doubt! The sight of the craggy summits of the Torridonian giants did nothing to allay my fears. As I pictured Hugh alone on the tops in the mist, rain and wind, the journey which was still only a developing idea began to look more and more like madness.

Maybe I sound too dramatic. After all Hugh was not considering a lone attempt on Everest or a canoe trip to the North Pole. Hugh was a good candidate for the task. If anyone could do it, he could. However it was immediately apparent that the terrain of the Scottish Highlands bears no comparison to the gentle training ground of our local Howgills. Even the rougher landscape of the neighbouring Lake District, Hugh's most frequented racing ground, does not approach the grand scale of the Munros. Hugh had spent many hours in all weathers running over the high ground of the Dales and Lake District, but he was by no means very familiar with the summits up north, having only scaled a handful of the more accessible Munros prior to our 'recce' holidays.

However the idea once born could only grow and there was an element of trying to justify the sense of it. Most of our mountaineering experience had been gained before our children were born. Hugh had spent student summer holidays leading adventure-seeking backpackers across the wilderness of Iceland over raging glacial torrents and misty ice caps. After leaving University we had spent over a year in India, teaching at the Lawrence School Sanawar in the foothills of the Himalayas. We had taken the opportunity to explore the high passes of Nepal and Ladakh.

The arrival of our family, Andrew, Joseph and Amy, had tamed our activities, but here was an adventure for us all.

I viewed the family's role in this venture with a mixture of excitement and apprehension. I was delighted at the prospect of spending the best months of the year in the most beautiful landscape of our islands. I anticipated the frustration inherent in being denied the summits. I consoled myself with the realisation that to be in the glens was certainly preferable to staying at home. I love to spend time with my children but to do so continuously without a break would be trying. The opportunity to have time to myself would obviously be minimal. As a family we had spent many long holidays travelling, but could we survive for four months living in a space no larger than the average bathroom? Would the children become ill/homesick/impossible to tolerate? Would Hugh become ill/injured/impossible to tolerate?

Lesson time. (H.S.)

Optimism prevailed and I believed that the joy of the landscape and being a part of such a wonderful achievement would serve to inspire me. The children were excited by the prospect, being kept well informed through meal-time conversations. There would surely be hard times but we would hopefully emerge a more closely knit and understanding family. It had to work. I had a strong desire to see the venture succeed.

Chapter 2   HOW MANY MOUNTAINS?

Mountains had always been an important objective in our holidays. Family holidays had taken us to the Alps, Pyrenees and the Rocky mountains of North America, but my experience of Munros was limited to running the Ben Nevis and Ben Lomond races and a brief trip on skis over the Cairngorms. I bought a few maps and was horrified at the complexity of the contour detail in Knoydart. To have any chance of succeeding in the now obsessive objective, I would have to improve my navigational skills, and equip myself to cope with vile conditions. I would also have to create some sort of structure to the route. With *Munro's Tables* and 22 Ordnance Survey maps I spent winter evenings plotting the 277 Munros onto three 1:250 000 maps which were eventually glued together to form the large reference chart for route planning.

I was now frightened by the number of mountains and by the awkwardness of the position of many. I stared at the chart for dozens of hours and could never find a natural line to link the peaks together. In weaker moments I looked for short cuts. One idea was to run the one hundred and thirty five 1000 metre peaks, but that would have been an admission of failure before the start. The 914m mark is not a natural one, but 3000 feet is, and this level will probably remain the mountain gauge in these islands for centuries after metrication.

In the spring of 1988, following the year of our stay in Glenelg, we rented a house in Diabaig by Loch Torridon. I spent some of the week running and looking at routes around the nearby peaks of Beinn Eighe, Slioch and Beinn Alligin. The snow and ice were hard, and again running shoes were inadequate for the task. The sight of Liathach from Glen Torridon was impressive but it was also like a giant towering over me, frightening me of my ambitions.

We returned home still not knowing whether I would ever get as far as Torridon on any run. For the second time, seven continuous days in high mountains had produced a lethargy in my legs. I wondered whether it was possible to sustain weeks of running in the Scottish mountains, without gradually wearing the body to a standstill. However, the Munro objective was now beyond the point of no return, and the year of the attempt was dependent on when I would be granted a sabbatical. My headmaster was very keen to help. He understood that I was growing older and that the task would become more difficult as years passed. In fact, the stamina of veteran fell runners usually stays well into the forties, but I preferred to take the challenge while the idea was hot, and the children were young.

One evening in December, at the end of 1988, I walked home from school with the letter of permission for 1990. The decision had been made for me. Pauline was thrilled, but I didn't tell her of my own fears which were far greater than that of being lost or exhausted.

We had fifteen months to plan the expedition. I had admired the exploits of Kelvin Bowers in running from Stoke to Sydney and Bruce Tulloh in crossing the States, but most of all the Crane brothers' run along the length of the Himalayas. Their bravery and sense of adventure in running 2000 miles without support and with minimal kit in an underdeveloped country had always astonished me. Adrian and Richard Crane had converted their monumental physical effort into help for the Third World through raising funds for 'Intermediate Technology'. I didn't want my efforts to be *wasted* on the rock and heather slopes. It was important to us too to translate manic exercise into funds for a worthwhile charity.

Early in January 1989, I spent a morning in Kendal Library, reading through charity registers and making notes of their aims and addresses. I found the peace of the library concentrated my attention on what I was planning. I came to realise that if I wanted to

With Richard Crane – a driving force behind Intermediate Technology's fundraising. (Sue Richardson)

make an impact worthy of stirring people to donate funds, then the Munro run would not be sufficiently national. It was at this moment that I started to think in terms of ascending the Welsh and English 3000 footers. Continuous Munros had been on my menu for a while, but continuous Mountains of Britain seemed to be a step towards insanity. I didn't like the idea of running through cities and along vast stretches of tarmac. Perhaps I could run the Welsh Mountains, sail or cycle to the Cumbrian coast, run the Lakes' peaks and sail on to Mull before starting the Munros. The cycling idea was tempting but once I allowed wheels, the rules of the game would change, and I would be tempted to cycle between Munros. I loved cycling, but it seemed to be a step towards mechanisation, when I wanted the travel to be on foot. A complete foot traverse would be impossible unless I could grow giant flippers and gills. The mountains of Skye

Passing Ribblehead viaduct with Sean Livesey – on the way to a Three Peaks Race victory in 1984
(*Simon Parker*)

and Mull make sea crossings necessary for all Munroists. I wanted the method of travel
to be pure – no grease, no bearings, no oil. Running and sailing seemed natural.

The extra few days needed to run the peaks of England and Wales would be minimal
in their additional effort, but probably of far greater impact for potential fundraising. It
was with this plan of running and sailing all the mountains of Britain that I composed
and sent a proposal to three favoured charities which between them help the
underprivileged in poor countries.

For six weeks our venture lacked direction as we waited for replies. We needed a
charitable purpose. Then, out of the blue, one afternoon, Richard Crane phoned us on

behalf of Intermediate Technology. At last a link was forged and it seemed that someone was interested in converting the manic run into a worthwhile fundraising exercise. Founded in 1965 by the late Dr E. F. Schumacher, Intermediate Technology (I.T.) provide advice and assistance on the appropriate choice of technologies for the rural poor of the Third World. Richard's enthusiasm and belief in the cause of I.T.'s work spread to us immediately and the work of planning a mountain run doubled into planning a charity venture.

Some fundamental decisions had to be made in the following weeks. To make the venture earn money for I.T., it had to have media appeal. Richard advised us to fix a start date and a target time. Without these, there would be little for the press to fix their attention on. Richard was also unhappy about the sailing – thinking that it would attract more interest than the actual running.

During Richard's first visit to our home, we were discussing the start date when his eye caught my oldest trophy on the wall. It was won with the Manchester Boys' Club team in the National Cross-Country Championships of 1969. Searching through my collection of diaries, I found that it had been won on April 19th.

I had been thinking of May 1st as a good time for the start in Scotland. However, any start date could be subject to wild weather. What difference would ten days make? The start date was fixed for the twenty first anniversary of this, one of my earliest races.

Now that I had dropped the idea of sailing, a target time of 100 days seemed realistic for the distance of a little under 2000 miles.

The April date was early, particularly after the run of late winters in Scotland. However, if I started on Snowdon and ran north, I could avoid most of the winter snows. I was now set on running the 296 Mountains of Britain and every bit of the way between them, except for the Skye and Mull crossings.

In the weeks following Richard's visit, I thought more about the direction of the run. I was unhappy about tackling long road sections so early in the trip. I could be tempted to run far and fast whilst fresh before the Scottish mountains. Roads are far more likely to cause stress fractures in the legs than the changing soft and hard ground of mountains. If I was going to get injured during the run then I would prefer it happened at the end. So by March 1989, I had settled on starting in the North of Scotland. The advantages of a North to South run outweighed the disadvantages and, as time went on, I realised that it offered the option of continuing after Snowdon onto the peaks of Ireland.

Chapter 3   HOW'S THE TRAINING GOING?

For ten years my training through the winter months had been between seventy and one hundred miles per week, run on the fells, road and countryside around our home town of Sedbergh in the Yorkshire Dales. I found that the higher the weekly mileage, the better I felt and the easier it became to do the everyday things of life including my work as a mathematics teacher. A by-product of running in the Howgills was success in competitive fell races, with the highlights being wins at Ben Nevis (1985), the Three Peaks (1984, –85, –87) and Ennerdale (1986, –88). Consistent running gives a feeling of being in control until the rhythm of training is broken down by circumstances. Most winters I picked up an infection which lasted for two to three weeks until I usually gave up the battle, stopped running and went to the doctor for a dose of antibiotics. There is a fine balance between healthy exercise and overdoing it. How could I strike such a balance in the summer of 1990 with so many miles to cover and mountains to climb?

By the spring of 1989 I was fit after a solid winter's training but for the third time in over twenty years of running I developed a long-lasting injury. My left ankle had dropped into a hole hidden by snow on Baugh Fell. The toes had stayed on firm ground so the tendon was wrenched as the heel dipped half a foot into semi-frozen bog. The tendon gave varying amounts of pain for the rest of the year, but most of all the pain was psychological. Decisions to rest or continue running are always agonising but with another Scottish holiday booked for more reconnaissance it was impossible on this occasion to stop. From our base in Glen Garry I stressed the tendon further with long trips into Knoydart and Affric.

On our first night in Glen Garry we heard strange noises coming from outside the house. Someone was prowling around outside! When we plucked up the courage to investigate we discovered Mike Walford, struggling in the darkness to find the front door.

We had come to know Mike both through his involvement in running and his work as an architect. In 1982 we had purchased an old stone barn, attracted by its position nestling on the gentle slopes of the high and remote valley of Grisedale (known as 'the Dale that Died'). We had combined work with pleasure, running the 10 miles over the rough bulk of Baugh Fell to visit the barn and discuss plans. These runs built the foundations of a two day mountain marathon partnership, spanning three successive seasons.

Mike had only been inside the house for a few minutes when he proceeded to fill the kitchen sink with something large and bloody. Using his penknife, Mike was cutting the skin from two deer legs and preparing them for the oven. During his stay in Glen Pean,

Training in the Howgill Fells (*John Forder*)

Putting markers out for the Howgill Challenge 1989 (*Eric Whitehead*)

he had found a young dying deer lying outside the bothy. After its death, Mike couldn't resist the temptation to chop off the choice joints with his ice axe. The children always remember him for this incident. We roasted one of the legs slowly for the best part of a day and it tasted delicious. The other, he took home to his family in Kendal. I saw dozens of dead deer during the week, with the smell of death producing a very unpleasant stench far around their bodies. The stalker at Kinloch Hourn said that it was a bad spring with the weeks of heavy rain being colder and more harmful for the deer than ice and snow.

Mike joined us for a few days and we spent the evenings studying dozens of maps trying to plan a sensible route from Ben Hope. Mike had climbed all the Munros during many previous winters and his experience was invaluable in providing encouragement, planning and humour.

I returned from Scotland happier about my knowledge of the locality yet still daunted by the task, stressed by the injury and worried by the publicity I was beginning to receive. The start date had been fixed for April 1990. Richard Crane had arranged for Intermediate Technology's London office to deliver a press release twelve months in advance of the run. The interest was strong and I appeared for interviews and photos. I didn't like having media attention so long in advance and wondered whether I really could reach 'The Peak of Endurance' and attain 'The Tall Order' which the papers talked

KENSINGTON PALACE

I am following with great interest your preparations for a record-breaking run of the mountains of Britain. As patron of The Intermediate Technology Development Group, I am particularly pleased that you and your colleagues are making such wonderfully imaginative use of your enterprise by helping to raise funds for the work of the charity.

Charles

19th April 1989

This letter was sent in support of Hugh Symonds fundraising effort, April 1989

about. I relied on Richard's experience, and was now, more than ever, dedicated to the idea of making the run raise big funds for Intermediate Technology. Richard advised us to organise a local event to begin fundraising and to arouse interest. Pauline, myself and Ann Parratt together with the Sedbergh School charity committee organised 'Help from the Howgills'. Hundreds of runners, hillwalkers and school children climbed between one and thirty-one of the 1500 foot Howgill Peaks over a period of two weeks in June, 1989. Sweat shirts with 'Mountains of Britain – Mountains of Help' sold well and funds climbed to over £10 000 in the summer of 1989. This money was handed directly to Andrew Brown, an I.T. engineer who went on to use the money to teach Nepalese blacksmiths and craftsmen the techniques of making electricity from fast-flowing water.

Taking power to Himalayan villages saves the cutting of trees for fuel, gives light to homes and develops the use of power-driven tools and machinery. The villagers are able to process their own products thus creating jobs and boosting the local economy.

Preparing for the Mountains of Britain run and the Howgill Challenge took vast amounts of time and just when many people were asking me 'How's the training going?' my training had in fact dropped drastically.

Pauline

During 1989 Hugh seemed to spend more time exercising his fingers at the typewriter than exercising his legs on the hill. Training seemed to have dropped to an all-time low, just when most people expected him to be training hard. The administration was taking over as a great deal of time and effort went into raising funds and sponsorship. After a day in January spent choosing our support vehicle at Madisons in Preston, I asked Hugh, 'Do you think actually doing it will be harder or easier than this?' He replied, 'to tell the truth I feel like I have already done it.' For much of the year Hugh was in poor health. I found him falling asleep in front of the television. This was so unlike Hugh and I was really worried. The point of hours of hard work going into arousing publicity in order to raise funds would be lost if Hugh was to be worn out by the preparation.

After a good season in 1988 with a win at Europe's highest race on Vignemale in the Pyrenees, the 1989 season was my poorest of the decade. We went to Switzerland in the summer and I had one of my worst ever races, finishing over an hour behind the winner in the Swiss Alpine Marathon at Davos. I was concerned that I might be harbouring a virus as well as the tendon injury.

Nevertheless, during the Autumn, plans began to fall into place and confidence grew. We found sponsors for food, shoes, maps, clothing and towards the motor caravan. Without this help the financial commitment would have been high and would have been an unwelcome pressure on the run. I found the interest of companies boosted my sense of purpose. I had to complete the journey to Snowdon to honour their commitment.

Through the darkness of Winter, my training picked up again as the need for administration dropped. I regularly went into the hills in bad weather and poor visibility to practise navigation. As I became stronger again, the tendon pains eased. Many fell running friends had now heard of the venture and were keen to help me in the hills. More than twenty came to a party in March. Maps and calendars were spread across tables as everyone booked themselves in to join me for some Munros. Fell runners help each other in their epics on the mountains. They know how to give support when the body is weak and morale is low. I knew that to tackle the Munros alone would be a much harder task. Further phone calls and letters ensured that I would have company for most of the run.

The route over the lonely plateau of Baugh Fell to Grisedale was also familiar to Paul Tuson, who took on the essential task of coordinating the support on the hill. All the joinery in our barn conversion had been his handiwork. As a Kendal runner, well known to prospective pacers and with an enthusiasm for the Scottish mountains, he was the ideal person for the job. We would telephone him regularly, keeping him informed of our position. Runners heading north would first phone Paul, who would ensure that they would be able to find us. Both Paul, and his wife Angela, spent a great deal of time on the telephone in the coming months.

In the days before leaving home, we spent most of the time packing the van with food, clothes and maps, ticking lists as each item was buried in cupboards. There was more media interest from the TV, and now, a year on from the first interview, I felt less nervous and more meaningful about the imminent challenge.

Just when everything was going so well, a bizarre incident occurred which put Pauline and I on edge for some time. I was crouching on the floor of the van, packing tools under the driver's seat, when I heard a strange noise. It sounded like a piece of taut

Easter Sunday. About to leave Joss Lane car park, Sedbergh. (*Eric Whitehead*)

elastic snapping. Maybe something strange had happened to the vehicle's electric system. Investigation revealed nothing so I carried on with my packing. Then I noticed it! A piece of lead shot was lying on the work top. Looking around I soon spotted the hole in the double glazing. The reality slowly sank in. I had been shot at! The pellet could only have missed my head by inches. This manic act could have put an end to my dreams. When Pauline arrived home from schoool with the children, I told her the story. She stared at me in disbelief, but the hole in the window soon convinced her. Subsequent interviews with the police took up precious time when we were extremely busy with the final preparations. Packing the high cupboards in the van involved standing right in line with the hole in the glazing; a very uncomfortable feeling.

By Sunday 15 April we were ready and we achieved the first deadline – departure. We were given a tremendous send-off by over a hundred wellwishers in Sedbergh and it was difficult to hold the tears back. We drove North to our first night's stop in the van. A lay-by on the west side of Loch Lomond gave a good view of Ben Lomond whose snow line was dropping by the hour. At last we were on the move. After a winter average of seventy miles each week I felt fit and healthy, but I now wondered whether I could more than double this mileage later in the week.

It had been a late and harassed evening. I had hoped to spend time looking at maps and doing more planning, but the van's internal water pump had broken down and we were without water in the kitchen and bathroom. We could manage with buckets from streams, but family life would be so much easier with water on tap.

Overnight snow had fallen down to sea level and driving conditions across Rannoch Moor were hazardous. I now wondered whether sticking to a fixed start date was wise. Runners had phoned Paul Tuson asking whether I was delaying the start as the snowfall was widespread and deep. Our second stop was at Roger Boswell's house, caravan site and garden near Fort William. We stopped to leave provisions to be collected on future transits of this northern outpost. Roger's help and enthusiasm flowed out of him like the snow fell out of the sky. We had hardly been in his drive two minutes when he had a hose inside the van trying to unblock the broken pump. Water was spraying everywhere in the back of the van. Eventually Roger declared the pump dead and cycled off to buy a new one. Later that evening he emerged from his workshop and our plumbing system was soon working again.

Pauline's Diary, Monday 16 April
Hugh has been very edgy all day. I think he may be worried! He blames it on the children, but they are no more problematical than usual. The tension will probably ease once the run starts. I must say it is worrying. Winter is very much here. It is actually freezing outside at the moment, although it is lovely and warm in the van. It will be easier once we are used to the van and have got over the teething problems. It takes quite a while to get organised. Everytime I open a cupboard I fear being bashed on the head by a low-flying tin of beans!

In the three days journey to Scotland's most northerly Munro, Ben Hope in Sutherland, we looked at overnight parking spots for future weeks, and made arrangements for access to Strathfarrar, a remote glen which we were to visit later. The radio telephone occasionally worked and whilst motoring through Dingwall, Radio Manchester taped an interview. It was hard for me to hide my apprehension as I stared at Ben Wyvis (Hill of Terror) plastered in snow. The climbing forecast warned of cornicing and wind slab, and I thought of Martin Moran's narrow escape from an avalanche on the same mountain. I had read a graphic description of this incident in *The Munros in Winter,* Martin Moran's book of his single season's climbing of all the Munros.

The van's wheel width just fitted the narrow road north of Altnaharra and we slowly closed the distance to Ben Hope. Our site for the night was a small gravel enclave one mile south of Loch Hope. I had been nervous riding north, as Pauline had been learning to drive the new large motor caravan. Now we had arrived at the first mountain, I felt a great sense of peace. Although I knew and had thought of the million and one things that could go wrong in the coming months, so many hurdles had been crossed just to establish ourselves here at base camp. I now felt ready to concentrate on the one thing that mattered: running the 'Mountains of Britain'.

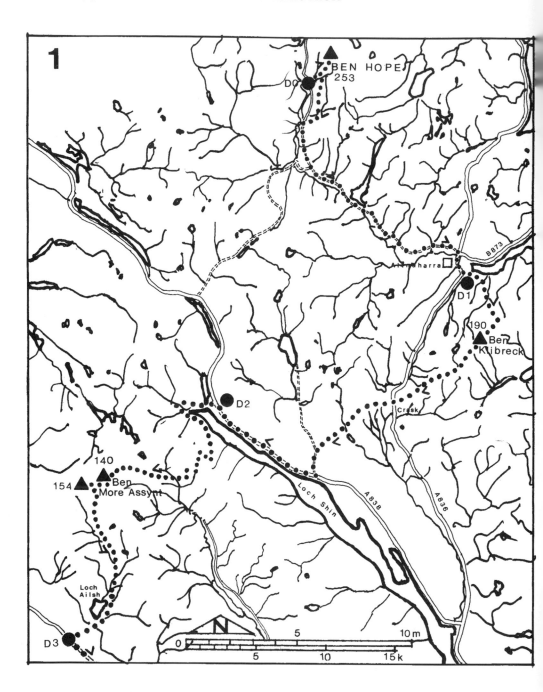

Chapter 4   THE SNOWS OF BEN HOPE

April 19–23, 1990

Dawn of day one was crisp and bright. Our small campsite had grown, with a small community of tents now dotted around in the bog and heather. There was no urgency to set off up the mountain. There was time to savour the wild mountain landscape of rocks and lochans, and time to talk to friends. Dr Bev Holt, who helped and advised us, particularly on nutrition, had come to weigh me, take blood and to share the start from the summit trig point. Paul Tuson and Dave Richardson had come to be with me on the hills for the first three days. Matt Dickinson, Jeremy West and Kees t'Hooft of Zanzibar Films had come for the first of many shoots. Matt had visited us at home in March and was amazingly enthusiastic about making a film about the run despite the risks of failure. At home he had made us understand that we had to have a commitment to the film if it was to succeed. The one to two hours per day of intrusion into our day-to-day life on the run would be a small price to pay for a record on film, and for future fundraising potential.

Before the departure from the cowshed south west of Ben Hope, a huge flock of geese flew north, high in the sky. I am not a superstitious man but Dave said, 'There's your omen.' The sound and sight of the geese is a permanent memory.

We took our time climbing to the summit. Time to give the film crew a chance to reach the top before us and time for me to gather my thoughts. I was wired into a small radio microphone carried in my bumbag. Jeremy collected on tape, sounds of my feet crunching in the snow and any thoughts that I put into words. It helped me clarify my own ideas about what I was doing. I slowed down for the final few hundred metres to the summit. I wanted to savour the feeling of anticipation. Like the one last mountain of the journey, there would only ever be one first mountain. So much time, thought and energy had preceded this day that I now felt a great sense of relief that I had finally arrived on top of Ben Hope.

The clear morning had been lost in the mist and the ground remained white and

1   THE FAR NORTH

Munro Number	Munro	Running Order
253	Ben Hope	1
190	Ben Klibreck	2
140	Ben More Assynt	3
154	Conival	4

frozen above 3000 feet. The view from the top was only of the iced trig point from fifty yards. Paul took the bottle of champagne from the sack and after a quick decorking and a swig each we left the summit in a snow flurry and headed south. The 'Mountains of Britain Run' had started.

Running on a compass bearing, we hugged the edge of the western cliffs occasionally retracing our footprints of the climb. Below 2000 feet the mist thinned and we stopped to view the snow and rock of Arkle and Foinaven – peaks which fortunately or unfortunately lay below the 3000 foot contour of Munro. During the next two days I passed sculptured mountains which lay close to, but not on my route. There had to be a

Leaving Ben Hope. (Paul Tuson)

defining line to this journey – it wasn't one of beauty – it was one of measure. To judge the beauty of mountains you have to see them first and I will be back to the far North West, not to 'do' the Corbetts or to 'do' the Munros but simply to enjoy interesting mountains.

We crossed the top of the waterfall of the Allt na Caillich and dropped into the wide Glen of Strath More by the Broch of Dun Domaigil. The sun was warm for the first support stop of the run. After bread, soup and a change of shoes and socks, I left the family happy and at ease, as the children were enjoying playing out in wild places. We were now in the process of establishing a rhythm.

In tee shirt and shorts I gently ran south along the single track road towards Altnaharra. Many fell runners have an aversion to road running but for me this lonely piece of tarmac was a way of seeing landscape change slowly without having to concentrate on a map and without having to watch every step of the ground.

Ben Klibreck came into sight after the climb up to Loch Meadie and Ben Hope's bold southern aspect became smaller. The movement from mountain to mountain empha- sised the start of the journey. I stopped every couple of miles to stretch the legs and admire the views towards Ben Hee and Ben Loyal. It would have been easy to have done too much on this first day. It was important to eat and rest between runs and to ease the body into hours of being on the move. By five o'clock I had run through the tiny village of Altnaharra, and Pauline had found a good patch of ground on which to park the van. The wide open site overlooked Loch Naver and the zebra-like snowy streaks on Ben Klibreck. So far north, the evening was light until late. The children enjoyed the environment around the van, collecting dead wood and making a bonfire.

Pauline's Diary, Thursday 19 April

Must admit to feeling a little harassed. Hugh ran 20 km (he may be doing the 3000 'foot' mountains of Britain but our left-hand drive motor caravan only measures in kilometres) in little more time than it took me to drive. This thin ribbon of tarmac, laid over the bog and heather of Sutherland is little wider than the van and passing places are virtually non-existent. At least I don't have to put up with Hugh looking nervous in the passenger seat any longer. Andrew is now firmly installed as the navigator. The barrage of enthusiastic questions from Joseph in the back makes concentration difficult. 'How high is that mountain?' 'Is Daddy going up that one?' 'Is that Loch Naver?' I find Hugh a little impatient at the end of the day. Understandable perhaps, but I feel that I have worked hard too. I feel like I have spent all day making cups of tea. I think that this is going to be exhausting. Am I up to it? Being supportive isn't my strong point. Will I get through it without murdering the kids? They have been very trying today, probably due to too many late nights. Activity in the van in the evenings distracts them at bedtime. Hugh obviously feels tired. Will he just get more and more worn out or will he get used to it?

I'm optimistic I suppose. Things will improve as we all get accustomed to the lifestyle. Today was especially difficult with several meeting points on a long slow road.

In the early morning of Friday 20 April, there was some strength in the sunshine. The radio reported that the best weather in Britain was to be had in the far North West. I was lucky. To be able to start the first few days in good conditions was a great advantage. Paul and Dave packed their light sacks and carried my clothing and food so that I could run without anything on my back. They could go home tired at the end of tomorrow but I had to always try to stay fresh for the next day. The pacers' job of carrying gear and keeping me company was paramount to the success of the run.

I had read of Klibreck as being a dull mountain, but it was far from that today. The eastern side had collected the wind and snow, leaving huge cornices overlooking Loch Choire. Under the bright blue sky in a sharp frozen wind, the mountain gave a crystal-sharp spectacle of empty Sutherland.

Descending on snow and rock, I tripped and gashed a leg, giving it a scar which remained with me for the whole run. It was an early but gentle reminder of my vulnerability. We stopped to munch nuts and raisins above Loch nan Uan. The bag was split and we looked like grazing cattle as we pecked the ground with cold fingertips and put the food to our mouths. We dropped off Cnoc Sgriodain and passed through some new forestry before meeting Pauline and the children a mile north of the Crask Inn. Andrew lowered deck chairs from the roof of the van and we enjoyed a lunch break in warmth that I hadn't expected for several weeks. The satisfaction in making a continuous journey over the Munros is in the feeling of travel. I have always enjoyed simply going from one place to another. It also often means that you see both sides of a

Dave Richardson at the camp by Loch a'Ghriama, under Ben More Assynt. (H.S.)

mountain. This afternoon it meant seeing a bit of Britain that would normally never be visited; from the Crask to Fiag Bridge. I ran as straight a line as possible without sinking in the bog. You would think that there would be little evidence of man in such a place, but I was amazed to find two wrecked cars half a mile from the road.

After joining the Lairg road, I ran on to the north end of Loch Shin. This put me in a good position for tomorrow – the first of many big mountain days. I wanted to spend nights with the family as much as possible and only camp out or make use of mountain bothies when the days from van to van were too long to be sensible.

Pauline's Diary, Saturday 21 April
Another beautiful morning but a hard frost. This part of the world in good weather is hard to beat. The gas doesn't function properly in freezing temperatures, so we couldn't light the fire, and the kettle took half an hour to boil! The campers must have been very cold. There is quite a little party here. Jeremy and Kees – the camera crew, Paul and Dave, Bev Holt and his son Chris. We are parked near the Merkland River at the head of Loch a' Ghriama – the first time that we haven't camped at the actual start point for the day, this being a few miles down the road.

There were bound to be occasions when it would be impractical to park for the night at the start/finish position. Although it's not exactly purist, there were a few places where I allowed myself a lift to the overnight spot and a lift back in the morning. So long as I touched a post or rock and retouched it in the morning, my running journey would be continuous. This would be more common in the towns and cities, but here by the locked gate to Corriekinloch, near Loch Shin, there was no space, so we moved two miles north to a spacious and flat spot which commanded superb views of the slopes of Ben More Assynt.

A tarred service road led to the power station in Glen Cassley. There we met Dave Peck who I had arranged to meet at 11 o'clock. It was a Saturday morning and Dave was enjoying a day on the hills after a hard week on the move working as a clinical psychologist in the Highlands and Islands. We had stayed at Dave's house in Tomich on the way north. His wife Ailsa had bundled our washing into a machine and solved our first dirty clothes crisis. Dave had taken us out for a drink but I had stuck to orange juices as I didn't want to start the trip off with an evening drinking routine. At the end of the first two days, Paul and Dave had gone to the pub with Jeremy and Kees at Altnaharra and Overscaig but I had resisted the temptation. Time in the evening was needed for looking at tomorrow's maps and getting food and rest.

During the first two days Pauline was able to meet me frequently. This had made it easy to change from road to fell shoes, but today I ran in one pair of shoes over the mountains and tracks through to Loch Ailsh and Glen Oykel. Running on tarmac in studded fell shoes isn't ideal but it is better than carrying an extra pair in the sack.

Climbing Ben More Assynt from the east, we looked over the multi-lochaned landscape to the north. It looked more suited to prehistoric monsters than to man. Above 2000 feet we were on hardening snow which made the mountain easier than it might have been. Quartz blocks stuck out of the snow giving a hint of the normal roughness of the mountain. The icy crossing to Conival was a joy under the rich blue sky. We stopped to eat and gazed at high frozen lochans, the weird mountains of Quinag, Canisp and Cul Mor, and beyond to the Outer Isles. The descent gave practice for Skye as my hands held on to rock on the Pinnacle Ridge leading down to Dubh Loch Mor. We left this blissful high setting with its towering buttresses and cascades and dropped down a widening path towards Ben More Lodge.

Pauline's Diary, Saturday 21 April
We met Hugh on the track from the Lodge. The children enjoy jogging along with him and he enjoys running the last couple of miles with the family – a good excuse to go slowly!

After three lengthy days, I enjoyed a leisurely morning eating and preparing overnight gear for a bothy trip. The mountains to the east of Inverlael are high and remote and the journey across them too long for one day from Glen Oykel. After a gentle road run to Lubcroy, I stocked up on more food before leaving the family for our first night apart.

Pauline's Diary, Sunday 22 April
Suddenly the scene has changed. The camera crew have said farewell – hopefully we shall see them again soon, they are so friendly and enthusiastic. Paul and Dave have also left. Hugh has a new partner – Ian Leighton, a seasoned hillman with an extreme case of Munroitis. Now I find myself alone with the children as Hugh and Ian are spending tonight at Coriemor bothy. It is strange to be on our own, but in one sense I don't really feel alone. I feel part of something much bigger – part of the show – the machinery keeping Hugh on the move. So many people are involved in this epic and the net spreads ever wider.

School starts tomorrow. This is how the kids want it. They want to do some work when school at home starts. Andrew seems to like the idea of using his normal books and he is going to do some 'Peak' Maths. We are parked by the sea shore just north of Ullapool so we will study the seaweed on the beach.

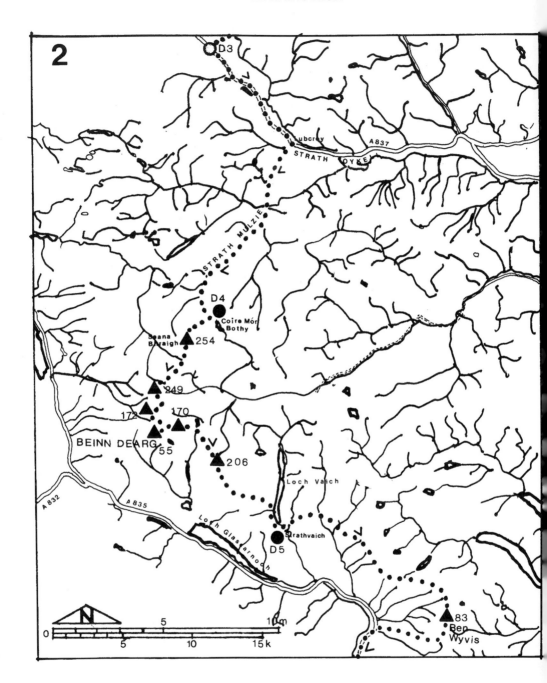

The children are fascinated by Suilven, especially Joseph. The scenery around here is wild and splendid; a joy to drive through but it would be an even greater joy to travel through on foot. I envy Hugh the pleasure but not necessarily the commitment he has made.

I didn't like this separation, but once Ian and I had crossed the rough ground to Strath Mulzie, the sheer beauty of the approach to Seana Bhraigh put me at ease. The isolation of Coriemor bothy and its position by the loch and under the pointed peak of Creag an Duine gave it an eerie atmosphere. A Brazilian man and a Greek woman were cooking black eyed beans on an open smoky fire. The man wore dark baggy clothes, pointed shoes, a strange hat and earrings. They appeared to be in residence for a while, as their food stores were hung high away from the mice. They seemed bizarre and out of place, so I asked if I could take their photograph. He talked of old Andean mythology and spirits being taken away by film. He eventually agreed, but only if he didn't look at the lens. My photo shows the man hiding behind the woman in an embrace, his long curly hair showing behind her head. I had an unsettled night on iron springs, disturbed by late foreign conversations and the thought of the camera disappearing during my sleep. Ian had a good night, outside under the stars. He is a wild mountain man who gives the impression of being able to survive any conditions.

We were away soon after seven the following morning and on the summit of Seana Bhraigh before 8:30. I had feared the next section for its tricky ground in poor visibility but the sky was clear and we could see the ground ahead to Beinn Dearg. This high terrain over unpronounceable Munros reminded me of Iceland. We saw hare and ptarmigan amongst the snows and high streams. The only evidence of man was a distant ship in Loch Broom. We passed through thigh-deep snow on the eastern descent of Cona 'Mheall and dropped rapidly to a fine waterfall at the south end of Loch Prille. The character of the sixth mountain of the day was different, with peat hags and little snow. Am Faochagach (pronounced Am Foogach according to Mr. Bennett, the stalker of Strathvaich) was a fine choice of a hill for friends, Mark Rigby and John Blair-Fish to have left a message and present of chocolate cream eggs. It brightened an otherwise dull hill and lifted my spirit. This uninspiring mountain can have few visitors, so the eggs which had awaited several days for my passage had been safe in their colourful wrapping, partially buried in the cairn. From this hill onwards I remembered to search for messages left amongst the summit stones.

Dropping down to Loch Vaich, trying to find footpaths in the thickening undergrowth, we picked up the studmarks of what we assumed to be John and Mark's visit. They helped us find a good route through to the dam, beyond which I could see the

2   THE BEINN DEARG GROUP AND BEN WYVIS

Munro Number	Munro	Running Order
254	Seana Bhraigh	5
249	Eididh nan Clach Geala	6
172	Meall nan Ceapraichean	7
55	Beinn Dearg	8
170	Cona'Mheall	9
206	Am Faochagach	10
83	Ben Wyvis-Glas Leathad Mór	11

welcome sight of the big white van, parked below Strathvaich Lodge; a sight which I got used to searching for and a sight which I gained confidence of seeing each day. The support team, with Pauline driving and Andrew navigating seemed to be working well.

Pauline

We left the excellent campsite near Ullapool with clean clothes, clean bodies and a good stock of fresh food. We were to meet Hugh at the head of Strath Vaich, just below the Lodge. Our route left the main road at Black Bridge, following a narrow, single track road up the Strath (Gaelic for valley). I came to love these journeys up wild, dead-end roads. They took us as far away from civilisation and as close to the mountains as is possible in such a large vehicle. The children would have freedom to play and explore, safe from the terrors of traffic. On this first journey off a through route, our way was barred by a closed gate bearing the sign, 'PRIVATE – NO UNAUTHORISED VEHICLES'. We decided not to let this put us off, after all we were due to meet Hugh three miles up the road. Picking out a house at random from the cluster of buildings nearby, we knocked on the door. A face appeared at an upstairs window. The lady advised us to drive up the valley and ask Mrs. Bennett, the stalker's wife, if we could stay for the night.

Mrs. Bennett had read about us in the paper. Not only was she happy for us to park in the valley but she also kindly gave a donation to Intermediate Technology and a donation of suntan lotion for Hugh's rapidly reddening face. The sunny weather had taken us by surprise.

Our liaison at home through Ann Parratt and Paul Tuson was working well. Ann took care of press and sponsorship enquiries and directed people to Paul if they needed our overnight position. A photographer traced us to the head of this private road and collected some images of me running by streams and over little bumps. Although this position was pretty and peaceful, it bore no resemblance to the wild and white terrain I had been over that day. In the whole trip I only met three photographers who took their cameras up high to capture the wildest of the mountain scenery. After several cups of tea, Ian left with the photographer to pick up his car and camp down the valley.

Tonight I felt a real sense of having started the run. Although only five days into the journey, my legs were strengthening and everyone's enjoyment seemed to be increasing. My only concern was for the sunburn on my neck. I hoped that there would be some clouds in the sky tomorrow.

Chapter 5 FIGHT ON THE FANNICHS

April 24 – 28

High fast-moving clouds indicated a change. As I approached Ben Wyvis, its summit became lost in swirling mist. The plan had been to run down the road to Garbat and meet Ian for a straight out and back visit to Wyvis. Mr. Bennett knew the country between Strath Vaich, Strath Rannoch and the Wyvis forest well and recommended me not to lose my height on the road down to Garbat, but to run across country to Tom a'Choinnich. I liked the idea of being on my own for a while. Pauline drove off to tell Ian that I was already on the mountain. This was one of only two Munros on which I had no company. No company except for the chatter of friends on the portable telephone. Being close to Dingwall, I thought there would be a good chance that the phone would pick up a signal. It would be a good way to catch up with news. Finding a phone box in the evenings was time-consuming and frustrating. I caught Paul Tuson at home working on his joinery accounts. He found the clarity hard to believe. He could hear the crunching of my studs in the snow, until I arrived and sat on the half-buried trig point. He had good news that Roger Boswell and Colin Donnelly were on their way to Fisherfield and were hoping to meet up with me at a bothy, but there was bad news from Colin that there was thought to be no shelter at Lochivraon – a resting place I had planned to use the following night! The descent to Garbat was tedious and steep. I was glad that I had chosen not to climb this route. In the following months there were just six mountains which I went up and down the same way.

The sixteen miles over mountain and country were followed by nine miles on road. I finished the day weary and lay in the back of the van amongst my kit and maps. The remedy for my lethargy was to eat monstrous amounts of food. The most difficult thing to do was to think about tomorrow, but without plans my days would end up in chaos. All the mountains had been plotted onto 1:50 000 maps previously. Each night I replotted the next day's mountains from the 1:50 000 onto the 1:25 000 maps. Sometimes this involved handling six maps on the small table at the back whilst Joseph and Amy would be asking questions and playing around me. I rechecked the crosses on the summits after the children had gone to bed. Pauline and Andrew used the 1:50 000 maps to find their way to my next position and I used the more detailed maps for the mountains. At first I found the scale cumbersome but as the days went by I found the extra information helpful, if not vital when the visibility was poor.

The previous winter, Ian and I had discussed at length the best way of tackling the Fannichs, Fisherfield, An Teallach and Slioch. In this region it would not be possible to meet up with the van as roads do not penetrate the wild glens of this vast landscape. The most remote Munro of all, A'Mhaighdean (pronounced A'Viechyan and meaning

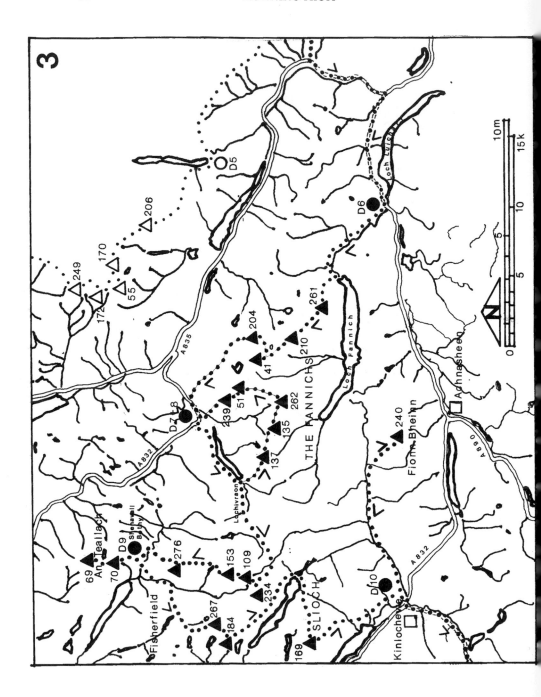

'the maiden') is situated in Fisherfield. We wanted to use two bothies for a three day trip over the 18 Munros. We couldn't risk the reputedly ruined bothy at Lochivraon so we made plans for one night's camp and a night in a bothy. We would cross the seven easternmost Fannichs together. Ian would then run from Sgurr nan Each to collect food and camping gear from Pauline, who would be parked in a nick in the road above the eastern end of Loch a'Bhraoin. I would run the two western Fannichs alone and go on to meet Ian by the ruined bothy where we would camp before moving west into Fisherfield.

Listening to the radio over breakfast we heard warnings of gales spreading from the west. A tanker was in trouble in high seas off the Hebrides. The sky was black and even the distant snow on today's peaks looked grey. We were offered a lift on the track towards Loch Fannich. In the coming weeks I got used to telling my story in a nutshell. The stalker understood and drove on with just our sacks. He advised us of a good line through the rocks to our first summit – An Coileachan. Twice on the climb we stopped to put more clothes on. The weather was worsening by the minute but we had no idea of the wind's real strength until we were exposed on top. The instant we faced the westerlies we were not braced for the blast. We were thrown backwards and over on the stony ground. Bending over double we slowly made the last strides to the cairn. It was hard to think with the noise of the wind battering my hood against my ears. We found some sort of shelter on the east of the cairn. We didn't talk, for our words would have been lost in the wind. Ian made moves to leave immediately before chilling off, but I knew that it was no day to make mistakes. I set the compass and counted the bumps in the contours before our next hill – Meall Gorm. Standing, exposed to the west again, we lent over to the left to try to keep our balance. Walking quickly up the climbs we were in control, but on the descents the wind took us to the right and blew us over several times. In trying to keep a straight course our path meandered tens of yards. Had the ridges

3 FISHERFIELD AND THE FANNICHS

Munro Number	Munro	Running Order
261	An Coileachan	12
210	Meall Gorm	13
41	Sgurr Mór	14
204	Beinn Liath Mhór Fannaich	15
137	A'Chailleach	16
135	Sgurr Breac	17
262	Sgurr nan Each	18
51	Sgurr nan Clach Geala	19
239	Meall a'Chrasgaidh	20
234	Beinn Tarsuinn	21
109	Mullach Coire Mhic Fhearchair	22
153	Sgurr Bàn	23
276	Beinn a'Chlaidheimh	24
70	An Teallach-Sgurr Fiona	25
69	An Teallach-Bidein a'Ghlas Thuill	26
267	Ruadh Stac Mór	27
184	A'Mhaighdean	28
169	Slioch-Trig point	29
240	Fionn Bheinn	30

been sharp, we would have been picked up and deposited in the lochs a thousand feet below.

On the previous days, I had stopped regularly to eat muesli bars, sandwiches and chocolate, but today it was too much effort to take the sack off the back. It wasn't good to get hungry but it wasn't good to stop either. I learnt to put food in pockets on future bad days. That way I could keep nibbling on the move.

In the thickening and lowering cloud, we couldn't see more than fifty yards ahead. The wind had brought a driving rain which added to the difficulty of looking at the maps. When a bearing was needed I bent double to create some sort of shelter in my belly. I wiped the map case with wringing wet gloves, the fingers now chilled to the bone. Running towards Sgurr Mór I suddenly found myself alone. Where was Ian? I couldn't look for him. I couldn't shout for him. I just stood waiting, getting colder and more worried. I stared into the mist but could only see the nearby rocks. Minutes went by. I dreaded the thought that he had been picked up by a gust and thrown over a crag. After what seemed like a long time just standing like a frozen statue, Ian's figure appeared out of the mist. He had been to relieve himself. I didn't envy him having to expose any part of his body in this, but I was annoyed that he hadn't told me first. We ran on to the huge pile of stones on the third peak. Six peaks to go and we were surviving.

The fourth peak, Beinn Liath Mhór Fannaich, is awkwardly placed for a single traverse of these mountains. The plan was to go east to the top and return to Sgurr Mór. The visibility had worsened and we couldn't find the narrow eastern ridge. Descending and not knowing whether we were on the ridge or not would be dangerous, as the slopes were steep and full of snow. We ran backwards and forwards searching for a narrow ribbon of rock that didn't drop sharply. The attempt to find a way became far more desperate when a gust whipped my right contact lens from my eye. It would have been pointless to have spent any time looking for it. Not knowing our position precisely, we went back to the summit of Sgurr Mór. With blurred vision I measured the distance to the ridge and took a reading on the altimeter. This time we would count paces; it could only be 200m away. The sense of relief when we found it outweighed the horror of losing a contact lens. My thoughts were now on aborting the day after the fourth summit. Ian and I had hardly spoken all day. We found a large rock to quieten the wind and talked of the options. Ian agreed that there are times when the best decision is to go down. This was no day to be in the hills at all. I was now glad that my loss of vision had put the blinkers on the day. The return to the van was essential to replace the lost contact lens.

We continued over Beinn Liath Mhór and dropped quickly to lower ground where the wind was less strong. The fierce weather had created a tension throughout the body and mind. This was now easing as we had the shelter of mountains. Across bog and heather we reached the road and ran on towards the van where Pauline was waiting to give Ian the camping gear.

Pauline's Diary, Wednesday 25 April

We are parked on a bend in the road, just beyond Braemore Junction. There is just enough room to park the van off the road, in front of the barrier across the track to Loch a'Bhraoin. Fortunately the van is parked parallel to the wind direction, but even so sitting here has something in common with being on a ship in a rough sea. The wind howls and the hailstones beat noisily on the van roof. The landscape has an

Life in the van. (H.S.)

appealing wildness; we are at a height of 1000 feet with no shelter. A mass of close contours on the map depict the many Sgurrs (meaning 'rough rocky peak'), which are on Hugh's list for today. Their speckled, snowy heads are in the cloud. Up there the wind must be horrendous. Amy is very disturbed by the wind and she has written in her diary, 'I am worried that Daddy might be blown off the mountain.' So am I.

We are almost trapped in the van as Amy can't take the wind. We did manage to spend some time outside collecting samples of plants for our bog garden which we made in a plastic-lined box. The variety is surprising. A patch of what appears to be a rather dull area of wet ground contains the most amazing number of different species of ferns, mosses and lichens, which on close examination are quite fascinating. Trying to identify them all is a nightmare.

Tonight Hugh and Ian are planning to camp. How can they put up a tent in this? I am waiting for Ian to collect the equipment. Will Hugh come with him as the weather is so bad? It would be good to see him. I don't like to think of him alone on the last two peaks of the day.

Ian and I had survived the most horrendous conditions. However, the day had put me ill at ease in his company. He had always conveyed an air of pessimism about what I was planning; a caution probably developed through his countless hours spent on the Munros. Having done them all three times, his reaction was understandable as he had a better idea than most, of the extent of the challenge which I had undertaken. However, his concern spread to me and I wanted to be rid of it. I knew that Ian wanted to help me for longer but I now preferred to go alone. To tell him was difficult and I felt bad.

I was glad to be with the family again but stressed by my rejection of Ian, worried by the mountains to come and concerned that I was now a day behind schedule, just one week into the run. I was worried that I might lose more days if the weather continued to be bad. At least my clothing had withstood the day well. I had been astonished at how warm and dry I had stayed whilst I was on the move. For future days of bad weather I had learnt that I needed nylon overmits, readily accessible food and that I would have to protect the maps more carefully than I had today. The maps had turned to blotting paper inside their case. For future bad days I cut relevant pieces of maps and stuck them together under transpaseal (clear plastic film). Tonight the van had turned into a drying room with socks, gloves, waterproofs and maps hanging from every available hook. I went to bed feeling glad that I wasn't camping out tonight.

I opted to complete the remaining five Fannichs in an anti-clockwise circuit. This way I would have the wind behind me on the high ground and I would go past the Lochivraon bothy or ruin early in the day, possibly meeting Colin and Roger who were supposed to be somewhere in the district.

Under clear skies, I ran along the stony path on the north shore of Loch a'Bhraoin. The wind was still strong but nowhere near as bad as yesterday. At least the clouds were now clearing, exposing a fresh layer of snow on the tops.

The bothy turned out to be quite usable. There was no glass in the windows, just plastic sheets, but the roof was solid. I walked in and saw a man dressed from head to toe in dirty orange waterproofs. For a moment Roger didn't recognise me and I didn't recognise him under his balaclava.

'Hugh!'

'Roger!'

'What are you doing here?'

Roger wasn't expecting me as he didn't think that I would have managed even one mountain yesterday. After coffee, boiled on the embers of the open fire, we left for the hills, wetting our knees on the way as we crossed the full river leading into the loch. Being in the mountains was so much more pleasurable now that I could see. The peaks of yesterday and tomorrow were in sight and I began to regain confidence and look forward to the days ahead.

Climbing Sgurr nan Clach Geala, the fourth peak, we met a man descending the icy slope, with a dog whose body was covered in frozen spindrift. He asked us whether we had seen a runner in the hills. I was shy to confess that it was me, as I was not running at the time. Raymond Anderson of Aberdeen is a journalist who had by coincidence met Pauline by the roadside. Seeing the advertising on the van, he knew that something was going on, and so he went in search of a story. We arranged to meet later in the comfort of our van.

The day felt short and easy in comparison to the day before. Roger and I were in the van by the middle of the afternoon, making plans and preparing supplies for the following night's stop at a bothy. Splitting the Fannichs into two days was not something that I had ever planned but it turned out to be fortunate as it rested me well before the next two long days in one of Britain's most remote regions. ·

After two nights on our wild and exposed patch of ground, we were all keen to move on. A ridge of high pressure had cleared the sky and I could see the jagged edges of An Teallach on the distant north-western skyline. I hoped to be on its summits later in the day, but for now, I was running south-west and into the depths of Fisherfield.

For the second time I ran along the peaceful loch shore to the bothy where Roger had spent another night. We distributed the weight between our sacks (Roger taking more than me) and ran off to the Bealach na Croise (*bealach* meaning 'a pass'), using deer trods to ease our passage through the rough ground. We left our sacks at the saddle west of Meall Garbh and climbed through a crunchy layer of snow to the top of Beinn Tarsuinn. The rugged scenery of wilderness reached out in all directions. I felt small and vulnerable. My journey was so subject to the elements. I would see or miss so many vistas in the coming weeks but perhaps none as great as this. I knew that I was lucky today and I had to push on to try to make An Teallach before dark. To climb An Teallach (Gaelic for 'The Forge') in wild weather would not only be to miss a great mountain but it would also be taking a big risk. We ran over three more mountains in the early afternoon; the high ridges and easy snow slopes speeding our passage towards the bothy at Shenavall. The two storey shelter was empty. We cooked instant Indian food for ten people and ate the lot before leaving for the last climb of the day.

Summit of Bidein a'Ghlas Thuill (An Teallach). (Roger Boswell)

With lighter sacks we climbed quickly onto the broad base of Sail Liath from where we could see the many turrets and towers of An Teallach, curving round to its far Munro of Bidein a'Ghlas Thuill. A layer of snow covered the sandstone rocks and made the route over Lord Berkeley's Seat look like a severe ice climb. We moved to the left above precipitous gullies cutting steps with a light axe. Fresh powder snow lay on ice giving a treacherous surface. One slip and the slide would have been long and almost certainly fatal. It took a long time to edge across the many gullies. I was worried for Roger who was following without an axe. Without turning round, I asked him how he felt. 'Safe as houses,' came the reassuring and chirpy reply. My size ten footholds were huge jugs for Roger's size seven soles. The careful movements were making the mountain a much longer trip than I had expected. I began to wonder whether we would return before dark. Below the first Munro, Sgurr Fiona, the ground became easier and we were able to climb directly to the top. Again the views of the North West were outstanding. There wasn't a breath of wind but a huge cloud bank looked ominous over the Outer Isles.

The sixth and final Munro of the day stood two metres higher, just half a mile away.

We dropped to the saddle five hundred feet below on more icy banks of snow. The final climb was simple and safe. It was eight o'clock and there was about an hour of daylight left. Our return to Shenavall was now waymarked by our footprints and was much faster with the ready-made steps. In the passage of this mountain in such beautiful conditions, I was amazed not to see any evidence of recent hillgoers. On our journey through Fisherfield and its surroundings we didn't meet or see anyone. Indeed, on the first thirty Munros, I only met seven people.

We returned to the bothy just as it was going dark. Colin Donnelly (three times British Fell Running champion), had come back from a long day visiting and surveying obscure 2000 foot peaks. Colin had collected vast quantities of bog wood two days ago during the bad weather. Tonight we burnt it till midnight, cooking rice, pasta, all sorts of packets of rubbish and a large christmas pudding. I was always conscious of how many calories I was burning and I knew that I would have to make an effort to replace them. On the third helping of pudding, Roger looked at me and said, 'These mountains are OK, I think I could manage them all right, but this eating is really punishing. I don't know how you can put that down every night.' Indeed it was hard to sleep on the wooden floor with such a full stomach. I heard the weather change in the night. The plastic bag covering the gap in the roof light was being driven hard by rain and the doors downstairs were slamming to and fro. I lay thinking of the day just gone. How lucky it had been clear and windless on 'The Forge'.

Pauline's Diary, Friday 27 April

We were glad to leave the freezing (literally) windswept site of the last two nights. The beautiful wooded valley of the Dundonnell River provided a sharp contrast to the wilds of Loch a'Bhraoin. We are parked at the foot of the track to Shenavall, although we are not expecting Hugh. The nearby river, the woods to play in, dead wood for a fire and space for running around, all combine to make this an excellent camp site.

We filled up with petrol in Dundonnell and for the first time used the letter from Calor Scotland in order to acquire free gas for the van. I had to get water from the burn as the water was turned off in the filling station loos. So far we have been drinking stream water with no ill effects. We have water, gas and petrol but no bread or milk. The nearest shop is in Aultbea, nearly thirty miles away. Luckily we have stocks of crispbread and UHT milk.

This afternoon we walked up the Shenavall track. The views of An Teallach were impressive if not alarming; snow covered its rock walls. It didn't help to chat to two men coming down from the mountain. They didn't make it to the top! 'Rather dodgy,' they said. 'Definitely a case for crampons.' I don't think Hugh has his with him. Will running shoe studs do? At least he has an ice-axe. Perhaps they saw the look of apprehension on my face for they proceeded to add comments such as; 'Perhaps he is more experienced than us', 'We are really very cautious' and 'On reflection it was probably OK.' I went to bed wondering whether Hugh had made it. It would be tomorrow evening before I would find out.

Roger and I left after coffee and muesli mixed with powdered milk. I didn't want to hang around today. It was Andrew's ninth birthday and I did at least want to see him for a few hours. Colin stayed behind to tidy up and to take our sleeping bags and excess kit back to his car at Dundonnell. We opened the bothy door to low mist, wind and rain. No views today. Just the constant sight of the map, compass and ground immediately before us.

A good stalkers' track took us quickly to a northern snow slope of Ruadh Stac Mór. We didn't stop for long on top; just time enough to set the altimeter and compass before scrambling down between the red rocks of a stone chute. On clear days I checked the altimeter and found it to be accurate to within 10m. Today it confirmed the height of the *bealach* between Ruadh Stac Mór and A'Mhaighdean. It gave me confidence. As the visibility was so poor, there were no obvious features in the terrain.

We climbed to the tiny pile of stones at the top of A'Mhaighdean – Britain's most remote Munro. We were blasted by wind, sleet and rain. Our pants were soaked in seconds. We ran to the shelter of a rock and struggled to pull our overtrousers on. Rocky cliffs disappeared into the mist, giving us a hint of the drop to the lochs below, but today we could only move on and just imagine the vistas of wilderness.

The trek round Lochan Fada was long and arduous. There were few deer trods in the peaty ground and tangled undergrowth. I was tiring rapidly and for the first time I didn't relish the idea of going up a mountain. Without returning tomorrow, there was no choice; we had to climb Slioch. On the lower slopes my nose bled and I began to feel dizzy. We stopped to rest and I soaked the back of my neck and face with bog water. I began to wonder whether the long days were wearing me down and these were the first signs of exhaustion.

I dragged myself up through crags, chewing glucose tablets to keep me going. We rounded the high horseshoe passing two tops on the way to the summit. I felt a sense of relief that it would now be mainly downhill to the van on a route which I had followed two years ago. This was the first mountain of the trip that I had been on before.

I had put the maps away and taken a vague bearing. We descended onto a steepening pinnacle of rock and looked down into a great void in the mist. We could hear the sound of water a long way below. This was definitely not the descent route. We retraced our steps and took more care on the second try. I wondered about the value of reconnaissance. There is no substitute for concentration and the map.

This time we found the path which took us to Loch Maree. We seemed to go down forever. I must have glanced at the altimeter through habit when we reached Kinlochewe River. I told Roger that it read zero. 'Does that mean energy levels?' he replied. I knew how he felt.

Back in the van, it was party time. The tables were taken over by toys and the walls decorated with cards. After a trip like this, the van was always a haven. It was our normal life; just on the move. Pauline kept a remarkable sanity in the claustrophobic conditions. With hot water, face cloth and soap, I removed the two days of sweat and dirt. Dressed again I reservedly made the first trip to a pub. I hadn't come far in terms of the whole trip but it felt like a milestone on the way. The temptation of Kinlochewe was too great. Roger and Colin were still in their five day old bothy kit, with black hands from sooty fires and brown clothes from peaty hags. I don't know why they didn't smell. They got a lot of funny looks from the bar. I enjoyed the three pints but couldn't help wondering whether my weakness was the beginning of the end.

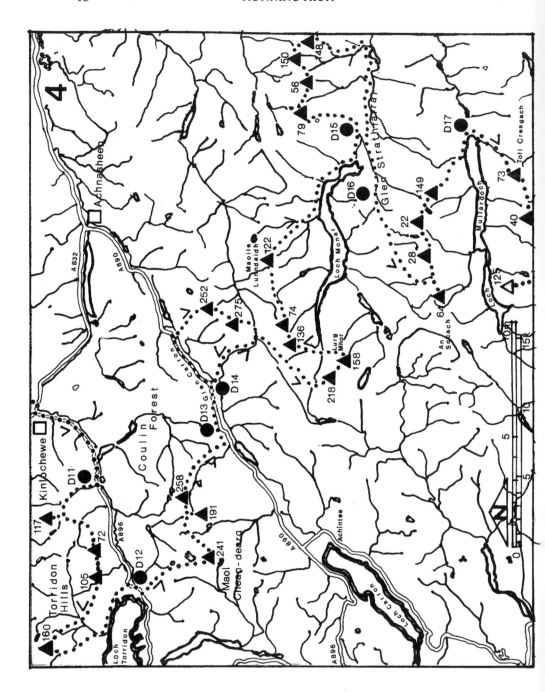

Chapter 6 'KEEP GOING, HUGH!'

April 29 – May 4

The isolated hill of Fionn Bheinn was well placed to give me an easy day after the previous excursions of twelve and ten hours. It would be unwise to keep pushing the body day after day. After all, this was not a race. The intention was simply to attain the target: Snowdon via the mountains of Britain. Back at home, today's four hour run would have been considered a long Sunday training stint, but after ten days acclimatisation to the scale of the Highlands any trip under six hours seemed short.

A track led us most of the way towards the north side of the lonely mountain. We passed many derelict buildings near the Heights of Kinlochewe. Colin and Roger couldn't pass a ruin by without making a quick survey. 'That one would be good if it had a roof,' said Roger, who made notes of potential bothies on his map. This was

4   TORRIDON TO STRATHFARRAR

Munro Number	Munro	Running Order
117	Beinn Eighe-Ruadh-stac Mór	31
72	Liathach-Spidean a'Choire Leith	32
105	Liathach-Mullach an Rathain	33
160	Beinn Alligin-Sgurr Mhór	34
241	Maol Chean-dearg	35
191	Sgorr Ruadh	36
258	Beinn Liath Mhór	37
252	Móruisg	38
275	Sgurr nan Ceannaichean	39
218	Bidein a'Choire Sheasgaich	40
158	Lurg Mhór	41
136	Sgurr Choinnich	42
74	Sgurr a'Chaorachain	43
122	Maoile Lunndaidh	44
79	Sgurr Fhuar-thuill	45
56	Sgurr a'Choire Ghlais	46
150	Carn nan Gobhar (Strathfarrar)	47
148	Sgurr na Ruaidhe	48
64	An Socach	49
28	An Riabhachan	50
22	Sgurr na Lapaich	51
149	Carn nan Gobhar (Sgurr na Lapaich group)	52
73	Toll Creagach	53
40	Tom a'Chòinich	54

already covered with a variety of coloured stars showing Munros, Munro Tops, Corbetts (hills of 2500 feet) and 2000 footers. It was easy to talk on the gently graded track. My impression of Colin was not of a hard-headed fell running champion, but of a man who loves being in wild mountains.

The only obstacle to the day's route was a pipeline running from Loch Fannich. In the middle of all the tussocks it was strange to be clambering over a large metal cylinder.

We climbed onto the summit of Fionn Bheinn. It was rounded and grassy and more like one of my local hills, the Howgills, than the recent mountains. We returned the same way to Kinlochewe. By mid afternoon, I was resting and thinking about tomorrow and the days to come.

My thoughts were now on how I could make up the lost day, and reach Mullardoch and Skye on the dates which I had given to friends. I had allowed two days for the Torridon mountains but after today's easy outing I felt ready to try them in one.

In the early evening I ran the five miles of empty road from Kinlochewe to the base of Beinn Eighe. The light in the sky stayed till late and there was a calmness in the warmer air. Whilst admiring the changing light on the distant rocks, we heard the drumming sound of a snipe diving from a height.

Pauline's Diary, Sunday 29 April

Hugh's out-and-back excursion up Fionn Bheinn gave the family a fairly free day today, as the van didn't need to move on to a new support position. We drove a mile up the road and set out on the Beinn Eighe Mountain Trail, a marked path on the slopes of the massif. This four mile trail, climbing to 550 m was an ambitious little project for the children, especially Amy. The literature suggested allowing three to four hours for the walk. I optimistically hoped that we could better this, otherwise Hugh would return to the campsite to find his home gone! Our route led upwards through one of the last remnants of the 'Great Wood of Caledon', to the rugged and rocky landscape of sparkling quartzite above the tree line. The rougher the route, the more the children enjoyed themselves, especially when we had to scramble up the steep sections. Here were mountaineers in the making.

We had a marvellous time noting the variety in the geology, plant life and climate. Here the children were learning in the real world. No need to sit down with the school books today. Amy is rapidly becoming a geological expert. Picking up a colourful rock she informed me:

'The shiny bit there is mica and the white bits are quartz and the pink bits . . . what are the pink bits, Mummy?'

'Feldspar,' I replied.

'Oh of course, feldspar,' she answered.

My enjoyment was tainted by the knowledge that Hugh would probably reach the campsite before us. 'Never mind,' I thought, 'Colin and Roger can always provide a cup of tea and cakes.' We arrived back to find a fuming Hugh lying on the grass in the hot sun, having waited for us for three hours. Colin and Roger had gone off to do their own thing. 'You knew that we were only a mile up the road,' I said. 'Surely if you can run the 'Mountains of Britain' you can make it just a mile up the road to reach the van?' Apparently not; not one ounce of energy was to be wasted. Just for once we had wanted to do a good long hike. So often we are short of time, or the terrain isn't suitable or the weather isn't right.

Monday 30 April

A beautiful warm sunny morning. Can't say the same for the family. Hugh is still sore about yesterday's mess-up and I am touchy about it, because I know that it was my fault really. I feel as though I haven't been doing my job properly. Hugh is also worried about his foot which is aching a little. Something happened to it during the last strides of last night's road run. The children are cross and argumentative; not enough sleep I expect. Paul arrived last night and is the only person worth talking to around here. I just hope that today's round of the Torridonian peaks goes well for Hugh; he should then be in a better mood. Sometimes I feel that I am battered from all sides.

Every day brought new mountains. Every week brought a change in company. The stimulation of both combined to keep me going. Colin and Roger had disappeared to a bothy in the depths of the Coulin Forest. I wouldn't see Colin again, as his nurse's training in North Wales didn't allow much time off. Roger's lifestyle gives him plenty of time to enjoy the mountains. His enterprise – selling satellite T.V. dishes around Fort William – is not demanding (none sold to date!). Roger would return.

Paul Tuson arrived for the second of many visits. As a self-employed joiner, Paul can be flexible about time off. However there are always customers waiting, and time off is time without pay. Paul's interest and commitment to the run was sparked years previously whilst on a training run in the Howgills. He had talked of today's Torridonian mountains as if they were great rocky prehistoric monsters reaching into the sky. This was a section that he didn't want to miss.

There were also new friends made on the mountain. Martin Moran had been introduced to me by Richard Crane. Martin had climbed all the Munros in one winter. Five years previously, he had spent the winter with his wife, Joy, living, like us, out of a motor caravan. They raised tens of thousands of pounds for Intermediate Technology. Since then, they have established a climbing school in the Northern Highlands. Today he took the navigation out of my hands. For the first time I was guided through the mountains.

Like Martin, I had chosen to test my skills on the Munros, but our style was essentially different. Martin, as an ice and rock climber, had chosen to face the dark evenings and rougher weather of the winter months. The prospect of confronting the mountains clothed in ice and snow excited him and was an essential element to his challenge. His target was not feasible without the use of transport between the peaks. I, as a fell runner, had chosen the optimum time of year in order to complete the journey entirely on foot. In terms of time taken to complete the round of the Munros, our journeys were not comparable. Discussing our similar but different nomadic ventures, we each came to the conclusion that the task of the other was the harder. Whilst I admired Martin's ability to cope with camping in the glens in the dark and cold months of the year, Martin considered that living in a van with three youngsters was a challenge in itself.

We climbed rapidly into the mist and onto the ridge of Beinn Eighe. It is hard to understand why such a massive mountain, with so many peaks has just one Munro summit. Unfortunately, today, we could not admire the peaks and *coires* (Gaelic for 'corrie' or glacial bowl). My footsteps followed Martin's along the stony spine to Ruadh-stac Mór, the named Munro summit. Behind me was Paul, carrying the sack with clothes, camera and sandwiches. The three of us moved quickly together in the cool clouds. We ran and scrambled down through cliffs and crags to the burn separating Beinn Eighe from Liathach, the next mountain. Most of our routes today were direct. The line up Liathach seemed impossible at first sight; almost vertical! We pulled our way up on rocks into the clouds again. Unlike Beinn Eighe, this mountain contains two Munros, all in the space of just over a mile. Between them lies an airy ridge of pinnacles. We dodged these to the left on an equally airy footpath which hung on to the edge of the southern cliffs. The thin path twisted round crags and in and out of gullies. Martin ran as confidently as if it were a high street pavement. He slipped on a wet patch of melting snow and appeared to slide to within inches of a precipice. He bounced back and ran on immediately as if pulled by a puppet's string. Paul and I looked at each other in amazement, and gingerly crossed the dangerous spot where the track had been washed away. Martin's skill and agility in moving quickly over rough and dangerous terrain was tested a few weeks later on Skye. He completed a solo traverse of the Cuillin Ridge in a record three hours and thirty three minutes. Most mountaineers struggle to complete the ridge in daylight hours in June.

We were moving fast today. After five hours we were on our way up the final mountain: Beinn Alligin. The heavy early morning cloud was now thinning. We ascended Alligin on a steepening slope of grass and rock. At last, for the first time since An Teallach, mountains were coming into view. The sun was strong and the sky a perfect blue on our arrival at the summit cairn. There wasn't a hint of haze or cloud in the sky. The Cuillins of Skye, Ben Nevis and perhaps a hundred other Munros speckled the skyline. Martin recited their names as Paul and I stood looking in awe in all directions. An Teallach looked distant and my first mountain, Ben Hope, was out of sight. The clearing of the clouds had been like an awakening; a realisation that now, twelve days into the journey, I had travelled beyond the horizon.

We dropped south towards Loch Torridon, the temperature soaring as we arrived at Martin's car. After a fruit juice and a change to shorts and tee shirt, I set off to run the last three road miles alone. I enjoyed these solo runs at the end of the day. I felt a calmness and confidence that my body was growing used to travelling distance and climbing height. Short road runs came easily. The body didn't need pushing. It was as if I was floating towards my destination. The weather was perfect, the scenery spectacular, and now for the first time since before the Fannichs, I was on schedule. Arriving at our camp by the Torridon Youth Hostel was like arriving in a paradise.

By seven in the morning on 1 May, the air was warm. It was as if the North of Scotland had been transferred a thousand miles south. The dozen campers at Torridon must all have been thinking the same thing that morning. It was too early for the midges, there were still great streaks of snow on the mountains and yet the climate was continental. This was Scotland at its best.

After the usual inspection of maps and guides, Paul and I left for the three hills between Glen Torridon and Strath Carron. Martin had advised us of lines of good approach to these hills before his departure yesterday. A good stalking track took us into the heart of this great mountain area. Stepping stones guided us across streams and between beautiful high lochs which reflected the mountain scenery. Leaving the track, we ran across short heather and bracken onto the final steep rocky slopes of Maol Chean-dearg, today's first Munro. The huge chunks of rock below the summit provided secure and entertaining scrambling which took us right to the huge summit cairn. A small plastic bag containing raisins and a message was weighed down by a stone. '35 KEEP' was written on a cardboard packet. Being my 35th Munro, I assumed it was for

Leaving Maol Chean-dearg. (Paul Tuson)

me, and that I should keep the raisins. We shared the raisins before descending a steep snow chute leading to the Bealach na Lice. There, we picked up another track which wound its way towards the next peak, Sgorr Ruadh. On top, tucked into the cairn was another piece of cardboard; this time with the words, '36 GOING'. We ran on in the heat to Beinn Liath Mhór where a third piece of cardboard read '37 HUGH'. By coincidence, 37 was my age. We assumed the messages had been left by Colin and Roger who were bothying in the district. The words, 'KEEP GOING HUGH' were later displayed inside the van alongside the multitude of good luck cards which we had received before leaving home. It meant a lot to have encouragement. At the time, I thought the Munro tally was high, but as the weeks passed by and I went through further milestones of 100 and 200 Munros, I looked back and realised how early in the trip these peaks were.

We ran in opposite directions from the stony summit of Beinn Liath Mhór. Paul returned to Torridon to collect his car and I ran south east to Achnashellach. The heat was more debilitating once I had lost height on the scree slopes. My pale legs were now turning red and I needed to drink frequently from streams. I was glad of the shade of the forest for the last mile of track to the van. I walked the last hundred metres and collapsed in a deck chair, calling for a million cups of tea.

Pauline's Diary, Tuesday 1 May

A glorious hot day from the start. Torridon must be one of the most beautiful places on earth in the sunshine. We were into shorts and tee shirts straight away. This site is luxury with hot showers and toilets. We all have clean bodies and shining hair.

Took a long time to decamp having enjoyed bacon and eggs for breakfast. We left at 11:30, driving round Loch Torridon (a beautiful route) and cutting across the Applecross Peninsula. We found a marvellous bread shop in Loch Carron (recommended by Martin Moran). For once we enjoyed real bread – brown and not sliced. We motored a little way off route to have a picnic lunch in the grounds of the ruined castle at Stromeferry. On the way back to Loch Carron we visited a Tartan Weaving Factory – small-scale production using old-fashioned machinery. Joseph would like a MacAllister kilt for his birthday. We now have a suitable topic for our artistic studies; designing the MacSymonds tartan.

We then collected the washing from the Morans' house. It was all hanging beautifully on the line in the garden. The children soon had it all neatly stacked inside a bin liner. Finally reached our parking spot near Achnashellach Station having investigated Gerry's Hostel and decided that parking there might mean being stuck there. The drive is steep, narrow and rough! The views from here are very fine and we have all we need– a water supply, a camping spot for Paul and space for the children to run around.

Thirty-six Munros lie between the Glens of Carron and Shiel. Groups of these are linked by high ridges which make route planning and navigation straightforward. Between the chains of mountains lie deep glens and the lochs of Monar, Mullardoch and Affric. In planning the continuous route through this region, the main consideration was where to start and finish each day. This was dictated by where Pauline could take the van. A backpacker using bothies or a tent can be flexible, and would probably take a different route. You don't have to be a mathematician to realise that there are a lot of different ways of putting thirty-six things in a different order – let alone 277 Munros. Here was a challenge within a challenge – to start near Craig in Glen Carron and finish by the

Cluanie Inn in Glen Shiel, passing over thirty-six summits, without wasting energy in travelling unnecessary distance or climbing unnecessary height.

Having been burnt to a frazzle the previous day, I didn't feel ready to run through to Loch Monar and Strathfarrar today. The seven mountains would be too much, particularly with the forecast telling stories of parts of Northern Scotland being hotter than parts of the Sahara. Without camping or bothying, the only option was to spend another night in Glen Carron.

Names and numbers of mountains were now beginning to confuse me. The heat was not just wearing on my body. A three hour circuit of Moruisg and Sgurr nan Ceannaichean was ideal to give me time to eat, rest and recover and to keep out of the sunshine. After a pleasant return trip over the two easy Munros I spent the afternoon slumped in the back of the van, catching up with my diary. Paul drove back to Sedbergh, to put in a few twelve hour working days and catch up with lost time. He loved these spells in the Highlands but his mood became sombre a few hours before each departure south. He took home with him a list of my proposed grid positions and dates for the next week. These were posted by Paul's telephone, ready for friends to receive before driving north.

Yesterday's easy day helped me to get things back in perspective. Having had time to take an overview of the next week, I could now concentrate on each day. Thinking back to Ben Klibreck, Dave Richardson had told me: 'Think about the mountain you are on.' This motto now meant a lot to me and I tried to recall it each day.

For the third time I passed the level crossing at Craig. Yesterday's steps were retraced for three miles before turning south west. Martin Moran joined me for this big day on his local mountains. To the east of Martin's home in Achintee lie at least five hundred square kilometres of high mountains and lochs. No roads penetrate this wilderness and there are few signs of paths or footprints on the hills. Without tracks, the choice of route is infinite. From boulder to boulder, and from burn to burn, the feet find their own way from mountain to mountain. How long will these sweeping regions of Scotland remain unmarked by man?

Whilst climbing over Beinn Tharsuinn en route to today's first Munro – Bidein a'Choire Sheasgaich (Gaelic for 'Peak of the Corrie of the Milkless Cattle' – called 'cheesecake' for short), we passed two tiny cairns. I was amazed to see Martin stride forward and destroy them, spreading their stones randomly. I listened and understood his reasoning well. Cairns on summits are a celebration of arrival, but cairns on the sides of hills can help to form footpaths, as they tempt people to pass that way. On so many of the popular hills, tracks have grown wider and wider causing scars on the landscape and deep mud on the ground.

The summit of Lurg Mhór was a mystery. Large blocks of stone lay split in half. Two channels the depth of a trowel radiated away from the cairn in sharp straight lines. Neither of us had seen anything like it before. On later mountains, I passed overturned trig points. Is there a gang of summit vandals or is this the hand of lightning or frost?

To Sgurr Choinnich, we could either try to maintain our height and contour round, or we could go straight. The former option would involve seven kilometres of rough ground with minor ups and downs, whilst the latter route of four kilometres was really far from straight. A giant V-shape would take us two thousand feet down almost to the shore of Loch Monar before reclimbing the same height. This is a choice which often faces the hillgoer. Today we opted for the direct route before plunging downward into a maze of streams draining into the loch. This way we could dip our heads into the burns and gulp vast quantities of water. The heat at this low altitude was stifling. I hardly wore more than shorts all day; just occasionally a tee shirt to keep the sun off my back. The steep climb was arduous. I tried to keep my mind off the physical exertion by concentrating on the sounds of birds. The single whistling call of the golden plover was common. Today there was a rarer sight and sound. There, near the top, were three dotterels fluttering around and chirping. They appeared to be enjoying the rare heat more than I was.

A fine narrow ridge led us to Sgurr a'Chaorachain before we dropped rapidly on a snowfield towards a high lochan in the northern corrie. In the shadow of the hill the ice and snow had survived. Even in this heat, huge blocks of ice floated in the perfect blue water.

A cross on my map marked the point at which I had planned to meet Dave Peck again. With a mixture of luck and good planning, we met at the pre-arranged time, 2:30. Dave was accompanied by Bill Gauld – the superbly fit British over 50s fell running champion. The four of us climbed Maoile Lunndaidh together before Martin returned to his car at Craig.

Dave, Bill and I ran the opposite way – down and south-east to Loch Monar. Now below the 1000 foot contour, the sun was fierce and the backs of my legs were stinging and tingling. Not having packed a sunhat, I had a handkerchief and headband relieving my head from the sunlight. However, I was wilting and slowing. I was getting increasingly concerned about the length of the heatwave. Although I could do with clear weather on Skye, I was beginning to doubt whether I would get there if this debilitating heatwave continued. The three miles of track to the Monar Dam seemed everlasting. Every undulation and kink in the path drained another vital ounce of energy. The heat had spoilt my appetite and fuelled my thirst.

Dave and Bill left in a hurry from the roadhead at the dam. They had half an hour to drive out of the Strath before the gate at the entrance would be locked for the night. Access to Strathfarrar is generally allowed only in the daytime. We had been fortunate in being granted special permission to spend two nights in the valley. I jogged and walked the last mile of tarmac, turning more dizzy with every stride. The sight of the van was like a shimmering mirage. I fell into a deck chair thinking that I couldn't go on tomorrow. This was far worse than battling against wind and hail.

The children had energy and wanted to play. They got used to me flopping at the end of the day. What a useless Daddy! Pauline's strength and understanding were astonishing. Just at the moment when I thought she'd expect me to take over, mind the children and do the chores, she produced a bowl of fruit salad with ice cream from the fridge. The beauty of the glen was a source of inspiration and energy for her. She didn't seem to mind how floppy I was at the end of the day. It was all worthwhile if we could all stay on the move and continue to live in such idyllic surroundings.

Pauline's Diary, Thursday 3 May
This is definitely my favourite spot so far. It is so peaceful. The lower reaches of the Strath are clothed in beautiful birch woods which shimmer and sparkle in the strong sunshine, creating a magical fairyland atmosphere.

I wondered why I was so tired until Pauline commented, 'What do you expect after 24 miles and 10 000 feet?' That comforted me a little but there was nothing I could do about the heat, except to hope for clouds.

An hour after the fruit and ice cream, I wandered over to the stream for a good scrub. The water was like magic, soothing stiffness out of my limbs and putting enthusiasm back in my mind. I now had the energy to eat. The fear of burning my body weight away caused me to eat and eat for hours. By bedtime, the pain had been transferred from my legs to my now bloated stomach.

Dawn, and still no clouds in the sky. I usually enjoy heat, but running in this was hard work. Perhaps I should have a day off? Any delay now would mean driving fifteen miles to the nearest phone box and giving Paul the details of changed plans. By forecasting my route to friends I had become committed to the days ahead. It was good in that it motivated me to keep going, but it could cause me to avoid a much needed rest. How long could I keep going day after day?

However, I knew that the next two days were in my short to medium category, about 16 miles and 5500 feet of ascent per day. I hoped they would provide the chance for recovery.

Dave and Bill joined me again for a gentle jog around the Farrar Four, a rounded group of mountains to the north of the glen. High ridges linking these hills kept us in cooler air. Although still weary, I was encouraged that I felt less drained than the previous afternoon.

Pauline's Diary, Friday 4 May

After a bacon and egg breakfast, seeing Hugh off, and doing some washing in the river, most of the morning had gone. I sat down with the children at 11:30 and we discussed the previous day's visit to the whisky distillery at Ord. Andrew has an excellent grasp of the fermenting and distilling process. He wrote a good piece on it. Joseph had a strong preference for playing by the river. I can't say that I blamed him. It was too hot for studies.

After a delightful day enjoying the sun, the peace and the river, we set out at 4 pm to meet Hugh, six kilometres down the road. Hugh's journey (almost a circular route today), was to finish at the head of the road by the Power Station. Andrew enjoyed running along with Daddy on the return trip to the junction just below the campsite. Our paths then diverged – Hugh taking a shorter cross-country route and the van following the road/track culminating at the Power Station beyond the two dams of Loch Monar.

I gave the map to Andrew and devoted my mind to a safe passage along a route hardly designed for large motor caravans. In any case, Andrew strongly objects to any assistance with navigation or even interest in the map on my part. He is keen to do the job properly and on his own.

The road took us across the two dams – the second being very narrow but manageable. Beyond the dams we took a left turn along a rapidly deteriorating track. The road surface was rough and bumpy and places to turn round or pass other vehicles virtually non-existent. At the back of my mind lurked the niggling realisation that should the road become impassable, the only method of retreat would be to reverse all the way back to the dam! After negotiating several pot holes and sunken stretches of track, we came to a halt before a large puddle of unknown depth. I stopped the van and got out to investigate. Better to be safe than sorry – this vehicle is essential to the success of the venture. At this point I consulted the map and rapidly came to the conclusion that we had taken the wrong turning at the dam. 'No wonder the road was so bad,' I thought, 'We weren't even supposed to be on it!' 'You've taken us the wrong way,' I said accusingly to Andrew. 'It'll take us ages to get back – we can't turn round, and Daddy will wonder where on earth we are.' My spirits sank as I contemplated the prospect of reversing. I struggled to contain anger and anxiety. 'Never mind,' I thought as I cooled down slightly, 'It may take ages but we can do it – just take care and keep calm.' After reversing a little way we came to a sort of miniature muddy lay-by. A possible turning spot, with help from Andrew. He got out of the van to give instructions. At this moment Hugh arrived from the opposite direction. After a few minutes it became clear that we were on the right track after all. The usual welcoming sight of the big white van had been absent when Hugh reached the Power Station. After waiting for nearly half an hour he had come looking for us, presuming that we had got stuck or gone the wrong way. Andrew, our navigator had done his job well, and I had read the map wrongly. I apologised profusely.

For the first time we had failed to reach a rendezvous point. How many times will we encounter this problem again?

Chapter 7   RUNNING BLIND
May 5 – 9

The heavy snows of mid-April had left great white slopes on the northern faces of the chains of hills that run east-west. Each new group of mountains appeared like a barrier from my northern vantage point.

In the boiling heat of Strathfarrar, Sgurr na Lapaich looked over a mile high. How else could it still hold so much snow? It reminded me of a small Icelandic ice cap, clinging to its snow through all seasons. It was a great relief that the weather had cracked in the night. The snow cap of Lapaich had vanished in heavy cloud. The weather had returned to normal for what is expected of Scotland. My energy had returned with it. The suddenness of the previous heat had left me no time to acclimatise and I was wilting by the hour. I longed for clouds to shield me from the sun, which was reducing me to an ember.

I gave Mark Rigby lots of clothes to put in his sack, before running west under the now obscured northern face of the Lapaich group of four. Mark was the fittest runner to join me on my travels. Like many, he enjoyed the opportunity for long runs on the wild mountains. He took his own tally of Munros to over 200 today. I was worried that Mark's fitness might force me to run faster than I should, but he was handicapped well by the weight of his sack, and he understood the pacer's job well.

Besides being one of the most successful fell runners in Britain, Mark has been a key figure in supporting other runners in recent years. Every summer, an attempt is made to increase the number of Munros climbed in twenty-four hours. Although records are assigned to the name of one person, it is like reaching the moon or the summit of Everest: there are lots of people helping on the way. Mark's experience and pace-setting had gone a long way towards the success of Jon Broxap's 1988 record Munro round – Jon had completed a circuit of 28 Munros in less than a day. Whilst traversing these peaks in the next few days, conversation with friends often referred in admiration to Jon's astonishing record. There was little doubt in our minds that the success of such ventures was as much in the planning and mental approach as in the pure physical exertion.

Thoughts and conversations combined to give a timeless passage between the mountains. I was frequently unaware of the difference between ten minutes and two hours. A five hour outing such as today's could seem short or long. In fighting heat or hail, time would be long. In the happy conditions of easy weather and good friends, time could be irrelevant but for the short darkness at the end of the day.

Mark and I ran on beyond the end of the glen and into the mists of An Socach. Closing on the summit we heard conversation. 'Think about the mountain you are on.'

There, sitting by the trig point, were Dave Richardson, Ian Rooke and Dave Bayliss. I had expected a party, being a bank holiday weekend, but what a place to meet! The friends from Kendal had guessed my timing from Paul's information. Astonishingly, they had only waited for ten minutes.

We doubled back and ran over the three other mountains in this high Lapaich chain before dropping down to Mullardoch in worsening weather.

The higher reaches of so many beautiful Scottish glens are scarred by the concrete and metal structures associated with hydro-electricity. The grass under the loch dam provided an excellent camp, but for the threat of the huge quantity of water held back by this monstrosity. A crane was working on the high ramparts above us and the now stormy weather was whipping the loch waters over the edge.

Pauline's Diary, Saturday 5 May

It's 6:45 and we are sitting in the van at Mullardoch in teeming rain. I feel dreadful – just as if I am getting flu. Who will drive the van if I am ill? I haven't said anything to Hugh – he is in such good spirits tonight – the liveliest he has been in the evenings for ages. Tomorrow is a mega day. One of the biggest, taking in ten Munros.

Bev Holt is here; putting off the evil moment when he will have to put his tent up. He arrived laden with three sunhats (explains the weather), and lots of lovely cakes baked by Shirley, his wife. A huge lemon cake disappeared in one gollop. Saturday night, and this is definitely the place to be. There is quite a party here (explains why the cake vanished). We are now struggling to pack away vast food stores brought by Eddie Dealtry and his wife Jen. How on earth did they get it all in their car?

The two previous days had helped me to regenerate interest and energy. Shorter days also gave me the chance to catch up with my diary. I was glad that friends had suggested I use a tape recorder. Even when I was exhausted I could usually lie in bed and put some of the day's feelings onto tape. Before leaving Mullardoch, this was the message:

Hugh's Tape, Sunday 6 May

'Each day is a challenge in itself. I set out hoping to do something, not knowing whether I am going to achieve it. Just like the whole trip. I've set out from Ben Hope but I don't know whether I'll get to Snowdon. Today is typical of that. The weather is bad and the target is to reach Dorusduain, hopefully over nine or ten Munros. Am I going to manage 1 . . . 2 . . . 3 . . . 4 . . . Munros today or what?'

Eddie Dealtry, Dave Richardson and I left Mullardoch in wild, wet and windy conditions. Our run was slowed to a walk as we fought our way through heather and tangled shrubs. Climbing higher onto the slopes of Toll Creagach, Dave began to be left behind. We were travelling too slowly to keep warm in the now-driving snow and wind. It was obvious that there was something wrong with Dave, and that if we maintained this pace we stood little chance of reaching Dorusduain today.

Dave had pains in his stomach, was weak and was certainly not up to a big mountain day. Between our first two peaks of Toll Creagach and Tom a'Chòinich, he left us for Glen Affric. I was unhappy that he was going alone, but at least he would soon be in the relative safety of the glen.

Eddie led on in deepening snow. The high ridges kept us in the clouds and only

Before departure from Mullardoch – from left Eddie Dealtry, Dave Richardson, Dr Bev Holt, Dave Bayliss, Ian Rooke, Mark Rigby. (H.S.)

occasionally did we get any hint of seeing into the distance. A lone runner passed us on the east ridge of Carn Eighe. We remembered that it was the day of the Glen Affric race, organised by Dave Peck. The sight of scantily clad runners racing by was bizarre in such conditions. I wondered about the sense of my own sport. How long would a runner in racing kit and few spare clothes survive if brought to a halt by an accident? Eddie and I jogged on, dressed to the eyeballs in thermals and goretex.

Beinn Fhionnlaidh was out of the way, two miles north towards the loch. This was just an effort without the reward of views. I hadn't decided to do the Munros for the sake of doing the Munros, but today I was doing just that. It was hard to look forward and look up: no scenery, just a face full of snow.

We retraced our steps towards the high Màm Sodhail and ran west to another An Socach. Dropping through crags, we curved north again to another outlying Munro – Mullach na Dheiragain. As if to wake me from my boredom, the dark, snow-heavy sky suddenly turned electric. I wondered at first whether it was just me. Eddie also heard the sparking. The wind had dropped, and the snow was falling vertically. There was a permanent buzzing, like the sound under pylons in a heavy drizzle. Unlike passing under cables, this unnerving noise didn't go away. There were no visible sparks and nothing glowed. There was no thunder or lightning, just the mysterious sound. It was like having a million insects clicking round the head. For most of the two miles to Sgurr nan Ceathreamhnan, the highly charged atmosphere put adrenalin into my weakening limbs.

The ridges of the Sgurr were now deep in snow. A brief clearing in the sky revealed the white slopes of Ben Attow. I had hoped to climb it today but there wasn't enough daylight, let alone energy. The climb of A'Ghlas-bheinn was hard enough. I had finished the food for the day:

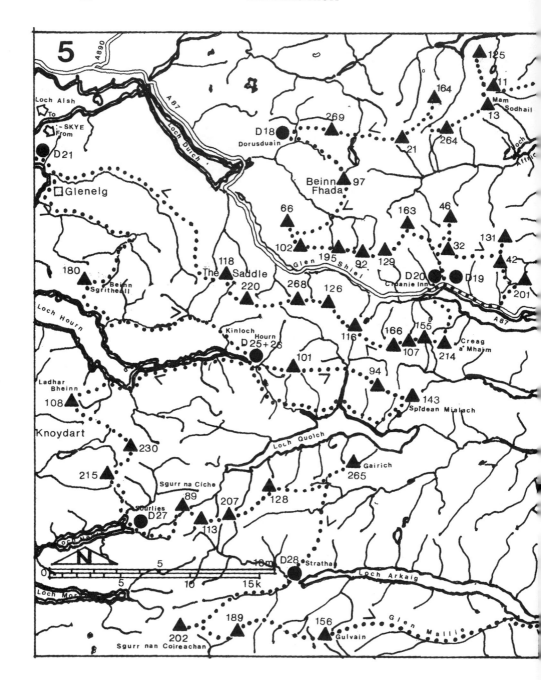

| Raisins | 500g | Nuts | 250g | Chocolate bars | 5 |
| Dates | 500g | Apricots | 250g | Cluster/Crunchy bars | 3 |

and was now surviving the ascent on glucose. Eddie waited at the northern *bealach* while I visited my second and final lone Munro.

5 AFFRIC TO ARKAIG

Munro Number	Munro	Running Order
11	Carn Eighe	55
125	Beinn Fhionnlaidh	56
13	Màm Sodhail	57
264	An Socach	58
164	Mullach na Dheiragain	59
21	Sgurr nan Ceathreamhnan	60
269	A'Ghlas-bheinn	61
97	Beinn Fhada (Ben Attow)	62
66	Sgurr Fhuaran	63
102	Sgurr na Ciste Duibhe	64
195	Saileag	65
92	Sgurr a'Bhealaich Dheirg	66
129	Aonach Meadhoin	67
163	Ciste Dhubh	68
46	Mullach Fraoch-choire	69
32	A'Chràlaig	70
131	Sail Chaorainn	71
42	Sgurr nan Conbhairean	72
201	Carn Ghluasaid	73
214	Creag a'Mhàim	74
155	Druim Shionnach	75
107	Aonach air Chrith	76
166	Maol Chinn-dearg	77
116	Sgurr an Doire Leathain	78
126	Sgurr an Lochain	79
268	Creag nan Damh	80
220	Sgurr na Sgine (Saddle)	81
118	The Saddle	82

for peaks between The Saddle and Beinn Sgritheall see Map 6 (Skye)

180	Beinn Sgritheall	95
101	Sgurr a'Mhaoraich	96
94	Gleouraich	97
143	Spidean Mialach	98
108	Ladhar Bheinn	99
230	Luinne Bheinn	100
215	Meall Buidhe	101
89	Sgurr na Ciche	102
113	Garbh Chioch Mhór	103
207	Sgurr nan Coireachan (Glen Dessary)	104
128	Sgurr Mór	105
265	Gairich	106
202	Sgurr nan Coireachan	107
189	Sgurr Thuilm	108
156	Gaor Bheinn or Gulvain	109

A score of nine on a bad day. I was happy and growing in confidence. 'Maybe this game is possible,' I thought.

I had a needle in my arm, just minutes after our arrival in Dorusduain. Bev was extracting blood for more metabolic tests. I didn't faint last time, but this just tipped me too far at the end of the day. The forests disappeared as I passed out and fell backwards.

Pauline

As soon as the needle struck, Hugh collapsed in a heap on the car bonnet behind. 'I'm only half there,' he repeatedly mumbled. He was right. The other half eventually returned and Hugh slowly got himself together again in the van.

When I came round, Bev proceeded to tell me that I really needed to take rest days. I was reluctant to rest right now, as I wanted to push on to Skye. There, I might be forced to rest, in waiting for conditions for The Ridge. I didn't want to attempt the most dangerous and dramatic part of the run in rain or poor visibility. I'd rather be forced to wait there, than rest now and miss good weather later. I promised a day off, if not before The Ridge, then after.

Bev drove home to Kendal, taking Dave, who had walked twenty-five miles on a day when he wasn't fit for one.

These long days were punishing to the end. Finding the time to eat pasta and puddings was hard, when all I wanted to do was sleep.

I was concerned that Bev would return next week with bad news about the quality of my blood. At least the weight measurements had shown an increase. The effort of eating was working. I wasn't wasting away – or at least not yet.

Most mornings we were woken up by Joseph and Amy. They loved to jump into bed with us for their morning cuddles. I would reach for the kettle whilst trying to stay horizontal. Before standing up, I would feel stiffness in my legs and wonder how they would cope today.

I had hoped to climb Ben Attow yesterday. I preferred to follow a long day with a shorter one. Instead I was now committed to two consecutive long days.

From our near sea-level position, I had to climb most of the 3385 feet of Ben Attow, before losing it all again in crossing the deep valley of the River Croe. It was another dark day. I was getting used to feeling my way through the mountains, an experience which I recorded on tape.

Hugh's Tape, Monday 7 May

'Seeing only 50 metres at a time, I count paces through the distance whilst reading ridges, contours and crags from the map. The eyes scan from the ground in front of me to the map, to the compass, and back to the ground in front of me. Occasionally, a hole in the mist exposes crags, maybe a mile away. It is confusing. Suddenly I wonder whether I am in the right place. I feel like a blind person suddenly gaining sight – the extra vision confusing the braille.'

Dave Bayliss and Ian Rooke had been very talkative on Ben Attow. It was comforting to hear their voices. They relieved the anxiety and pressure of these long, continuous hard days.

Gradually the day's eleven and a half thousand feet of climbing reduced the chatter.

The sound of voices was replaced by rain and wind battering against my hood. East of Sgurr Fhuaran, paths took us up and down like a big dipper. Easy access to these dense mountains has made them popular and today, despite the rotten conditions, I met several people. We had arranged to meet Eddie in the *bealach* west of Saileag. He lay there shivering in his bivvy bag. His company replaced Dave and Ian's. They dropped down to Glen Shiel and returned home, not to be seen again until Mull.

Eddie and I strode on over more snow-topped peaks of Kintail. Again, I felt that I was just going through the motions. Not being able to enjoy the beauty of these mountains, I was merely pushing myself towards Skye and hoping for better weather.

A Mars bar and a letter from Paul Tuson lay on top of today's final peak – Ciste Dhubh. The chocolate told a story of how the weather had changed. Having lost shape and turned whitish, it appeared to have been melted and frozen. Today, it came close to destroying my teeth as I chewed the ice-hard block.

A huge snow slope aided a rapid descent towards the Cluanie Inn. This was a miserable place to park. The rain heaved down on the roof, giving a sound like deep-frying chips. The forecast had been for showers but rain had been continuous all day.

The fourth consecutive day of heavy rain. Vast quantities of transpaseal were being used every day to keep the maps dry. How long could I keep going without the inspiration of seeing the mountains? I retraced yesterday's steps towards Ciste Dhubh before turning east for the five mountains north of Loch Cluanie. These strange-sounding Munros form the 'Cluanie Horseshoe'. They provided a welcome day of just six hours.

Eddie felt a responsibility to help me find my way round these mountains. Whilst standing at the Bealach Choire Chait, he pointed at a *bealach* on the map and proceeded to talk me through where he thought we ought to go. Whilst frequently wiping his snow-covered spectacles, he would move a finger along the map to what he thought was the next peak. He did this several times and was rarely pointing at the right part of the map. It didn't seem to matter, as Eddie's knowledge of the area was much better than his vision through his glasses.

During stops for navigation, my feet became cold today. The goretex socks which had been keeping my feet warm and dry in the snow, were beginning to leak after three weeks of constant use. I was relieved to leave the snow and hail of the five summits and to be able to return to the van by Loch Cluanie.

Pauline had moved three miles east of the Cluanie Inn to a rendezvous point under Carn Ghluasaid – today's last Munro. After hot soup and a change of clothes and shoes, I set off on the short road run. The fast traffic sprayed me and my nose bled again. I stopped several times to wash my face in puddles. In torrential rain, I returned for our second night parked by the Cluanie Inn.

One good thing about being close to some form of civilisation was the phone box. I contacted a boatman in Glenelg and provisionally arranged to borrow his boat and row to Skye, at midday in two days time.

I was weak and worried about the nose bleed. However, I was now looking forward to a change of scene. I recorded my feelings on tape.

Hugh's Tape, Tuesday 8 May
'The last four days have not excited me. I feel that I am just waiting for Skye, and its

dramatic Cuillin Mountains. Tomorrow I am moving west instead of permanently changing direction and picking off hills. The anticipation fuels me with an energy which perhaps my body hasn't got.'

The east face of Sgurr na Sgine. (H.S.)

The shorter day allowed me to rest and go to bed early. I hoped that there was sufficient physical energy for the mental drive to be of any use.

It had rained heavily for most of our time in Glen Shiel. It was a novelty to leave the Glen without being dressed in waterproofs. Today looked more hopeful with some hints of breaks in the clouds.

Seven peaks of over 3000 feet join together to make the Cluanie Ridge, which forms the southern barrier to Glen Shiel. The distance from first peak to last is hardly ten miles, and the undulations never dip lower than 2000 feet.

Again, I ran into the clouds. Being a popular range of hills, there is a path running most of the length of the ridge. In poor visibility, tracks can be misleading, so the map was still used to confirm the route.

Whilst running up the third and highest peak – Aonach air Chrith – the clouds swept eastward, suddenly releasing the claustrophobia of darkness. For twenty-seven consecutive mountains I had been running blind. Now, for the first time in five days, I could actually see the Highlands. To the north lay the mountains of yesterday and Kintail. To the west were Beinn Sgritheall, Ladhar Bheinn and Sgurr na Ciche – great mountains which I could look forward to, after Skye.

Refreshed and excited by the clearing in the sky, I ran on beyond the end of the ridge. Old iron fence posts led over a Sgurr below the magic 3000 foot mark. Some of the rusty posts had been bent over horizontal! I wondered how. Surely even the winds of the Highlands couldn't manage that? Picking my way carefully through loose rocks, I closed on the bold shapely Munro of Sgurr na Sgine (peak of the knife).

Each additional peak of today's nine, was a step nearer Skye. The magnetism of the island seemed to fuel me with energy. For a change, I never felt weak today. It didn't matter that the summit of the Saddle was lost in clouds and rain. I was now nearly there.

A steep thousand foot climb took me through snow and rocks to the summit cairn marked as 1010 metres on the map. There I found some fruit before setting off along the Saddle's summit crest. The second top lay just over 100 metres west. Also marked at 1010 metres one could be forgiven for visiting the wrong Munro summit. No mistakes today. A felt pen message written onto thick cardboard was weighed down by a stone on top of the cylindrical trig point.

> HUGH
> Don't forget the other
> summit – it's got the same
> spot height and buried
> treasure in the cairn.
> GOOD LUCK!

The anonymous message left me wondering who had traced me to this spot. Perhaps Paul could tell me later. By October, the message had been traced to Martin Moran.

A rocky ridge took me west and then north over lower peaks and bumps. The ground was awkward and rough through to the *bealach* by Loch Coire nan Crogachan. From there I followed a path west, and down into the forest by Glen More.

Pauline

The family atmosphere deteriorated with the weather. When the sun was shining, our cramped living space was irrelevant. The world was our garden and the children used up surplus energy running, climbing and exploring. In the open landscape of the Highlands, children can be so free. When the rain came we were all cooped up together.

A short spell of rain could be pleasant. We were cosy and dry in our luxury mini home, listening to the rain drops drumming on the roof. Andrew, Joseph and Amy spent hours being creative with Lego in their miniature bedroom above the cab – well out of the way of the constant cooking and tea-making operations. Much more school work was done on gloomy days. As we were all kitted out with waterproofs and stout boots we could venture out to explore the swollen rivers and muddy puddles.

However, after five days of continuous rain we were all beginning to suffer. It was becoming increasingly difficult to occupy the children. Lego had lost its appeal. Frantic arguments developed over who was entitled to the last pair of wheels, and tiny pieces would come raining down into the bolognese sauce cooking on the stove. Tempers became too frayed for school work. My imagination was nearing its limit – we had looked at everything we could think of under the microscope. The evenings were the most fraught. Everything seemed to happen at once. Hugh would arrive with his pacers, all sodden and wanting tea and cakes. The van would be full of dripping gear. The children, in their usual noisy fashion, would be eating tea/writing diaries/getting ready for bed. They had that special gift common in the very young, of making adult conversation impossible.

It was a relief to leave the Cluanie Inn, indelibly associated in my mind with constant drizzle. We treated ourselves to fish and chips in Shiel Bridge before heading over the Ratagan, the high road to Glenelg.

The road alternated between the beautifully surfaced and graded improved version and the narrow, rutted and steep old version. We took most of it in first gear and the van temperature rose to over 90 degrees centigrade for the first time. We stopped half way up to admire the view and cool down. I always enjoyed these journeys – the more minor the road, the more enjoyable was the drive. Ensuring safe passage for the vehicle over these difficult routes was an adventure for us.

On the descent we filled our three five-gallon water-bottles from a mini waterfall forming a perfect fast-flowing tap. In Glenelg the village shop supplied our fresh food needs and a new bottle of gas.

After an afternoon of fun on the beach we met Hugh at Moyle. I noticed a sudden change in Hugh. His weariness was on the wane. I noted in my diary,

'Hugh seems to have boundless energy – he's got three thousand footer fever! It seems that he can't wait to cross to Skye and test his skill on the Cuillin Ridge. Does this impatience all stem from a desire to get that particularly tricky bit of the route behind him?'

I was relieved to see that Pauline had managed to get the van over the arduous Ratagan Pass. After 23 miles and nine thousand feet of climbing, I was ready to rest and eat.

Our meeting point was at the road end near Moyle, and by good fortune, there was a telephone box within a mile. Pauline ran off to confirm arrangements with the boatman, Dave Smith, while I put the children to bed. I was looking forward to an easy morning – just six miles of road to the jetty by midday, and then perhaps, a few miles towards Broadford on Skye in the afternoon.

Pauline returned running fast and looking anxious. Any idea of a lie-in was shattered. Since my earlier phone call from the Cluanie Inn, Dave Smith had checked his tide timetable. The only time we could cross was 6:45 in the morning. For a few minutes, I looked for alternatives. It was now 9:30 and getting dark. Pauline had told Dave to expect me at 6:30 unless he heard otherwise. Gradually, I came to the conclusion that there was no choice. I had to run to the jetty tonight.

Six miles of road in darkness that was becoming darker. Pauline had set off for the jetty, and I had forgotten my head torch. I was running blind again. There were no cats eyes, white lines or street lights. I just hoped that the road didn't cross any cattle grids. I sensed the line of the road from different shades of black.

I knew to turn right by the cemetery. It was next to the cottage we had rented three years ago. I couldn't have done this without some familiarity. Steep cliffs reflected the sound of water. Lighthouses reflected their beams in the sea. Occasionally, I walked for fear of stepping off the road. I passed shapes that slowly moved out of my way. The sound and smell of the sea came closer. I felt my way round a sharp bend and there, below me, was a dark image of the jetty. The van was parked just yards from the sea. My first mainland stint was over, and an hour before midnight, I had finished for the day.

Chapter 8 THE DREAM OF SKYE

May 10 – 12

The alarm woke us at 5:45. Amy peeped through the curtains in disbelief. 'I didn't know that we slept here. It's nice isn't it?' Amy had slept through last night's movements. Looking across to Skye, we could see the narrow stretch of water was calm but for a section in the middle of the straights, which was like a fast-moving river.

Soon after 6:30, we heard the slow chugging of an outboard motor. A seventeen foot boat with two men and a dog rounded the corner and turned towards the concrete ramp. Dave Smith and Chris, the landlord of the Glenelg Inn, stepped off and introduced themselves.

Dave pointed to the fast stretch of water and said that it would slow in the next half hour. During slack tide it would apparently be safe to row across, although Dave admitted that he had never done it.

Before leaving, I waited for the forecast at 6:55. It sounded good for two days but less promising for Saturday – the day I had planned for The Ridge.

The engine was pulled out of the water and two huge oars placed in their locks. I kissed the family goodbye and jumped into the boat with Dave, Chris and the dog. My back now faced another jetty, 500 metres away at Kylerhea, on Skye. I followed Dave's instructions, pointing ourselves into the now – slow tidal flow. Half a dozen seals bobbed their heads up, the dog barked and the seals slipped back into the sea. This happened several times, the dog and seals being as curious as each other.

There was a tranquillity in the sea and calm in the air. Despite my aching arms and

6 SKYE

Munro Number	Munro	Running Order
259	Sgurr nan Eag	83
222	Sgurr Dubh Mór	84
147	Sgurr Alasdair	85
211	Sgurr Mhic Choinnich	86
159	Inaccessible Pinnacle of Sgurr Dearg	87
186	Sgurr na Banachdich-North Peak	88
181	Sgurr a'Ghreadaidh	89
266	Sgurr a'Mhadaidh-South West Peak	90
198	Bruach na Frithe	91
236	Am Basteir	92
187	Sgurr nan Gillean	93
251	Blà Bheinn (Blaven)	94

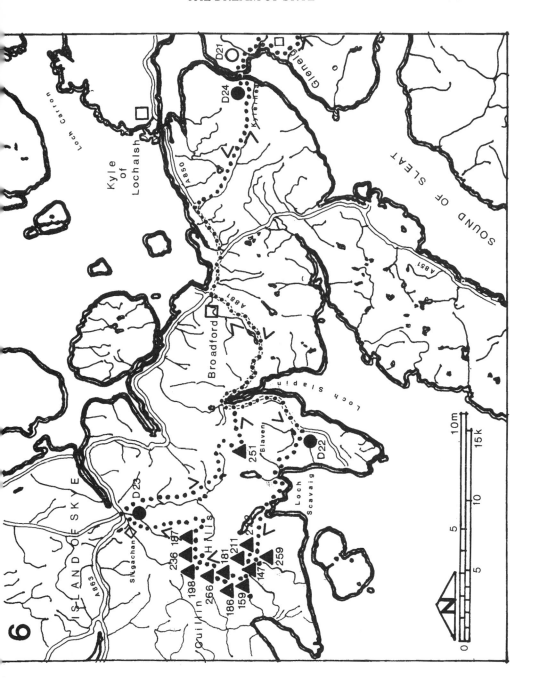

blistering fingers, this was another touch of paradise. I had been anxious about this arrangement with people I didn't know – but now things seemed to be falling into place. All I wanted now was dry weather for The Ridge. Before leaving Dave at Kylerhea, I asked him to expect a call for the return trip in three, four, or five days time. I didn't want to commit myself to a fixed length of time for completing the mountains of Skye.

Pauline

The Glenelg Ferry once linked Skye to the mainland. In this perfectly peaceful setting, the concrete ramp was the only evidence of the activity of summers past. Although only 500 metres of smooth but racing sea now separated us from Hugh, we had to travel 30 miles to the Kyle of Lochalsh in order to cross with the van. We watched the boat glide silently across the narrows, as we hurriedly crunched our muesli. There was no time to linger. It was highly likely that Hugh would reach Broadford, our next rendezvous point, before us. We arranged to meet in 'the most obvious parking spot'.

On the entire journey from the first of the Scottish Munros, Ben Hope, to the last, Ben Lomond, there were only three days without mountains. Today was the second, and it gave me a day of road running, which seemed easy, after three weeks' running on rough terrain. I seemed to float along at seven miles per hour without expending any energy. There was no hurry to run the twelve miles to the next meeting point at Broadford.

I was glad that I wasn't lying in bed as originally planned. The early morning was beautiful. Just following the road and being on my own, I had time to think about the days to come. I wondered whether I could make use of this good weather, and traverse the Cuillins before poor weather returned. I had always thought of climbing the single mountain of Blà Bheinn before the Cuillins. This would have given me a welcome short day before the traverse of Britain's most arduous and dangerous ridge. I now began to think about reversing the order, and traversing the Cuillin Ridge while the weather was good.

Friends from Kendal were joining me for the twelve Munros of Skye. I knew that they were on their way, but I also knew that they weren't expecting me to tackle The Ridge until at least Saturday. Paul had been told that I had landed on the island, but I didn't know whether Mike Walford and Phil Clark had got the message. I ran on towards Broadford, just hoping that we would meet today.

It took me an hour to run from Kylerhea to the main Broadford road. Just four cars passed by on the open single-track road. The loneliness and isolation was emphasised by the calls of cuckoos and lapwings. Things were different on the main road. No longer could I run down the centre. I was now hugging the kerb, avoiding fast cars and buses. However, the scenery made up for the disturbance, and I ran safely on to Broadford to meet Pauline at the far end of the bay. It felt very satisfying to have come so far and be halfway to Skye's mountains – all before breakfast!

The van was parked in a prominent position overlooking the sea and the island of Pabay. The children played happily with rocks, a roll of electricity cable and some horizontal lamp posts. They can walk or balance for hours along narrow planks or poles.

Whilst frying bacon and drinking real coffee, a car full of mountain men and camping gear rolled up. Mike Walford, Phil Clark and Keith Barber had found us. They had expected me to be still on the mainland today, but last minute phone calls to Paul had put them right.

It was now warm, still and sunny. It would have been a good day for the mountains. Mike and Phil didn't need any convincing that we should go for The Ridge tomorrow. There was a great air of excitement as we talked over the maps.

Having spent three hours of the middle of the day stationary, Amy began to wonder what I was doing. Children are creatures of habit: 'Daddy, why aren't you going anywhere?' she asked.

There were ten more miles to be run today. I jogged slowly to conserve energy for tomorrow. Again I was on a single-track road and at peace with the surroundings. Mike, Phil and Keith had driven on to set up their tents by the roadside as close to The Ridge as possible. From there they would spend the afternoon taking a rope, climbing harness and some food through to Coruisk. That would give us an easier start in the morning.

I ran on through the timeless village of Torrin. Turning a corner towards Loch Slapin, Blà Bheinn came into view. Under a perfect blue sky, I watched the huge walls of rock grow as I slowly approached the mountain. Blà Bheinn and its huge, rough ridges were a barrier to any view of the main Cuillin Ridge. I wondered what was in store for me tomorrow. I had heard so much about the narrowness of the crests and the steepness of the mountain faces. What was it really going to be like?

The Cuillin Ridge from Blaven. (H.S.)

I knew that if there was one section of all the Munros that I should have researched, then it was this. I hadn't dared to for fear of it putting me off. I trusted my friends who had spent scores of climbing days on Skye.

The alarm woke me at 4:30 am. I stepped carefully out of the van, so as not to wake the family. Mike, Phil and Keith were outside under the dawn sky. They were eating breakfast and packing last pieces of kit. Together we finally left at 5:10, leaving Keith to decamp and move round to Sligachan. For the next week, not only did I have a support team in my family, but the pacers had support in Keith Barber. For Mike and Phil, Keith was the mover of car and kit, stores manager, cook and entertainer. The campsite atmosphere was always lively when Keith was around. If he wasn't playing practical jokes with the children, then he was telling crude ones to the adults. It must be something to do with the mentality of plumbers.

I didn't know why I wasn't tired so early in the morning. I began to think that fatigue was all in the mind. I had covered fifty miles in the two previous days but didn't feel any worse for wear.

We followed a track across a ridge, to the grassy haven of Camasunary. It was tempting to stop often to admire the Isles of Rhum and Soay, which stood across the calm waters of Loch Scavaig. We followed the coastline into the bay by Loch Coruisk, passing the infamous 'Bad Step' en route. Here, the path is broken for about fifty feet by a section of cracked slab hanging over the sea thirty feet below. The beauty of mountain, sea and loch was stunning.

Phil collected the gear which he had hidden yesterday, and we started the climb towards The Ridge. It soon became obvious that this was not going to be an ordinary day out. Our route was upward through An Garbh-choire; a huge boulder strewn mess. The rock was rough and of all different sizes. At times it was impossible to run as we dodged round boulders the size of buses. I looked up to huge castles of rock and wondered what on earth was in store.

At eight o'clock, we arrived on the crest of The Ridge, which throughout its seven miles of length rarely falls below 2500 feet. If we had carried straight on we would have plunged hundreds of feet into Loch Coir'a'Ghrunnda — its rough-sounding name resembling the scenery surrounding it. To the left and right lay The Ridge – the dream of which I had had visions for years.

At first, I was pleasantly surprised. It didn't look that hard or dangerous. No knife edge, and my hands hardly touched rock on our route south to the first Munro – Sgurr nan Eag. We retraced our steps, dodging round a huge turret of rock before climbing to a peak which formed a fork in The Ridge. Phil continued left to fix a rope for an abseil. Mike and I turned right to gain the summit of Sgurr Dubh Mór – the only Munro which lies off the Main Ridge. My hands were already becoming roughened by the course crystalline gabbro rock. We returned down crags and over the forked peak to see Phil perched a hundred feet above. Sat facing us, he called down giving instructions for handholds which lay above and out of sight. My pulse soared, and it wasn't for the speed of running. I had climbed and scrambled a little before, but this was the first time I came to terms with the meaning of 'exposure'. With firm handholds, I stepped left on footholds the size of fists. Underneath lay a huge drop down to Coir'a'Ghrunnda. I was tempted to look, but it was for no more than a blink. Pulling higher, with my eyes now firmly on the rock in front of me, I slowly closed the distance to Phil. I was relieved to sit down on a firm boulder, before I looked left and saw a deep vertical cleft – The Thearlaich-Dubh Gap. It was as if a chisel had been carving away at a piece of wood. One by one we abseiled thirty feet into the dark abyss. At first sight we seemed to be trapped in this cold sunless hole. Vertical rock lay straight ahead and huge blocks tumbled away forever on the right. We escaped to the left on screes and moved quickly into the warmth of the west side of Sgurr Alasdair – Skye's highest mountain. We scrambled up a chimney and onto a narrow arête which led us to the top of Alasdair.

From this superb viewpoint, I began to realise the magnitude of the task. Behind us, just a mile away was today's first peak. The traverse had taken two hours! Ahead lay a most bizarre array of bumps and pinnacles which strung round to Sgurr nan Gillean –

today's proposed last peak. As the crow flies, Gillean was just three miles away, but this was no ordinary place for birds to fly or runners to run. The scenery changed slowly as we edged towards each waiting obstacle. This was not a day to rush. Even though I was now gaining in nervousness I knew that the day had to be savoured. This was a special day in a lifetime.

As on An Teallach, I knew how lucky I was. There, I had been in calm winter conditions, and now, exactly two weeks later, it was a perfect summer's day. No longer the heat of Strathfarrar, it was just warm, windless and clear. In the 23 days of running, the weather had oscillated like a swinging pendulum. By chance, the beat was right just when it counted.

We descended and reascended to gain Sgurr Alasdair's twin – Sgurr Thearlaich. From there we descended to the Bealach Mhic Choinnich before moving carefully onto Collie's Ledge – a route which, for a change, looked much harder than it really was. The narrow shelf hugs and climbs the nearly sheer west wall of Sgurr Mhic Choinnich – a Munro which we doubled back to from the north-west to save near vertical and overhanging direct climbs.

My sense of security fluctuated every few hundred metres as we moved from firm, healthy stands to positions of delicate balance. Below us lay the great amphitheatre of Coire Lagan which drops into Loch Brittle and the sea.

On the way up the Inaccessible Pinnacle (*Eric Whitehead*)

Now the infamous Inaccessible Pinnacle was in full view. A tiny purple dot was climbing the jagged east ridge. The 'In Pinn' stood, demanding to be looked at for most of the day. It is as if aeons ago before mountaineers or Munroists existed, a jester had plunged a serrated bread knife upwards through the mountain. As if to tease and entertain, this thin blade of rock juts out higher than its main mountain of Sgurr Dearg. Having scrambled our way up through screes to the base of the Inaccessible Pinnacle, the voice of the purple dot we had seen earlier, called down to us. It was friend, climber and photographer, Eric Whitehead from home. He had been commissioned by the *Guardian* to photograph me on the In Pinn. Seeing him above relieved my fear for the early steps, up the narrow arête of the east ridge. I tried not to think about or look at the two thousand foot drop on the right. Instead, I followed the instructions written so clearly on Mike's hat – 'JUST DO IT'. Watching where Phil placed his hands and feet, I followed closely, steadily climbing higher to positions of greater exposure. Eric was three quarters of the way up, and at this point he asked me to stop for a photo. Not satisfied with this (photographers never are!), he abseiled off the steep west side and got into a position for different photos from the base of the In Pinn. I hung on like a rider on a vertical motorbike without handlebars. For ten minutes, I was gripped in a position unmatched in my prehistory. I just hoped I'd have a future in which to tell my story. Both legs clung sideways over vast voids, and my hands, now scratched by the gabbro, hung tight to protrusions of stone. Phil offered me a rope. I declined, thinking that I'd be more likely to fall off whilst tying myself on. A jovial atmosphere eased the tension as we watched Eric take a position below on the firm rock of the proper mountain. At last I could move on again, and up to a firm ledge at the top. A long time ago, Mike had said to me that there was only one Munro you couldn't climb with your hands behind your back and this was it. For this reason, I was jubilant on top; I thought that I had seen the worst that exposure and Skye could offer.

Tied on to a huge boulder, we abseiled sixty feet down to meet Eric with water and cakes. It was time for a midday break. Five Munros down and six to go. I felt that the back of the day must have been broken. Sgurr nan Gillean looked even closer now.

High spines took us over Sgurr na Banachdich and Sgurr a'Ghreadaidh – 'peak of the mighty winds'. Occasionally tracks misled us, and we had to return, to try again. We were frequently poised on slabs which sloped away and down towards the corries. I had learnt to trust the great grip of the gabbro and we were moving faster now.

We passed small flat spots where rocks had been removed to form crescents. Bivvy sites, I was told. Places for people to sleep if they didn't make The Ridge in a day. The boulders were there to stop people rolling off in the night, but they looked more like Druid sites to me.

We were now faced with the four peaks of Sgurr a'Mhadaidh. Only the first is a Munro, but we needed to cross the lot to follow The Ridge. We often had a three way choice. Straight on and vertical, to the right on a path, or to the left on a path. We tried the easier options first, but they always petered out and turned back – copout routes! These were doubly worn, for everyone would go and have a look and then return realising that they go nowhere. Sometimes old crampon scratch marks on the rocks would give clues of the right route. The vertical options were far harder than the In Pinn, and certainly not possible with hands behind the back. The exposure wasn't great but even a fifty foot fall wouldn't be nice. I didn't like putting all my weight on a wobbly rock. On one such hold, Phil said reassuringly, 'It was just the same last time I was here – two years ago!'

It was now that I began to realise that the day was far from over. Our progress had been slowed again, and I looked across at Gillean wondering if there would be a sting in the tail.

We avoided the main crest for a while by dropping to the left of the three-pronged peak of Bidein Druim nan Ramh. Boulders and scree choked our route but we were given a break from delicate moves. Regaining the Main Ridge, we climbed higher on better ground to Bruach na Frithe. This is the only Cuillin mountain with a trig point, and the only one where you could have a dance on top. They are wise with their concrete, these OS men!

Abseiling off the Inaccessible Pinnacle (*Eric Whitehead*)

Choosing to vary our route a little, we traversed on a snow slope before dropping through rocks to the base of Am Basteir – 'The Executioner' – today's penultimate Munro. Our route to the top was blocked by the axe-head lump of The Basteir Tooth – a non-Munro appendage to Am Basteir. My tolerance of exposure was wearing out. I didn't want to do any more than just look at the wide vertical wall leading to the top. I had had enough. It was as if I had been overtaking juggernauts in a mini all day long. I had survived every manoeuvre so far, but one more could be my last. Phil sensed my concern, consulted his guidebook and led us down some scree to avoid the problem. We lost a lot of height towards the Lota Corrie but I was happier to do this and stay on safe ground. We regained height on a wide ledge which led us to a split between The Tooth and the main summit. I sat down and waited while Mike and Phil scrambled to the top of The Tooth. Part of me regretted not going as well, but I had to save all my nerve for whatever was remaining. Mike and Phil returned and we carried on higher, gradually revealing great vistas to the north. Just when I was thinking everything was fine, we came to a short overhang. We had used the rope twice for abseils but now was the first time for a climb. Earlier in the day we would have managed without, but now with weakening limbs and nerves, the extra protection was useful. A short pull up and we were on top in an airy position. It was safer than the In Pinn but five hours on, I felt less safe now as I was beginning to lose my bottle.

Ten down and one to go. Sgurr nan Gillean was now little more than a stone's throw away, but a stone could drop forever on many of the gaps between us. Planning to return to the *bealach* to the west of the Sgurr, we left the gear there to climb unhindered. I summoned the energy for the last. Running alternated with slow awkward moves, but things seemed to get more difficult as we climbed higher. Phil said, 'This is more exposed than I remember. I am beginning to regret leaving the rope.' He had given words of reassurance all day long, his calmness and control helping me tremendously over difficult steps. But now his words did nothing to calm me. We had arrived at a hole in the route. A huge thumb of rock known as the 'Gendarme' had fallen away three years ago leaving a void. Phil didn't know whether the amendment to the route was an improvement or not. In previous delicate positions, it had been possible to avoid looking at the drops, because they were usually behind or to one side. However, here we were forced to look below. Stepping across gaps, it was necessary to look forward and down for footholds. There, in the same direction, were vertical precipices, thousands of feet to the corrie below. I knew that I didn't want to return this way. I had now overtaken too many juggernauts and I was beginning to shake. Phil now offered reassurance again by saying that he would go back alone to collect the kit. Mike and I would continue east after the summit, on the so called 'tourist route'. On the Cuillin Ridge, this term takes on an entirely different meaning. It is merely a route for those not seeking to enhance the already dramatic nature of the traverse.

The top of Sgurr nan Gillean gave superb views in every direction. Back along The Ridge we took a last look at the cheeky In Pinn, now little more than a pin head. Even now the day wasn't over. From this high pedestal, Mike and I gingerly descended east on blocks slanting towards the Lota Corrie. A path toured through boulders and past cairns, down and then north three miles to the campsite at Sligachan. Some 'tourist route' this!

Pauline
We drove into Glen Brittle from where The Ridge could be clearly seen, standing sharp

Phil Clark and Mike Walford running by Loch an Athain en route to Blaven. (H.S.)

and proud against a cloudless sky. Using our powerful binoculars, we made fruitless efforts to spot tiny figures on the skyline, seeking reassurance that all was well. It was not foolish to try – we later learnt that Keith had indeed detected our party earlier in the day. We had trouble deciding how to bide the time until we could return to camp and await Hugh's arrival. An unsettled, uneasy feeling prevailed, knowing that Hugh was attempting a route outside the scope of fell running and more in the department of the climber. I was very well aware of the dangers. My comfort lay in knowing that Hugh was in good company and can usually be relied on to keep his head. I just hoped that he'd keep his body. There was nothing we could do but wait.

For a while we entertained ourselves sketching the intricate outline of The Ridge. After a short walk we returned to the site at Sligachan and made use of the showers. Andrew, with a little 'help' from Joseph and Amy, put up tents for the night. I decided it could be an excellent idea – at least we would not have to listen to them not getting to sleep at night.

We had been told to expect Hugh, Mike and Phil at 6 o'clock. It was no surprise that well after this time they still had not returned. I had grown used to late arrivals – times were only guidelines – a deadline for the support crew. Today was different. I wanted to see Hugh safely at sea level once more.

At 8:30 pm I noticed two runners heading towards the campsite – Mike and Phil! Where was Hugh? A catalogue of horrors flashed through my mind as I hurried to put this question to Mike and Phil.

'We told him,' said Mike, 'But he took no notice of us.'

'He insisted that he had seen the van parked further down the road and ran off towards it,' added Phil. 'We told him you'd be here.'

After a few minutes Hugh rolled up. If only the film crew had been there. This was the day for the ultimate welcome back to camp.

We had been lucky – no long wait for the clouds to roll back or the rock to dry. Good friends had lent their knowledge, skill and humour. But above all Hugh had shown that not only was he swift of foot, but also sure of foot and steady of nerve. He had mastered the most serious ridge traverse in Britain. We felt both a sense of gratitude and achievement.

It was a joy to touch green grass once more after hours spent on hard grey rock. From camp to camp we had been away for fifteen hours. Even now, I didn't feel tired, just relieved to be on firm ground again. The day had been wonderful – a mixture of excitement and terror, fuelled frequently by natural adrenalin. The only signs of wear were from the gabbro – one pair of dead running shoes and a highly scratched set of fingertips.

The camp at Sligachan was idyllic under the pure blue sky. I went for a shower at Eric Whitehead's rented pad. He was cooking Kashmiri chicken and vast quantities of rice. I had a plateful with wine before returning for dinner at camp. The Sligachan Inn was irresistible that night. After three pints of Murphy's I returned to the van, and ate another Christmas pudding.

It was Saturday morning, and an appropriate day for a lie-in. The Skye Ridge had given me a 'high' and I felt no pressure to run on, even though there were just 93 Munros behind me and 203 more before Snowdon.

Five miles east of the Cuillin Ridge, stands Skye's only other 3000 foot peak – Blà Bheinn. Had I stuck to the original plan of climbing Blà Bheinn first, I would have been faced with a long run on the busy and fast Portree to Broadford road. Instead Mike, Phil and I now enjoyed the peace and beauty of Glen Sligachan. We took our time to savour the views west to The Ridge – stopping frequently to take photos and recall yesterday's peaks. Under the perfect blue sky, Blà Bheinn's great walls and gullies were now reflected in the waters of Loch an Athain. We climbed into Coire Dubh, with rocks and boulders gradually replacing the heather of the lower slopes. The stony gully led us to a saddle which was a perfect resting spot before the final push to the top. Here, amongst all the multitudes of rocks, lay a small patch of grass known as 'The Putting Green'. From here, we picked our way round great slabs of stone and climbed vertically for two short sections. Putting weight on my arms again, I felt soreness from yesterday's efforts. I enjoyed the climbing much more today, knowing that the exposure was only for minutes rather than for hours. A ten foot wall and a twenty foot chimney led us to the main footpath to the top.

From 3044 feet on the summit of Blà Bheinn, The Ridge exposed its full length and beauty. I was more than glad that I could admire it now, having done it. My thoughts now turned to the future. Looking east, we could see back to the mainland.

I had promised Bev Holt (the Doctor) that I'd take a rest day, before or after The Ridge – but now, I didn't want one. I had gained a momentum and joy of mountains that I didn't want to break.

We jogged down a rough ridge and onto a good footpath which took us to the road. There waiting for us were Pauline, Keith, Bev Holt and his daughter. Bev proceeded to tell me that the blood count was fine. Mike Walford chipped in, 'What about the sperm count?' Bev could see that my spirits were high and my health seemed good. He put me under no pressure to take a rest. Knowing the British mountains well, he talked of the future and said that the Cairngorms would be my greatest problem now – their size and number being a psychological barrier.

Mike, Phil and Keith drove to the mainland to meet me in the morning. I had planned to end the day at Broadford, but it was a bad place to start the next day. There was the tide and the next mountain to consider. The plan now was to return to Kylerhea and row across at first slack tide in the morning.

Ten miles of glen and mountain lay behind me and now seventeen miles of road stretched ahead. Andrew shared the first mile. We waded the top of Loch Slapin amongst drift wood and oystercatchers. In the warmth of the afternoon, I returned through Torrin, passing a tractor so old it didn't have a letter on its registration. I was now floating again, along a single track road under a perfect blue sky. I wondered where my energy was coming from. I seemed to be freewheeling in running shoes – just drifting back towards the sea and the mainland. These last miles of Skye were identical to the first, except anticipation was replaced by thrill. I had always imagined that I would have needed rest days before and after The Ridge. Instead, it had fuelled me with drive, before, during and after.

I couldn't resist phoning home from an isolated phone box by the sea. My father said, 'I'm glad you've done those wretched Cuillins. I really didn't think you knew what you were doing there.'

Before dropping down to Kylerhea, I turned to take one last look at the now silhouetted mountains. Skye had gone like a dream, and now there was one last sleep before the row in the morning.

Chapter 9   NIGHT OUT IN KNOYDART

May 13 – 18

Shouts from across the water disturbed our breakfast in the sunshine. We couldn't understand a word, but it was comforting to know that Mike, Phil and Keith were on the other side. Otherwise, the end of this no through road was a peaceful place. The only traffic was the occasional trawler passing through the narrows. They made great waves in the sea, waves which rocked the boat as I returned with oars in hand again.

Sometimes it takes a second look to remember a face from the past. Whilst rowing back to the mainland, I asked Chris whether he had been the landlord of the Glenelg Inn in April 1987. One night of that month, I had entered the pub and was faced with a bizarre sight. Dozens of people were in fancy dress. Hardly had I ordered my pint, when a cowboy shot me three times with a toy gun. Chris seemed to have an eccentric nature – I asked him if he had been this character from the wild west. He remembered the occasion well and confessed. It was a pity that it hadn't been as easy to identify the Sedbergh gunman of April 1990.

Phil met me on the mainland and we ran one mile to meet Mike and Keith at their idyllic camp in Glenelg Bay. There was no one in sight, so we felt uninhibited playing loud music on the car stereo whilst drinking coffee and looking at maps on the beach. 'Relax – Just Do It' by Frankie Goes to Hollywood hit the right note, and I ran off with an injection of new fuel.

Gliding along the next two miles of coastline this quiet Whit Sunday morning, I passed a retired Geordie couple camped in their own paradise. They had made a temporary rock garden to surround their motor caravan. I asked them how long they were staying – 'October,' they replied. In this sunshine and warmth, they had found a tranquillity which would be hard to find on the Riviera or Costa Brava.

The route took me on a grass path past the massive ruins of Bernera Barracks and on tarmac to the 2000 year old Pictish Brochs of Dun Telve and Dun Trodden. A mile beyond these half ruined round towers, the tarmac turned to dirt track. We left this to head up into the wild eastern corries of Beinn Sgritheall. This was a gentle and beautiful approach on which we saw large herds of deer trying to escape our attention. They ran off round rocky ridges at speed and with a sureness of foot that we couldn't hope to attain. From the summit, we saw a lone walker heading towards the North West Top – a subsidiary peak just 500 metres away. He had left a thermos, sandwich box and shirt by the cairn. It was tempting to take a drink and a buttie. Somehow, because we knew that the man wouldn't see us, we had a strong urge to make our presence felt. Realising that the food was probably quite important to him, we settled for a trivial and childish trick. Carefully looking to see if the walker ever turned his head, we lifted the sweaty shirt that

Returning to the mainland from Skye. (P.S.)

was lying to dry on the stones of the cairn, and moved it ten metres to spread it over the trig point. Whilst running away rapidly, so that we wouldn't be seen, I wondered whether the walker would realise that his shirt had been moved, and if so, if he would ask why and how? A stupid game really, when we knew that we would never know the man's thoughts.

The descent to Arnisdale on the southern side was loose and steep. This summit of 3196 feet gains all its height in a distance of just one mile from the sea. We rested on the beach in Arnisdale, admiring the grand shapes of Beinn Sgritheall and Ladhar Bheinn which lie on either side of Loch Hourn.

Seven miles of footpath now separated me from tonight's camp at Kinloch Hourn. I enjoyed this journeying from place to place. Arriving in the narrow head of the loch, I sensed a strong transition from the wide open spaces of Skye. I was now approaching the remote region of Knoydart, and entering a new stage of the run.

Pauline

When the memories of a long journey begin to fade, there are always tiny sparks which continue to shine. I shall always have strong recollections of both the tranquillity of Strathfarrar and the haven of Kinloch Hourn.

The road to Kinloch Hourn is narrow, steep and bumpy. For thirty miles the traveller is transported through the woods of Glen Garry and up to the bare landscape beyond. Here the road is open and the deer run wild. The inevitable dam holds back the waters of Loch Quoich. The road hugs a delightful shoreline clothed in rhododendron and the bright yellow gorse which generously decorates the Highland roadsides throughout the spring.

Unlike so many of our forays up the glens, our route today took us above the dam and on beyond Loch Quoich. The road wove its way between the rocks of a low pass through the mountains before descending sharply down to sea level at the head of Loch Hourn.

This final descent came at the end of a long day. Although, as the crow flies, the distance from Kylerhea to Kinloch Hourn is a mere 12 miles, we had travelled 80. In contrast, Hugh's journey took him about 20 miles over Beinn Sgritheall. After climbing out of Kylerhea to reach our crossing point at Kyle of Lochalsh, we had driven east up the length of Glen Shiel and almost as far as the Great Glen, before we were able to round the barrier of the Cluanie Ridge and turn west towards our destination. This was one of those days when the journey filled the day, for the roads were slow in a vehicle such as ours.

I was gaining confidence with the van and beginning to realise that a marked tarmac route on the map would be passable for us. However, today's journey had a sting in the tail. We edged our way down the final steep descent, gripped tightly between the low wall on our right and the rocks of the cliff on our left. I had to remind myself that Amy and Joseph's bedroom rested above my head – so easy to forget the extra height when passing overhanging rocks or trees.

Once again I was having fun. For me the challenge lay in ensuring that when Hugh reached his destination, a comfortable resting place would be there, on time.

During the whole journey, I met many friends from recent and not so recent times. Most of these planned their arrival and were of no surprise to me. Occasionally, people kept their intentions secret, and arrived out of the blue. Kinloch Hourn was one of the last places I expected someone to search me out. But this evening, a stranger arrived and stared me in the face.

'I know who you are; do you know who I am?'

'Don't tell me,' I replied.

'Think back twenty years,' he answered.

I recalled Bill Richardson correctly as one of my Maths teachers at William Hulme's Grammar School in Manchester. Having read an article about the run in his local Aberdeen press, he was determined to find me somewhere while I was in Scotland. Through phoning Intermediate Technology, he finally tracked me down to the end of this long road to the sea. Bill had a lot to answer for, as he had been one of the main instigators of my early long distance charity challenges of the late sixties. I remember him serving me hot drinks in the middle of the night whilst walking from Mold to Manchester. That had been a success as I had jogged and walked the fifty miles in the comfort of running shoes. The previous year I had learnt about footwear the hard way. In a sponsored walk from Lancaster to Manchester, I had struggled forty miles to Bacup and then dropped out with blistered feet caused by heavy walking boots.

Our camp by the burn was a wonderful place to recall these memories. We sat round a bonfire which the children had lit, its smoke deterring our first midges of the season.

Pauline

We spent three nights at this perfect camp as Hugh's plans for the next two days involved an out and back trip followed by a night in a bothy. The grounds of the estate offered a perfect grassy site next to a sparkling river. There is nothing like a rocky mountain stream for keeping children happy. Amy and Joseph took off all their clothes and paddled while Andrew amused himself building fires for the evening.

As Hugh set off on his return trip we donned our boots, and together with Keith, set out to explore. We could do as we pleased as the van need not move. Hugh covered 18 miles of mountain and track in the time it took us to walk and scramble less than three miles. Our route took us round the head of the loch where the thrift and scurvy grass were in flower, past the magnificent woodland surrounding the Lodge. Eucalyptus trees towered above the flowering rhododendron. Our path climbed through birch, oak and conifer woods above the clear blue green waters of the loch. On treks such as these I would always carry a pile of reference books to help us to identify flowers, birds, rocks, butterflies, fungi, and insects. On each mini expedition we gained a little more knowledge.

The steep wooded hillsides and narrow waters of the loch were strikingly reminiscent of the typical scenery of a Norwegian fjord. How could it be that the electricity board had chosen this very special Glen to bear the marks of the giant pylons carrying the high voltage cables to Skye? The stalker's cottage rested next to the lodge, beneath the power lines. Ironically it is powered from its own generator. Despite the bounty of power overhead, the cost of a transformer to enable the cottage to tap into the national grid is astronomical.

Here, over 30 miles from the nearest shop, the stalker singlehandedly manages 6000 acres of land, keeping check on the deer belonging to the estate and grazing sheep of his own. Proceeds from Bed and Breakfast supplement his none too generous income. The landowner lives in Norfolk. Although we were enjoying the delights of this sanctuary at its best, it was not difficult to imagine the harsh realities of life in the winter months. When the sun is low in the sky, the steep and narrow glen is hidden from its warming rays. One hundred and twenty inches of rainfall in an average year. Eighty seven inches had already fallen in the first three months of this year. With the exception of two days, it had rained every day from 1 January to the end of March.

Links with the outside world are tenuous. Television reception is non-existent. As the cottage is built close to the hillside, radio reception is hopeless, although this luxury can be enjoyed from a vehicle a little way down the road. The telephone is via a radio link across Loch Quoich. The transmitter batteries are charged by solar panels on the roadside, one mile above Kinloch Hourn.

I could think of no better place to pass a few sunny days in the spring. It must take a very special person to enjoy a lifetime so far removed from the entertainments of the modern world.

Phil and I climbed the 3365 feet of Sgurr a'Mhaoraich via its steep western slopes. This bulky, grassy hill stands in an excellent position giving a panorama of the Knoydart hills to the south and west and the Glen Shiel hills to the north. The day was warm and clear, just perfect for enjoying the hills. Crossing the mountain in a direct line, we descended on a snow slope into a burn which led us to Glen Quoich. It wasn't hard to see and meet Mike who was wearing fluorescent yellow tracksters. He stood out a mile in the green landscape of bracken . It is hard to justify visual pollution on the hills but for once this garish clothing had a use. Mike had left the car two miles away and had run up Glen Quoich to meet us with sandwiches and to take over from Phil for the afternoon run.

We followed the zig zags of a good stalking track to the summit of Gleouraich. A cairn artist had recently converted the top stones into a series of balancing triangles. I saw at least a dozen of these during my traverse of the Munros. They resembled a type of Buddhist prayer emblem but I don't think that they would survive for long in the normal winds of the summits.

Picking our way through great fields of stone, we descended 800 feet to a saddle. We passed two walkers and a dog and ran on across more stone towards the summit of Spidean Mialach – 'The Pinnacle of the Wild Animals'. Whilst climbing the last few hundred feet, Mike and I turned to see one of the walkers catching us rapidly. We wondered why he was travelling so fast, as though he wanted to talk. His chatter was in a strong Durham accent. Having spent my university years in Durham, I had come to recognise and love the clean and honest accent. We stopped and talked at length in the summit warmth. Although Ron Davison and I had never met before, we had many friends in common in his own club of Durham City Harriers.

We left Ron and his dog (Corrie) to wait for his friend. Through rock and on path, we descended to Loch Quoich. Six miles of winding road led us back to Loch Hourn. The heat had returned, but this time my body didn't complain. I was now almost four weeks into the journey. I had experienced all sorts of weather and my body and mind were becoming accustomed to the extreme conditions. Today's 7000 feet and sixteen miles seemed easy. I was developing a confidence and learning to relax and enjoy just being amongst the mountains.

In the mid May evening warmth, the odd midge menaced us as we sat out under a slowly darkening sky. Andrew lit another fire and Mike took the opportunity to dispose of his latest pair of decayed running shoes. The mixture of hard rock and wet ground that pervade Scotland, rots and wears away running shoes within three hundred miles. The sides become torn and soles slowly lose their studs – although on Skye this all happens within one day. Mike saved the labour of taking his old shoes home by burning them on the bonfire. The burning rubber and black fumes temporarily poisoned us, but at least it deterred the midges.

However, it didn't deter the arrival of another friend and supporter from the Lakes. Tony Cresswell, Youth Hostel warden from Buttermere, arrived whilst Phil, Mike and I were organising piles of food, cooking equipment, sleeping bags and clothes for the two day journey into the 'Rough Bounds of Knoydart'.

This big hilly peninsula lies between Loch Nevis and Loch Hourn. Mountains and crags drop sharply into the sea throughout its 36 mile coastline. The ruggedness of its interior has prevented penetration of roads. However, stalkers' tracks give access on foot. Without these the approach would be extremely long and arduous.

We departed early, expecting a hard day. It was a luxury to have three friends to carry my kit. My only burden was a small camera carried in a bum bag. In a disappearing watery sun, we followed a track west towards Barrisdale Bay. Above the narrow inlet of Loch Hourn, the path twisted its way below crags and through woods. We watched Ladhar Bheinn – Knoydart's highest Munro – disappear under an increasingly threatening sky. I had been looking forward to this section as one of the highlights, but unfortunately, dark skies had returned and I was to be robbed of any views from the tops.

Most of the Munros of the west of Scotland are between 3000 feet and 3500 feet high. Often this height is gained directly from sea level, in contrast to the Grampians of the east. We left Barrisdale Bay and climbed the unrelenting 3343 feet to the summit of Ladhar Bheinn. A zig zag track led us up and into the huge Coire Dhorrcail, although there wasn't any chance of seeing the tall rock faces today. A narrow spur took us further west towards the summit. Nearing the top, we passed a small group descending. It was too windy to talk but I couldn't help but notice their clothes. No bright colours, no goretex and no fancy kit. One lady was in a long dark tweed skirt which blew up in the wind, revealing a pure white petticoat. This was another occasion when I wondered whether I was dreaming in the mountains.

I was confused about the ridge on the stormy mountaintop and wondered whether the compass was being disturbed. To make sure that we had reached the Munro summit we ran on to find the lower trig point, just 200 metres away to the north west. This confirmed our position and we returned to pass the summit cairn again. There was little evidence of being on top of the mainland's most westerly peak, and we would have had to wait for two days for the vista to open. I promised to return.

Descending on dark rock and earth we crossed minor *bealachs* and knolls before crossing the main Mam Barrisdale. This high pass at 1450 feet provides the main thoroughfare across Knoydart, from the harbour village of Inverie in the south to Loch Hourn. For this main route it is the high point but for us, crossing at right angles, it was our lowest stage before the next ascent.

Lying on grass enjoying a picnic, a brief clearing exposed some of the ground to the south. I now understood why the region is known as 'The Rough Bounds'. I pointed and said, 'Look at that – it's 50% rock and 50% grass!' Tony Cresswell replied with his normal witty speed, 'No – I'd say that it's at least half and half.' This set the mood for a continuous series of jokes during the next half hour's climb of Luinne Bheinn. Mike Walford was leading a route up by some old rusty fence posts when he said; 'The art of getting up a mountain is to avoid climbing.' The spirit of the hill was with us. Its closest pronunciation in English being 'Loony Bin'. The summit also marked the 100th Munro of my journey. There were minor celebrations and further jokes before we ran on over complicated ground. The half rock/grass makes movement awkward in the mist. Without footpaths, nothing guides the route and the rock and grass always compete for your steps.

The light-hearted atmosphere caused me to lose my grip on the navigation. Fortunately a hole in the clouds revealed Loch Quoich coming closer. We turned around and headed towards Meall Buidhe – today's third Munro. Stopping for another rest gave us a chance to reconsider our position. Discussing the various scales and qualities of maps, Tony said,

'Mine's a 1:50 000 but it only cost me £1.15.'

'I've got a one inch one,' Mike replied.

Quick as a flash, Tony chipped in, 'Marjorie Proops doesn't think it matters.'

Two people walked by and must have been as surprised as us. I rarely saw people on the mountains in poor weather. It was a shame not to be enjoying Knoydart in its full glory, but I suppose I witnessed it in its normal state.

Through crags and past fast-running streams and waterfalls, we lost all our height to the sea again.

Passing the ruins at Carnoch, Phil recalled having seen a ghost there three years previously. In broad daylight, he witnessed a person vanish from the footpath in front of his eyes. We walked the last mile by Loch Nevis, picking up driftwood for an evening fire. We expected Keith (the mad plumber) to have walked in and tentatively reserved some sleeping places in the bothy at Sourlies.

The small well-built shelter was almost full. We don't know what Keith had told the occupants before our arrival, but there was a stony cold reception as four sweaty runners breezed through the door. Perhaps Keith had subjected everybody to an hour's verbal diarrhoea. We squashed in and sat down for a few minutes but felt quite shy to talk and disturb the peace. It had stopped raining so we moved outside and established an Egon Ronay kitchen outside the west-end gable facing the sea. Outside we could spread ourselves out and listen at ease to Keith's endless jokes. It was impressive that he had walked the eight undulating miles from Glendessary. His all-up load including tent and food must have been at least eighteen stones. I was glad of the tent, particularly as Keith had managed to roll out his own sleeping bag in the bothy; his snoring is reputedly so bad that its occupants wouldn't be guaranteed much sleep.

I was amazed at the population of walkers – an ordinary Tuesday evening and there were fifteen people at Sourlies. I wondered what it would be like on a Bank Holiday weekend in good weather.

Mike Walford was really at home in this situation. Crouched on all fours, he kept bellowing at his cooking pots as if he was breathing fire. I spent most of the evening eating and coming to terms with my new label of King Henry VIII. On occasions like this, my many-coursed meal would consist of several packets of quick-cook rice dishes, three angel delight puddings, followed by three quarters of a christmas pudding – the remainder tonight going to the real King Henry VIII look-alike – Keith.

The day had taken eight and a half hours and had been less arduous than anticipated. However, tomorrow there would be more mountains and a total height approaching 10 000 feet. I retired early, to the soft bed on the grass.

Sgurr na Ciche at 3410 feet competes with few other mountains in Britain for the single greatest climb straight from the sea. Expecting today's five mountains to be hard going, we departed at seven. We were now a group of five. Late the previous evening, Frank Thomas had arrived, knowing my position from Paul. People were finding me in more and more absurd places.

Mike's technique of gaining height without climbing had an element of sense. He really meant going up a mountain without losing unnecessary height on the way. Seeing what I thought was a good line through some crags, I scrambled upward on a poor mixture of rock and vegetation. In the mist it was difficult to gauge the gradient. About 100 feet above a terrace, the ground was approaching vertical and the heather I was holding was tearing out of the ground. The stone was unstable and dangerous. Phil's wise words made me return and lose height. Meanwhile, as I seemed to be about to break a limb, Mike was calling up to me, 'A hundred Munros isn't enough.' We moved round on easier ground and pushed our way to the top of Sgurr na Ciche to be blasted by a fierce westerly gale full of rain. I saw my companions turn their backs and run for the shelter of rocks. I didn't react as quickly as them. After four weeks of contrasts, I didn't mind the weather whatever it threw at me. Having a face full of rain was just a natural way of having a wash. So long as I had the right clothes on, I was comfortable and no longer felt vulnerable or exposed to the elements. It was as if I was enjoying the combination of the roughness of the ground with the roughness of the weather.

The bare mountain rock was wet and greasy. Care was important on all the twists and turns between today's five Munros. One slip could bring a sudden end to my dream. I found the 1:25 000 particularly useful in intricate terrain such as today's. Checking the directions of walls and fences, and counting paces for distance, we traversed the summits of Garbh Chioch Mhór, Sgurr nan Coireachan and Sgurr Mór. We contoured round the south of Sgurr an Fhuarain and stopped to watch a large herd of deer below

Wrong route on Sgurr na Ciche. Phil Clark and Tony Cresswell with hat. (Frank Thomas)

us. Pointing towards them, Tony Cresswell said, 'It must be a hard life spending ten months trying to find something to eat and two months dodging bullets.'

Gairich – 'peak of yelling' – still offered no views; just a roaring from behind us on the ascent and into our faces on the return.

It was now five miles of wet ground to the next roadhead. I was concerned that Pauline might not reach Strathan to the west of Loch Arkaig. I knew that our proposed meeting point was beyond the end of the tarmac. I also feared for her escape from Kinloch Hourn where the route out was narrow, steep and on loose stones.

We crossed Glen Kingie and called in at the Kinbreack bothy. Mike Walford had a fire burning in no time and was searching the bothy for something to make a hot drink with. He found a kettle and took water from the burn, but searching every nook and cranny produced no tea bag or grain of coffee. However, there was an old bottle of chilli sauce with a quarter inch left in the bottom. Sometimes, wild men of the hills do wild things, but this was ridiculous. He poured boiling water onto the dregs and drank it straight from the bottle. When leaving the bothy, we saw a dead sheep in the stream, just above where Mike had collected the water. Mike has guts, or at least he used to.

We met Keith at Strathan before 4 o'clock but there was no Pauline and no van. I knew that the Arkaig road was tortuous and particularly so with a large vehicle. It was difficult to relax in the hour spent waiting.

Pauline

Strathan is a distance of 10 miles south of Kinloch Hourn. Yet once again we had first to travel east to the Great Glen in order to reach the Glen of Loch Arkaig. Our route took us 85 miles, 60 of these on single track roads.

Hugh had suggested that we warm up the engine before setting out up the steep climb out of Kinloch Hourn. The engine could be very temperamental when cold – I didn't fancy stalling half way up. 'Choke' was a very apt term for the function of that particular part of the van's anatomy. Having been accustomed to a diesel VW I never did get used to it. After a good ten minute warm up, I slotted into first gear and went for it. Thank goodness there was nothing coming down as passing points were non-existent and we needed our momentum.

On reaching the turn off to Gairlochy, our access to Arkaig, we were met by a sign – 'ROAD CLOSED, TWO MILES AHEAD'. We decided to investigate. A three foot trench barred our way. A detour taking us almost to Fort William was unavoidable – an extra 20 miles.

The children couldn't resist the bright lights and succeeded in dragging me into the town. It was such a novelty for them to look around lots of big shops full of interesting toys. In the bookshop we found two more Highland fantasies by the excellent author, Mollie Hunter. We had so enjoyed her book The Haunted Mountain *with its startling tales of 'Ben Macdui' and the 'Lairig Ghru'. I read these stories to the children every night.*

We took the opportunity to use the cashpoint having discovered that this was the only sensible way to obtain money in Scotland. The banks charge up to £2 to draw out £50 at the till. Quite often we asked friends to bring up cash for us as we passed through few towns large enough to boast a cashpoint.

Fort William was exciting for the children but stressful for me. Amy and Joseph constantly threatened to get run over or lost in the crowds. We left the town after a delightful surprise meeting with friends from Sedbergh. Jackie and Ian Higginbotham

*just happened to be on holiday with their family, camping in Glen Etive. We found
ourselves motoring along the shores of Loch Arkaig rather late in the day.*

*Loch Arkaig is unusual – there is no dam. The road, which closely hugs the loch
shore, was in a bad way. The edges were falling into the loch. The surface, though
tarred, was very uneven having subsided patchily. Here and there repairs have been
carried out, but on the last mile of road a totally new surface had been laid – what a
difference. We reached the sign declaring 'END OF PUBLIC ROAD', and parked. In my
usual cautious fashion, I decided to investigate the last bit of rough track on foot – no
need to take risks. We all walked the last half mile into Strathan, where Hugh was
waiting (we were not late – he was early). Everyone agreed that 'Ben' (our name for
the van) could manage the bumps and 'Ben' did.*

In planning the schedule for 296 mountains, I could only make guesses and produce
guidelines for a one hundred day run. However, I had always imagined needing days
with short excursions or with complete rest. Expecting to be tired from the tour of
Knoydart, I had provisionally scheduled a short trip to the two mountains south-west of
Strathan. Had our camp been attractive and a good place to settle for two nights then I
might have stuck to this idea. However, Strathan was a bleak spot and my energy levels
seemed good enough to consider another long outing. In fact the two previous days had
both been less than nine hours in length. After the long days of the far North West,
anything less than ten hours seemed like a normal day – not too long and not too short.
By combining the two Glen Pean mountains with the isolated peak of Gulvain, I could
advance the schedule and allow myself a day off in Fort William on Saturday.

The approach to Sgurr nan Coireachan and Sgurr Thuilm was via a gently graded
track leading into Glen Pean. It was a wonderful start to the day. The heavy black clouds
of the two previous days had thinned and moved higher, revealing the surrounding
peaks.

We joined the narrow ridge linking the two Sgurrs, and left our kit to climb the 'peak
of the corries'. The peace was wrecked by the sudden roar of an aeroplane. Flying
towards us it appeared to be as low as the Glenfinnan viaduct, four miles to the south. I
felt sure it was going to crash into our ridge as it raced up the glen without climbing. At
the last possible moment it heaved itself upwards and disappeared behind crags below
us. I expected the return to the *bealach* to reveal the burnt-out remnants of our sacks.
This was one of the few occasions I heard or saw low-flying aircraft. Perhaps most of
them train in the Lakes and Dales, where I am used to suffering them most clear days of
the week.

There had been no panorama from Knoydart, but now was an opportunity of a
panorama of it from here. Sgurr na Ciche had recovered from its storm and now revealed
its distinctive rounded summit beacon. To the west lay the deep blue Loch Morar and
vast tracts of lochaned landscape surrounding it.

We returned in search of the sacks and crossed Sgurr Thuilm before long and
exciting snow descents on the eastern slopes. The revised route saved me the return to
Strathan but I didn't miss out on the luxury of a lunchtime brew. Mike wasn't with me
today; he was resting for the weekend's Scottish Islands Peaks race – a mixture of
sailing and running the mountains on Mull, Arran and Jura. Keith and Mike walked two
miles up Gleann a'Chaorainn to set up a pit stop and camp fire. Again, Mike's lurid
yellow pants came in handy in searching out the spot.

From here, our route to Gulvain rose and fell twice. I enjoyed these non-guidebook routes. It was satisfying to strike over ridges and across burns, unguided by previous experience. Plodding across peaty bog, I lost a shoe deep in the black stuff. My right arm dipped to the elbow in tugging it out of the ground.

The final climb to the summit was steep for over a thousand feet. I enjoyed the change from running – just pulling up through the stones and streams using all fours more often than not.

I couldn't understand where Gulvain ('faeces') got its name from, but it led me to a new christening of Glen Mallie in the afternoon. The twelve miles were hard work after the three summits. In increasing heat and fatigue, we named the glen after the mountain – 'soil-pipe alley'. After a seemingly endless valley, we rounded the end of Loch Arkaig and found the mobile base.

Pauline had parked the van by a waterfall at the end of 'The Dark Mile' – so called after the dense line of beech trees. Every camp had its atmosphere and you knew it straight away. For me, the tell-tale sign was whether the children were playing happily or otherwise. Here there were felled trees to play and balance on, and the sound of the rushing water added to the air of contentment.

Between breakfast and lunch, I made a quick circuit of the two 'Lochy Hills' to the north-east of The Dark Mile. Sròn a'Choire Ghairbh and Meall na Teanga stand at least ten miles from the nearest other Munros, but their position gives them an outstanding view of the Central Highlands. In clear skies and warmth, I sat on the tops looking back to the mountains of Knoydart, Glen Shiel and Affric. I had reached a transition in the journey. Behind me lay 111 mountains of the maritime north-west. I was on the last mountain before the crossing of the Great Glen that divides Scotland from Inverness to Fort William. Casting my eyes south and east across the glen, I was looking forward to the inland mountains of the vast Grampian Region.

The next ten miles emphasised this natural break in the journey. It was one of the flattest runs to be had until Cheshire. Returning across the end of Loch Arkaig, a short cut off the main road took me through the Achnacarry estate. There were hundreds of copper beeches and the rhododendrons were in brilliant bloom. Any undulations in this easy afternoon run were completely ironed our after joining the Caledonian Canal at Gairlochy. This man-made section of the Great Glen runs alongside the River Lochy, and with a large series of lochs, it allows boats and yachts to pass through Scotland. It allowed me to drift towards Fort William, and a rest day before the big mountains of the Ben and beyond.

Chapter 10   THE AGONY OF NOT RUNNING

May 19

I touched a traffic light on the swing bridge over the canal and jumped into the passenger seat of the van for the first time in four weeks. Riding in the van made me feel as if I had opted out. The swing bridge marked my opt-out point for the next twenty-four hours. Tomorrow I would touch the traffic light again and return to normal. In the meantime, things were abnormal.

The party was over. One by one, friends had left during the last two days. We were now alone without an entourage. It was time for rest and for organisation.

Nearly five weeks after our first visit, we returned to Roger Boswell's house, garden and caravans. The snow had melted, the grass had grown long and the trees were flourishing. The sharp contrast of seasons and the journey behind me, made me feel that we had been away for months rather than weeks. Roger welcomed us with his usual dynamism. He was boiling kettles, offering us baths and showing us the way to our boxes of food, all whilst filling the washing machine and feeding the cat. We parked ourselves for the night and I looked forward to an easy and unhurried Saturday.

Pauline
The sight of Roger's washing machine took me back to my pre-school days, when my mother would stand over the large white drum on legs, pushing down the washing with a posser. It was somehow in tune with Roger's nature not to have the modern switch-it-on-and-forget-about-it type machine, but to have this 1950s model complete with mangle. Armfuls of grubby running gear and children's togs were agitated by this archaic contraption and the resulting black sludge horrified even Roger. Managing the mangle was an art in itself – disastrous if anything had been left in pockets. Amy's precious stone came to grief in my Rohan shorts pocket. It says a great deal for the garment that the crushed rock merely burst a few stitches, leaving the material intact.

After a few hours it was only possible to negotiate Roger's garden by ducking under the spider's web of washing hanging in the hot sun. How did all those clothes fit in the van?

The day began slowly, and after the fourth cup of coffee, I eased myself into action. The morning was filled with chores. Stepping in and out of the van a hundred times must have amounted to half a Munro. The sorting and cleaning seemed to tire me more than running up hills.

Pauline drove us to Fort William. We stopped at a garage to give the van a good look over. I became frustrated by air pumps that either didn't work or didn't register the high pressure required for the van's weight. We tried three garages before getting it right. I realised how easy a life it was just to wander about the hills and how hard a life Pauline had in the day to day running of the family and the van.

By mid afternoon, we had reorganised ourselves and were ready for some relaxation. Pauline took the children to the swimming pool, while I visited the shops of Fort William, trying to gain sponsorship for Intermediate Technology. I met managers of climbing shops and left sponsorship forms behind. Thinking that 111 Munros might show people that I meant business, I had hoped for a good response. However, my story didn't seem to excite anyone. At one shop I complained about a leaking map case which I had bought there five weeks previously on our way north. The shop accepted no responsibility for it and told me to go to the hardware store over the road and buy a plastic bag. These incidents added to my feelings of remoteness and isolation on the streets of Fort William. I didn't seem to be able to communicate with anyone. Whilst on the hills, conversation with friends or strangers came easily, but here in the town, people just passed me by.

I normally like Fort William. Its factories, hydro pipes, lack of skyscrapers and its open views to mountains give it the feeling of a North Norwegian town. But, today, I just wanted to be off the streets and on the mountains.

Pauline

The addictive nature of running is well known. Hugh's addiction had grown with the years, to the point that a daily 'fix' had become essential to his well-being. No matter what the difficulty, Hugh would always try to fit a run into the day. If the day was full, he would rise early or run in the dark. If a day trip out didn't involve a race or any other exercise, we would drop him off at some outlandish place on the way back, so that he could 'run' home. Running and Hugh were inseparable. Problems arose when for reasons of injury or illness, Hugh couldn't run. Fortunately these occasions were rare. Not given to being openly bad-tempered, he would become quietly miserable, irritable and fidgety. In attempting the 'Mountains of Britain Run', he was indulging in the ultimate 'high' whilst hopefully steering clear of an overdose.

I both admired and envied Hugh's freedom to indulge – to be able to devote himself to his task with such single-mindedness. As every mother knows, life with a young family is a bitty affair. In the face of catering for the needs of the family one's own interests tend to fade into the background. I had accepted from the start that there would be precious little time on this trip for purely personal activities. Having recently learnt the flute, I had packed it in the van hoping to do a little practice. I played only a handful of times. The days were filled with travelling and children – the evenings with feeding Hugh, paper work and planning the next day. There was little evening relaxation as Joseph and Amy usually chatted until late! However, there were compensations which more than outweighed the aspects of life put into temporary storage. To travel the Highlands in a luxury motorhome was certainly a pleasure to be savoured and to be an important part of such an ambitious project was very rewarding. Major support of such a venture is a mixture of sacrifice and privilege.

The so-called rest day produced the ultimate 'low'. 'Rest' is probably a misnomer as Hugh was very busy. It may be that Hugh could have done without the rest, but we did need the chance to reorganise. To clean the van, ourselves and our clothes. To re-stock with provisions kindly stored by Roger and to plan the next stage. Hugh spent hours on the phone. The children watched a little television for the first time in five weeks. It was noticeable that they soon tired of it. Roger's home provided the perfect venue for all this activity and Roger himself couldn't have been more helpful.

Hugh was like a fish out of water and looked very out of place on the streets of Fort William. His high level route had kept him well away from all but the tiniest villages for nearly five weeks. He was at one with his travelling environment but very uncomfortable with the town. I was very relieved when the time came for him to don the studs once more and life could get back to normal.

The day off had made me feel very uneasy and out of place. Perhaps I shouldn't have taken one at all – after all I was far from exhausted. If there had been any value in the day, it was in telling me to avoid days off in the future.

Chapter 11   BIG DAYS
MOVING EAST

May 20 – 29

In the early evening, I returned to running shoes and the Caledonian Canal's swing bridge. The tensions of a frustrating day were eased as I ran three miles towards Fort William and Ben Nevis. Passing through the Claggan housing estate, I called to see Joe and Jeannie Robson, with whom I had stayed many times for the annual Ben Nevis race. They were amused that their house was on the way from Ben Hope to Snowdon.

The summit of Ben Nevis from the Claggan stadium was a familiar route. Six times I had raced to the summit and back to the highland games arena. Every year, on the first Saturday in September, five hundred runners converge from all over Britain to compete on the nation's highest mountain. I had had varying degrees of success, depending on how suicidal I felt for the steep descent. My strength had always been in my ascent speed. Only once, in 1985, did I manage to throw all caution to the wind, throw myself off the mountain and win the race. Speed and agility are instantly lost as soon as thought is given to what could happen in a fall against the rocks. As soon as firm preparation began to be made for the Mountains of Britain run, my sense of self preservation increased and my downhill racing speed fell. My competitive drive to race dropped dramatically in the year before the run.

Today I could take my time on the mile of open road leading to Achintee and the base of the Ben (as Ben Nevis is often known). It was like a fresh start. There were new mountain ranges to look forward to, and tomorrow, for the first time, I wouldn't be turning at the top of the Ben. The compass was now set East for a hundred miles towards Aberdeen. There were fifty-two Munros before the next turning point – Mount Keen – the most easterly Munro.

My appetite for a big day had grown after the pavement slabs of Fort William. Today was well suited for a return to the mountains – ten Munros with 12 500 feet of ascent. Roger Boswell had been busy arranging company from Lochaber Athletic club. The details were left under the van's windscreen wiper before 6:00 am.

THE SUNDAY NEWS
Delivered to your door.

I shall be doing the Ben at 6:00 am with Peter Travis (so look out for us coming down as you are going up). After I've finished that, I am going to cycle from the Youth Hostel to collect Cammie's (Ronnie Campbell's) van, then I'm going to nip into Ft Wm to collect Phil Hughes, and drop him off at the end of Glen Nevis. Phil will then run up to the *bealach* between Carn Mór Dearg and the Aonachs (or possibly the *bealach* between the Aonachs

Towards the summit of Ben Macdui. (Matt Dickinson)

Right. Pauline preparing to go.
Below. Over a hundred maps.
Far right. Summit of Ben More Assynt. (Dave Peck)
Below right. Filming in the bog country – west of
Crask. (from left – Paul Tuson, Dave Richardson,
Jeremy West, Kees t'Hooft) (H.S.)
Overleaf. Sunset on the Munros – Loch Lomond
and Ben Lomond. (P.S.)

Left. Phil Clark on Collie's Ledge (Inaccessible Pinnacle on left). (H.S.)

Below left. 'Is that an eagle?' – Glen Carron. (H.S.)

Left. Sourlies bothy. Phil Clark, Keith Barber, HS and Mike Walford. (Tony Cresswell)

Below. Shelter Stone Crag and Loch Avon. (Paul Tuson)

Breakfast on the go under Liathach in Torridon. (H.S.)

and the Grey Corries) where he will intercept you and then run with you and Davie Rogers all the way to Fersit.

Meanwhile, I shall drive round to Fersit in Cammie's van and run back in to intercept you. Cammie's van will then be available at Fersit to bring everybody back to Ft Wm.

It would be a great help to Phil if you could give an estimate of when you're likely to arrive at the 2 *bealachs* – could you leave a note of the times under Cammie's windscreen wipers so that I can pass the times on to Phil?

Best of luck.

Meanwhile, Roger's own weekend left little time for him to attend to his washing machine. Throughout Saturday, he had manned a first-aid post for the 'Rock and Run' two day mountain marathon, which was being run in the Mamores and Grey Corrie mountains to the east of Fort William. At the crack of dawn on Sunday he accompanied fell runner, poet and writer Peter Travis up and down the Ben. It was a wonderful coincidence that Peter's charity hop over the three peaks of Britain should happen to cross paths with me on the lower slopes of the Ben. Peter ran up and down Ben Nevis, Scafell Pike and Snowdon all in 10 hours 56 minutes, linking the base of each mountain with an Army Air Corps helicopter. There was no time to talk as Peter was racing down the hill towards a beating chopper. However, there were plenty of shouts of encouragement in both directions.

The two hours taken to scale the 4406 feet of the Ben was double the normal race time. There was time to talk to Eddie Campbell and Davie Rogers as we twisted our way up through the zig zags. Eddie, triple winner of the Ben Nevis race in the early fifties, had climbed the mountain at least a thousand times before. Eddie has kept his fitness and youthfulness when most runners have hung up their shoes. Davie Rogers, more than thirty years younger than Eddie, was keen to learn about training. A recent winner of the Ben Lomond race, he looks to have a bright racing future and has the most important ingredient – enthusiasm. We discussed speed training, hill repetitions and the most important ingredient of training – long trips into the mountains. Today's outing was certainly in that category and probably at least double the normal training requirement of a racing fell runner.

The summit plateau was covered in a hard layer of snow. The whiteness merged with the thick layer of mist and care was needed to avoid the huge icy precipices and find the steep bouldery slope leading to the Carn Mór Dearg arête. Picking our way slowly down the vast rock field, we passed a sign: 'Abseil posts – 50 feet intervals – for roping down only' . Looking over the edge into the depths of Coire Leis, we could see lots of poles jutting out of the steep bowl of snow that led to the valley bottom. Our route now maintained its height as we followed the fine rocky line of the arête to the next summit. Looking back to Ben Nevis, the mist was clearing and exposing the massive cliffs and gullies of the north eastern side of the mountain. The narrow crest widened and climbed to the summit of Carn Mór Dearg, which just claims the 4000 foot mark. A thoughtful person had left some cakes and an anonymous message: 'Please leave for Hugh Symonds. 10:00 am Sunday. Only 10 Munros – just savour it.' I knew that it had to be Phil Clark. The word 'savour' had been in vogue through Skye and Knoydart. I had also seen him the previous evening at Achintee. He had given me valuable information on the snow conditions of the north side of the Ben. This had saved me the effort of

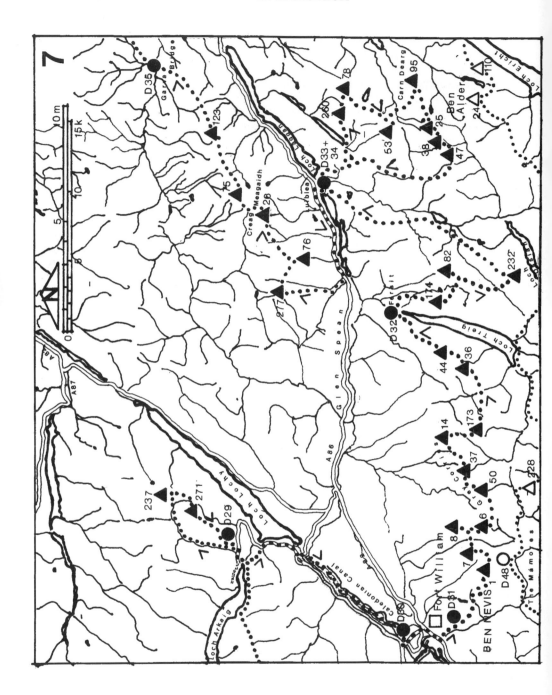

carrying an axe. It is quite common for these heights to be snow and ice bound until the end of May. The original and alternative plan had been to cross from the Lochy to Laggan hills if May was still gripped in winter above 4000 feet.

Eddie had added another one to his tally of Ben Nevis ascents, and now returned home for lunch. We met Phil Hughes at the first of the *bealachs*. Roger's intricate plans always worked. We scrambled up a steep bank towards the Aonachs. I had to look several times to judge whether I was hallucinating. My friends confirmed it. There was a man walking across the snow-speckled landscape in a pair of swimming trunks. I had seen a *sadhu* (saint) do this in the Himalayas, but not a Scotsman on a day which could hardly be described as warm. He turned out to be a man from Radio Scotland with a very good sun tan and a good knack of getting people to talk to him.

East of Aonach Beag, there were vast quantities of snow and I began to be concerned about having left the axe. Visions of long detours flashed through my mind as I saw steep, iced slopes running east towards the next Munro. I didn't want to take any risks, but I didn't want to go back either. Edging closer to a precipitous drop, the snow became slushy and in places it had melted away to expose firm rock. A narrow line led us through a gap in the snow. Looking back towards the summit, we could see huge cornices hanging off the edge of Aonach Beag. The blend of snow and rock, revealed through windows in the now clearing sky, gave a tremendous feeling of scale in this, one of the densest areas of high mountains in Britain.

---

7   LOCH LOCHY TO LOCH LAGGAN

Munro Number	Munro	Running Order
237	Sròn a'Choire Ghairbh	110
271	Meall na Teanga	111
1	Ben Nevis	112
7	Carn Mór Dearg	113
8	Aonach Mór	114
6	Aonach Beag	115
50	Sgurr Chòinnich Mór	116
37	Stob Coire an Laoigh	117
14	Stob Choire Claurigh	118
173	Stob Bàn	119
36	Stob Coire Easain	120
44	Stob a'Choire Mheadhoin	121
174	Stob Coire Sgriodain	122
82	Chno Dearg	123
232	Beinn na Lap (Loch Ossian)	124
260	Creag Pitridh	125
78	Geal Charn	126
53	Beinn a'Chlachair	127
95	Carn Dearg	128
25	Geal-Charn	129
38	Aonach Beag (Alder District)	130
47	Beinn Eibhinn	131
277	Beinn Teallach	132
76	Beinn a'Chaorainn	133
26	Creag Meagaidh	134
75	Stob Poite Coire Ardair	135
123	Carn Liath	136

The day was growing warmer over the next four mountains of 'the Grey Corries'. Amongst the vast expanses of quartzite screes, snow patches relieved the stark greyness of the scenery and provided some relief for my thirst. It is slow sucking snowballs, but given a cold ten-minute chew, it is possible to ease dryness in the mouth.

Two stobs (pointed hills) now lay between me and the van at Fersit. Although not a long day in terms of time (10 hours) and distance (22 miles), it was massive in terms of ascent (12 500 feet). Without camping out or using a bothy, there was little alternative to committing myself to the 10 Munros. The day would have been hard to execute in atrocious weather; I had been lucky again.

Closing on the summit of the penultimate peak, I saw a man pacing up and down by the cairn. His hand stretched out to welcome me to the top. Heavy mountain clothing disguised the identity of a figure that seemed familiar. Emptying his rucksack of tea and cakes, I recognised the man as an old friend. I had seen little of Dave Wells since we had been group leaders for Dick Phillips' Icelandic walking holidays. Like Bill Richardson at Kinloch Hourn, Dave had gathered information from Paul Tuson and had estimated my arrival time. He had only waited ten minutes. The support of friends gave me a tremendous boost throughout the run. Many drove hundreds of miles and took days away from home and work to be with me in the Highlands.

At Fersit, our camp had grown to two motor caravans. Friends from Kendal, Mike and Sue Parkin, had joined us with their toddler and baby.

Pauline's Diary, Sunday 20 May

We are now waiting for Hugh to come down at Fersit. The children are enjoying the company of Ben Parkin and Snip the dog – someone new to play with. Up until now they have had to rely on each other. I spent ages chasing a delectable Orange Tip butterfly with the camera.

We went up the Aonach Mór Gondola today – the mountain was a mess. The Forestry Commission's wholesale felling devastated the lower slopes whilst snow fences, tracks, ski posts and other odds and ends destroyed the upper slopes. A most uninspiring mountainside. Amy refused to walk, so Andrew carried all the gear in a large rucksack enabling me to carry Amy. We managed to reach a snow-filled gully where the children enjoyed investigating snow bridges with the marker sticks that had been left lying around.

Observations from the Gondola sparked off an interesting little study. When does the cable go over the pulley wheel and when does it go under? We designed our own cable systems – the Design and Technology lesson for the day!

Fourteen Munros lie sandwiched between the Lochs of Treig and Ericht. The plan was to tackle ten of them in the next two days and save the southern four for the return trip to Glen Nevis. Despite coming as close as two miles to some hills, they would be left for at least two weeks. The tactics were to sweep the Grampians in a roughly clockwise direction, and as usual make day to day decisions on where we could usefully park the van. It was like a giant score orienteering course. I had to double and triple check that I never missed a peak from my map of random speckled red dots and numbers. Check lists were ticked and maps were marked each day with a pencil line of the route. Evening administration took over an hour and sometimes it was more of an effort than donning the running shoes.

Pauline

Whenever possible, I gave the children tasks which were both educational and functional. Every evening, Andrew ran a little wheel along the pencil line which Hugh had marked on the map. He could experience his Daddy's journey through the lines and contours. Reading off the appropriate scale, he would make note of the distance which Hugh had covered and work out (no calculators allowed!) the cumulative total. Andrew developed an expert understanding of maps through this exercise, and through his role as navigator when I was driving. Andrew and Joseph both helped me to work out the height which Hugh had climbed, using the contour detail on the map. This could be quite a complicated exercise. It was Joseph's job to make a note of the distance travelled by the van and calculate the cumulative total. All these figures were recorded on a custom-designed daily form. It was often an effort to knuckle down to these tasks along with essential arrangements to be discussed for the following day. I took care to write down all meeting points together with expected arrival times so as to avoid any misunderstandings.

Leaving Chno Dearg. (Sue Parkin)

Mike and Sue alternated their days of running with me and today it was Sue's turn. In sharp and comfortable weather, we took our time to enjoy Stob Coire Sgriodain, Chno Dearg and Beinn na Lap – 'boggy mountain'. The last hill was far from boggy today. In places near the summit, the peaty ground had dried and cracked. Perhaps it was psychological, but I frequently felt more weary on the shorter days. Seven miles of stony track left me jaded after an outing of just over half yesterday's time.

Tuesday – a dark and threatening day. Seven mountains, on a circuit designed to ease my return passage to Glen Nevis in a fortnight.

A wide track led Mike Parkin and I towards the three Munros of the Ardverikie

Forest. Vast expanses of high wilderness are often termed 'Forests'. Centuries ago, these areas were covered in oak, birch and scots pine, but since their destruction, grazing has prevented regeneration. In the thick mist, these hills were unexciting until the descent from the third – Beinn a'Chlachair. Bounded by steep crags for most of its long southern wall, it was a tricky task to find a route into the huge glaciated trough which separates this area from Carn Dearg and the Aonach Beag Ridge. A brief hole in the cloud increased visibility beyond fifty metres and a line was found down through a scrambly mixture of rock and vegetation.

The next high ridge of four Munros gave a fast and interesting traverse. Closing on the second Geal Charn (white cairn) of the day, there appeared to be several cairns grouped around a larger heap of stones. In the thick blackness of the mist, it was impossible to identify these objects until they were virtually walked on. There, sitting by the summit, were three walkers wearing deer stalker hats. They blended well with the grey fog, stones and slush. Motionless, I wondered why they had chosen such a cold place for a rest, particularly without any view. I expect they wondered why I only stopped for a few seconds to reset the compass before running off towards Aonach Beag.

Occasional clearings gave glimpses of the huge massif of Ben Alder to the south; although only two miles away, this mountain was timetabled for next month. This whole region was a hub in the route. Tributaries and rivers point in all directions, some twisting their way to the Spey and the North Sea, and others to the Spean and the Atlantic. The ordering of these peaks in the core of the Highlands had puzzled me for a long time. There was great satisfaction in not only visiting the mountains but also planning their day-to-day execution.

Returning on the track to Luiblea, I glanced at my watch and said to Mike: 'It's only been an eight and a half hour trip.' Mike replied: 'Only!' I realised how my sense of a long run had grown over the weeks. Nearly within sight of the vans, we saw three runners approaching. I wasn't expecting anyone, so again, I thought some secret tracking had been going on through Paul. No, not this time! This was pure coincidence! Friends – Adrian Belton, Hélène Diamantides and Rex Stickland were off on an evening jaunt to recce the Aonach Beag Ridge. Adrian was planning a 30 Munros in 24 hours route over the Grey Corries, Mamores and mountains to the East. Although unsuccessful in two attempts during the 1990 season, his enthusiasm and experience from failures should give future endeavours a good chance of success. We stopped to chat, and plans were made to meet the following day for the run over the hills to the north of Loch Laggan.

Three miles of road past Moy started the next day. I was alone but for the company of Snip – the Parkins' dog. I wondered about the sense of this – not being an experienced dog trainer. Snip kept well to the right, avoiding the traffic until Mike and Sue's van passed by and stopped to pick him up. They drove on to Roughburn where we met for the climb of Beinn Teallach. Only a Munro since 1984, this mountain had grown in O.S. terms from 2995 feet to 3001 feet. Perhaps I should have been running all peaks over 2995 feet (or 2994 or 2993?), just in case they grew overnight.

A strong westerly wind blew us along five Munros, with the greatest height of the day reached on Creag Meagaidh. Bright sunlight broke through the billowing clouds and the snow of the high ridges became blinding. The sound of the studs breaking through the crunchy surface was like crushing cornflakes. 'The Window', a hundred foot steep notch in the ridge, gave great views into the deep cirque below. We stayed to rest and stare, cutting a Cumberland Rum Nicky into five slices with a compass. This rare delight, donated by 'The Village Bakery' in Penrith, accompanied me on the hills when there were groups of four or more people with me. So filling, it was impossible to do one justice between just two or three. Following the ridge to a grassy descent we arrived at the River Spey and the overnight stop by Garva Bridge.

Pauline's Diary, Thursday 24 May

The whole scene has changed in terms of both landscape and atmosphere. The country has become much more open – the sky much more obvious. Billowing cumulus float across the bright blue above. The valleys are wooded with glistening birch and the grass is very green. There is quite a large camp here. The film crew have returned – Jeremy and Kees. Runners, Paul and Roger have pitched their tents nearby and Mike and Sue have parked their van next to ours.

For the second time I took advantage of Sue's offer to look after the children and went for a run! Tempted by Sue's example, I had a bath and hair wash in the icy River Spey – it wouldn't surprise me if such activity has been known to cause brain damage. The effect of dipping one's head in freezing waters has to be experienced to be believed. The resulting feeling of 'joie de vivre' more than compensates for the previous tortuous experience.

On Creag Meagaidh. From left Sue Parkin, HS, Adrian Belton. (Hélène Diamantides)

Roger Boswell and Paul Tuson returned for a stint. With Mike Parkin and Snip we climbed through heather onto Geal Charn – the first of the four Monadhliath Munros. The day was raw with a strong northerly wind blowing snow flurries and chilling us to the bone. Snip, the dog, was without any body warmer but handled the freezing twenty miles with ease. The vast expanse of space called for careful navigation. It was tricky even in good visibility. Indistinct low rolling hillocks were spaced out by lochans and a multitude of drainage systems. Cairns and old rusty fence posts guided us but sometimes caused confusion. This was a long transit today and the feeling of distance and travel was emphasised by the clear views to Ben Wyvis, Strathfarrar and the Cairngorms, which were topped with a fresh icing of snow. It was thirty days since I had been on Wyvis. Since then, I had grown to understand how far I could run in a day and still be able to run the day after. Before Ben Hope, I had imagined needing a short day to recuperate after the Monadhliath. The low-level ten mile run from Newtonmore to Glen Feshie would have been ideal for this before the big days in the Cairngorms – but now I was planning to combine the two days and advance the schedule again.

We met the Zanzibar film crew on A'Chailleach – 'The Old Woman'. Partially buried in the stones of the high cairn of this mountain, Roger found a colourful magazine with pictures of naked and not-so-old women. It kept the support team entertained while I did another summit interview to film. The magazine posed a dilemma. We didn't like rubbish being left on the hill, but no-one liked the idea of being found with this pornography in their rucksack. It was reburied in the cairn to be found by a friend and teacher from Sedbergh School just three days later. I was later accused of having left the offending article.

From Newtonmore, the run through to Glen Feshie was split in two. The Parkin family had returned home and Roger Boswell had departed on Paul Tuson's bicycle, for a windy fifty mile ride without a puncture repair kit. The movements of supporters were often complicated. If they came with a car, then moving it or collecting it could be problematical; and if they came without a car, the difficulty was in reaching the liaison point in the first place. Roger and Paul had spent at least half the run over the Monadhliath contriving solutions to their own movements in the next few days. Paul always came with a bike in the boot of his car. This had simplified his own movements in the past in Sutherland and Torridon. Today, Roger was returning home for a few days before cycling back to collect and move Paul's car round to Braemar the following week. Meanwhile, Jeremy West and Kees t'Hooft – the film crew – had one small car for themselves, tents, tripods, cameras and food. Jeremy was sometimes able to move another car to the next filming point. Paul was the only supporter now, as we ran through Kingussie and across the Spey. We were expecting Les Stephenson, another runner from Kendal Athletic Club, but had little idea of how or when he would get to

---

8 THE MONADHLIATH

Munro Number	Munro	Running Order
256	Geal Charn	137
219	Carn Dearg	138
263	Carn Sgulain	139
247	A'Chailleach	140
34	Sgor Gaoith	141
111	Mullach Clach a'Bhlàir	142

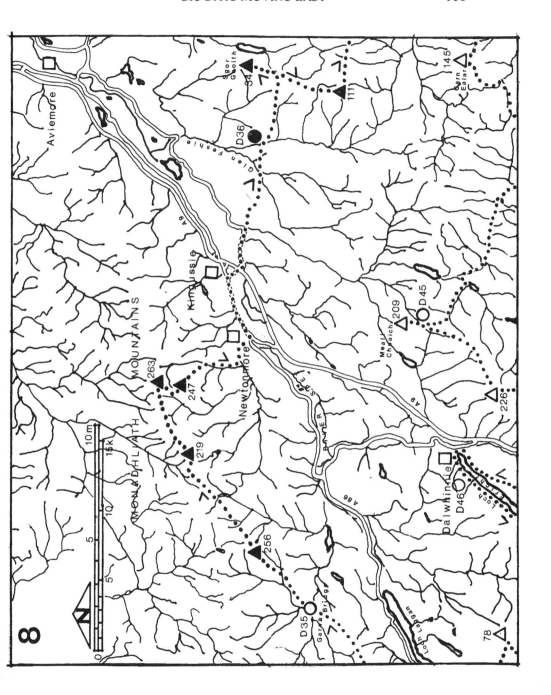

Glen Feshie. Unbeknown to us, as we were running through the forests east of Glen Tromie, Les Stephenson had jumped off a train at Kingussie and had bumped into Pauline at the tea break point at Tromie Bridge. This was all happening just a few minutes behind us. Relieved of his rucksack, which he had dumped on the van roof rack, Les set off in hot pursuit knowing from Pauline that we were not far away. Paul and I were astonished when we heard and saw a striding runner catching us up. This occurrence couldn't have happened better if it had been planned.

A cool wade of the Feshie was all that separated us from the night's stop at Achlean and the start of the Cairngorms.

Pauline's Diary, Thursday 24 May

We arrived at Achlean, at the head of Glen Feshie, to find a familiar red Renault parked there. Its occupant, Dave Wells, was fast asleep. Throughout the trip he appeared at frequent intervals, often unexpected and always in the right location – on the top of mountains with hot herbal tea and sandwiches for Hugh or in the Glens with luscious trifles (his wife, Pat's speciality) and delicious cakes. This was to be a quick visit and as he was returning in a few days time he offered to relieve us of our dirty washing and return it clean. Wonderful! Dave warned us that the occupant of the last house of the valley was none too keen on company and would most likely turn us away. I hoped for the best.

'The light was right', and so a filming session took place inside the van with Hugh and Dave discussing routes. It is not easy to put children to bed when the van is full of people, film cameras and 'Dougal' (the large and woolly microphone which accompanied Jeremy everywhere). A late bedtime again inevitably led to a late meal for Hugh and me. As we tucked into our fillet steak (a rare treat), we began to entertain the thought that we might be overlooked by the unhelpful character who had already turned away our entourage with their tents. After all we were not camping – just parking. No such luck! Yes, we could finish our meal but then we must move two miles down the road into the forest. Once again we moved camp with Joseph and Amy tucked up in bed.

Forty-nine Munros lie to the east of the A9 which cuts the eastern Highlands from Inverness to Perth. I had struggled to plan a route over and through these Grampian mountains and had made a rough guess of two weeks for the complete traverse. This time would allow me at least one rest day if the continuous battering of my body caused it to weaken or break down.

Seventeen of these Munros lie in the main Cairngorm massif. This is the largest area of high ground in Britain; the vast granite plateaux containing four of the five highest Scottish mountains. The extensive wilderness is split in three by the two long north to south passes of the Lairig Ghru and Lairig an Laoigh. Encouraged by the knowledge that friend and supporter, Mark Rigby, had previously completed a round of all seventeen Munros in under 24 hours, a scheme was devised to top all these peaks in three days. Mark didn't have to run the day after his solo epic, but I had to keep fresh enough to be able to continue East towards Mount Keen.

The plan was as follows:

> *Day 1*   (7 Munros)
>   To climb the peaks west of the Lairig Ghru and finish the

Cairngorm Day 1, Friday 25 May (company: Paul Tuson and Les Stephenson)
A stony track led us from Achlean up 2000 feet to the wide featureless expanse
separating the two westernmost Cairngorm Munros. Yesterday's topping of snow was
melting and evaporating in the morning sunshine. The effect produced a thin layer of
mist which hovered just a few feet above the ground. Blowing and swirling in the wind,
it looked like a staged dry ice scene. The film crew were overjoyed and spent over an
hour shooting near the steep eastern rock slopes of Sgor Gaoith (peak of the wind).
Yesterday's view of the Cairngorms from the Monadhliath had been deceptive. The
gentle velvet slopes of the west hide great eastern slopes which drop precipitously into
deep blue lochs.

We left the mosses and lichens of the rolling western mass and ran four miles due
east, in and out of a deep valley and onto the third mountain of the day. Beinn
Bhrotain's desolate summit was slow going. The vast field of rounded boulders made
running difficult and the scale of the day was now dawning on me as the hours were
beginning to tick by. Steered by Monadh Mór (Big Hill), we avoided losing too much
height and contoured as best we could towards the Devil's Point. This pyramid peak,
although 3303 feet high, is dwarfed by its surrounding Munros. On the thousand foot
climb to Cairn Toul, I ate my last scraps of food and Les Stephenson complained of
fatigue. 'Never have I wanted a pint of beer so much in all my life,' he said. The route
was now beautifully guided by the craggy rim passing over Angel's Peak and the high
plateau. At last we found some water to drink above the Falls of Dee, but we had now
eaten everything. For the first time in five weeks, I had run out of food and I was
bonking – the runners' and cyclists' term for getting hunger knock, not a form of
nocturnal activity. The day was chilling and the high summit of Braeriach was frozen.

The snow was crisp and the summit stones were encrusted in an icy coat. The great
corridor of the Lairig Ghru looked a long way down and even five miles to the van now
seemed distant as I was becoming more hungry with every stride. Somehow, Les
managed to find an apple in the depths of his rucksack, and the one third share seemed
a big improvement on fresh air. At ten hours, thirty miles and 10 000 feet, the day was
one of the hardest I had had, and I feared for myself over the next two. The sight of the
van was more welcome than usual but even then the last mile through thick long
heather was slow and rough on the legs.

Pauline's Diary, Friday 25 May
*Today is a long day for Hugh. It is nearly 7:30 and he still hasn't appeared at the
Cairngorm ski car park. The phone works very well up here. It is frustrating not to be
able to use it. I have lost my voice!*

*We visited the wildlife park at Kincraig today. It was fascinating for the children to
see past and present animal life of the Highlands. Although the park is well laid out
and spacious, it still hurts to see creatures captive.*

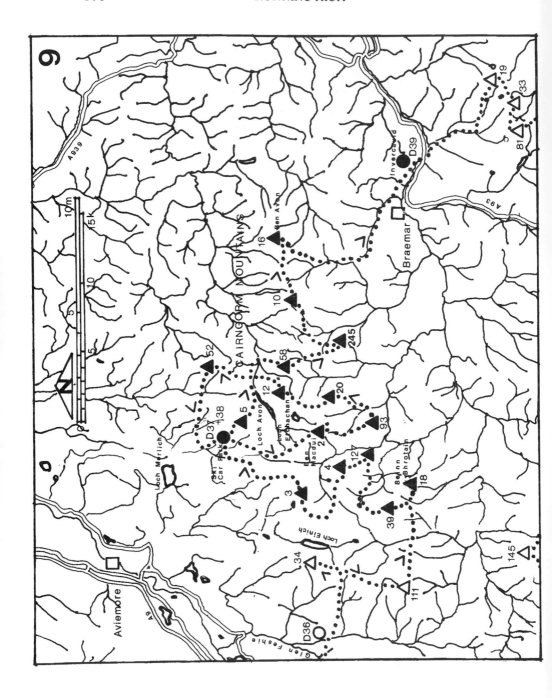

Aviemore was a real culture shock. Very busy and tiring. I persuaded Andrew to take charge of Joseph and Amy in the van, so that I could do the shopping as quickly as possible – fresh food for the next few days, sunblocker for Hugh's beetroot nose, calor gas and petrol for the van. It was a relief to escape to the clear air of the ski car park – a quiet spot at this time of year.

That night, after the usual lengthy feast, I lay in bed experiencing strange sensations. A strong tingling feeling was moving around the inside of both legs. It gave them a feeling of lightness and strength. I hadn't had this before and thought it was probably the muscles refuelling with glycogen after the day's exhaustion. Marathon and distance runners sometimes employ a pre-race training and diet system which boosts their energy supplies. By exhausting the glycogen from the muscles, the body is tricked into wanting more carbohydrates in return. By eating lots of starchy foods, it is possible to build up more reserves than usual. This can make a crucial difference in the closing stages of a race. Unfortunately, the human body grows wise to this deception and the trick can only be done once every few months. Tomorrow would tell me whether the unplanned bonking and eating regime had done me any good.

Cairngorm Day 2, Saturday 26 May (company: Paul Tuson and Les Stephenson)
Packing the sacks with more food than usual, we set off for Ben Macdui – at 4296 feet, Britain's second highest mountain. By coincidence, it was my 148th and the halfway peak to Snowdon. Matt Dickinson, the film director, had flown up to shoot some sequences and interviews on the summit. The two hours spent on the top gave Paul, Les and I the chance to pick out the dozens of distant peaks from the panorama viewfinder-stone. The sky was blue and sharp. Arrows pointed to the Bens of Wyvis, Hope and Klibreck. This was the thirty-ninth day on the mountains, and now the first hills were visible again. This halfway point bestowed a sadness that the journey was now on its way out. The hills to the South and East didn't look as interesting as those to the North and West. My legs seemed to have grown stronger from yesterday's glycogen depletion. I had grown a bond with the hills and I wanted the journey to last forever. The halfway mark had come too soon. I didn't have to travel at the speed I was going; but I

---

9 THE CAIRNGORMS

Munro Number	Munro	Running Order
18	Beinn Bhrotain	143
39	Monadh Mór	144
127	The Devil's Point	145
4	Cairn Toul	146
3	Braeriach	147
2	Ben Macdui	148
93	Carn a'Mhaim	149
20	Derry Cairngorm	150
12	Beinn Mheadhoin	151
52	Bynack More	152
5	Cairn Gorm	153
58	Beinn a'Chaorainn	154
245	Beinn Bhreac	155
10	Beinn a'Bhuird-North Top	156
16	Ben Avon-Leabaidh an Daimh Bhuidhe	157

Towards the summit of Ben Macdui. (Matt Dickinson)

had learnt that I didn't want to take days off; and the positioning of the van at the roadheads often dictated the length of my tours into the hills. I had gained a momentum which I was enjoying, but which I knew would bring about the end too soon.

Descending gingerly on the boulder-strewn southern face of Macdui, we ran onto the fine ridge leading to Carn a'Mhaim. Lying parallel and above the Lairig Ghru, this rare Cairngorm ridge gives superb scenes across to the eastern buttresses of the Devil's Point and Cairn Toul.

The summit tors of Beinn Mheadhoin. (Paul Tuson)

Dipping 2000 feet in and out of the Luibeg Burn, we lunched by the sprinkling waters before the traverse of Derry Cairngorm. Above the high Loch Etchachan, Dave Wells intercepted us to make the second of several surprise pit stops. The additional cake and tea made doubly sure that we wouldn't run out of food on today's tour. Scattered around the rich blue loch were a handful of tents – a superb situation to escape the crowds of the Bank Holiday weekend.

Beinn Mheadhoin (pronounced vane) provided a short scramble onto its summit tor and a slow melting northern snowslope gave a standing glissade towards the day's final peak.

The short heather leading to Bynack More yielded much faster and easier running after the million rocks of the previous hills. Five miles and the deep Strath Nethy separated us from the Cairngorm Ski car park. Expecting this to be a drudge, a narrow gorge gave a welcome and interesting surprise. Enclosing a land of mini geography, little hills sheltered a rocky and narrow steep stream. Climbing this to its source, we came to a cove of shattered rock. I enjoyed these routes off the beaten track between the mountains, as much, if not more than, being on the summits.

From this hidden gem, we climbed to a saddle and used sheep trods through the heather to take us to the lower Cairngorm Ski car park. These northern slopes of Cairn

Gorm have had their soul stolen by monstrous constructions of concrete, metal and cable.

Pauline's Diary, Saturday 26 May

Having a whole day free coupled with the excellent weather, we decided to go on a long walk – a trip to the Lairig Ghru and Lurchers Crag. We were also able to see Ben Macdui, Hugh's halfway mountain and the subject of Mollie Hunter's thrilling book, The Haunted Mountain. *Joseph was quite thrilled to see the features of which we had read so much just a few weeks earlier. It was difficult to handle the incessant questions in the open air with a lack of working vocal chords.*

The budding mountaineers decided to leave the path and shoot straight up the very steep, rocky, heathery hill to Lurchers Crag. Amy and Joseph amused themselves travelling from café to café (created in their imagination from the configurations of boulders on the hillside). Feeling pretty ropy, I dozed for half an hour at a safe distance from the crag, whilst the children played in a make-believe quarry. Their capacity for amusing themselves using the available natural materials plus a good dose of imagination, is growing.

We returned by a route which was blocked by a steep, concave snowslope. Andrew was all set to shoot straight down, but I judged it unwise and we followed its top edge on grass and rocks until we could see the runout. Andrew displayed great skill at skiing down on his boots. Joseph was very game but quite uncoordinated.

The start of the day wasn't nearly so promising. A trivial argument over the type of spoon with which Amy was to eat her breakfast brought to a head the whole process of child discipline. Are children to get their own way simply by making enough noise? Hugh, having first decided that she must use the spoon she was given, backed down when screams and protestations ensued. To me this was a perfect example of his opting out of the issue of discipline. It was one of those occasions (and there have been few), on which his one-track-mindedness irritated me. 'Mountains of Britain' or no, he is still a father with a responsibility towards the children. Yesterday was a long day for him and he was tired – the whole thing was trivial in a sense, and I should have been more understanding – but it is difficult to handle boisterous youngsters without a voice. I am tiring of having complete responsiblity for the family all day and every day and in addition not feeling one hundred percent. In a fit of anger I threw Hugh's running shoes out onto the hillside. One landed in a stream and I suddenly realised that it could be washed away and lost – I could do real damage! This was not the intention. I rushed to the stream and retrieved it. By the end of the day feelings had cooled down.

Just as we were settling down to dinner (late as usual) Jeremy and Kees turned up – 'The light was right' again – a stunning sunset. Hugh left his meal to be filmed running along the car park with the setting sun as the back-drop.

Cairngorm Day 3, Sunday 27 May (company: Paul Tuson and Chris Davies)

The two faces of Cairn Gorm couldn't contrast more sharply. The climb under the ski tows was sheer physical effort. There was certainly no pleasure of nature. Drinks cans, old shoes, cigarette packets and broken bits of ski gear littered the mountain with more than just posts and winding tackle. Over the top and all this was suddenly out of sight. Dropping sharply between cliffs, we came to the shores of Loch Avon and stunning natural splendour unblemished by man. Under a cloudless sky, the Loch took different shades of blue – from the pale shallows near sandy beaches to the darkness in the deep centre. At the far end of the waters, Ben Macdui was guarded by extensive snowfields and a line of crags broken by the massive portcullis shape of the Shelter Stone Crag.

Having crossed the previous day's route and the stepping stones over the River Avon, we climbed onto the easier ground of the slopes of Beinn a'Chaorainn and Beinn Bhreac. There were wide skies and wide open spaces with plenty of room for deer to run free. We closed on a large herd which sensed us unusually late. When less than fifty metres away they were startled and ran away towards our next peak – Beinn a'Bhuird (pronounced 'byn a voort'). We approached again whilst the deer grazed for a while. Again they ran away and again in the direction of our route. Only on the fourth occasion did they run north and away from us forever.

Over the North Top of the day's fourth Munro and past more deep eastern corries, we ran on to the fine high ridge of 'The Sneck' that links the former mountain with Ben Avon. The summit tors of Avon were busy this Sunday afternoon. I took the opportunity to distribute Intermediate Technology sponsor forms, and promised to send postcards to people who made donations.

The ten mile route to the van was a joy. The fertility of the lower ground contrasted sharply with the desolation of the higher. The scent of plants and trees nourished me with life force. In many places the track was soft and peaty but not wet. It was a natural thick pile carpet for the running shoes. I floated downhill effortlessly towards the overnight camp at Invercauld.

The day had been another marathon at nearly twenty-six miles. Although shorter, at seven and a half hours, it had been the fourth consecutive big outing. I couldn't understand why I felt so good and so strong. Nevertheless, it certainly didn't worry me. I had become a running, eating and sleeping machine and even now, 157 Munros into the run, I wasn't doing it for the sake of doing it. I was savouring it while it lasted.

Pauline's Diary, Sunday 27 May

We have spent the day in the company of Carol Davies. Her husband, Chris, was running with Hugh. It is a great asset to have some support! Carol has a way with the children. Also I enjoyed some adult company during the day.

At the rendezvous point we met up with Ann Parratt, our liaison officer from Sedbergh. She had come up with her two children, Gemma and James, to chat with us about progress so far.

It was obviously going to be impossible for our large group (our family, runners and film crew), to camp at the meeting point. Just up the road we could see the perfect campsite – the grounds of Invercauld House. I decided to be bold and optimistic. Leaving the children behind with Ann and taking Carol for moral support, I drove the van up the dirt track leading to the grand house. We were using the tradesmen's route, not the more impressive main drive. After an awkward five point turn round a nasty bend, followed by a rough and steep descent we arrived at the mansion. Picking out the most used-looking of the many entrances, we knocked at the door. A dark, balding gentleman answered. I gave a brief summary of the 'Mountains of Britain' venture and politely asked if a large motor caravan, five tents and several cars could spend the night on the estate's land. The gentleman was a little uncertain as to his capacity to give permission, but seemed keen to help. Eventually he said, 'Well, I suppose it will be all right.' At that moment an elderly lady arrived – we didn't quite catch the name. We both had a strong feeling that there was something special about this delightful old

Discussing fundraising with Ann Parratt at Invercauld, near Braemar. (P.S.)

lady. Although she apologised for being deaf and almost blind, she seemed bright-eyed and quick-witted. In a most friendly and helpful manner she offered us camping space, providing that we remained on the back road. As we left, thanking the lady, we offered her a sponsorship form and she made the comment, 'Keep it up – strong girls.' Did she think that Carol and I were running?

Wishing to avoid the nasty bend on the return journey, I decided to reverse up the steep slope. After a while an unpleasant smell filtered up through the open windows followed by fumes emerging from under the bonnet! What on earth had happened? After years of driving, I was only now discovering the penalty of reversing any distance whilst slipping the clutch – a burnt-out clutch plate! There is no noticeable after effect at the moment – Roger assures me that the plate can afford to lose a few millimetres of rubber, but I am still worried that I may have caused permanent damage. I will obviously have to change my driving technique!

This camp is ideal. Hugh has spent much of the evening discussing arrangements with Ann, and signing a large number of postcards to be sent to individuals who have sponsored the venture so far. It is a great encouragement to know that back at home, a great deal of work is being done by Ann and others helping her, to make our fund-raising a success.

Having a huge, safe, open space to play in, Andrew, Joseph and Amy have made the most of their playmates, Gemma and James Parratt. The sun is shining, the company is so congenial and my voice is on the mend. I feel that I could live this way forever.

Pauline's Diary, Monday 28 May

As we were packing to leave, a landrover drove up and stopped next to our camp. The driver started talking to Jeremy. Even from a distance I could see from his expression that he was very hot under the collar, so I decided to go and find out what the problem was.

'Do you have permission to camp?' he demanded.

'Do you know that this is a private estate? What are all these tents doing littering the place up?' he continued in the same irate fashion.

He informed us that the estate office knew nothing about us.

'Have you seen the Laird?' he asked. When I had the chance to speak, I explained that we had been up to the house to ask permission and we wouldn't dream of trespassing. In any case we were about to leave. Flinging the comment, 'You can stay all week, if you have permission,' he drove off to find out, making it quite clear that he would be back inside fifteen minutes if we lacked authorisation. That was the last we saw of him!

Later we visited Braemar Castle. After an informative conversation with the gardener there, it soon became clear to us that the charming old lady who had so generously allowed us to camp on the land was in fact Mrs. Farquharson, the Laird's wife. The family own Braemar Castle along with Invercauld House as well as a castle on the Isle of Mull. Mrs. Farquharson originated in Seattle, America, but added the gardener, 'She is as Scottish as the Scots now.'

Over fifty runners accompanied me during the complete run. This Bank Holiday Monday, I was with Les Stephenson, Chris Davies and Roger Boswell (sometimes). I had come to know most friends through training and racing on the fells in the 1980s, but the friendship with Chris Davies dated back to 1956 (when I was aged 3), way before running days. We were next door neighbours in Altrincham, South Manchester. Chasing each other round the gardens at the age of five led to first-ever training runs on Altrincham's pavements at the age of fourteen. Chris ran ten Munros with me, from Cairn Gorm to Glen Muick. There was plenty of time to reminisce. Meanwhile, whilst we were taking it easy on the broad Lochnagar plateau, Roger Boswell was scooting into the distance collecting the sixteen Munros and tops (subsidiary 3000 foot peaks) of the area to the west of Loch Muick. It was an indication of the ease of these mountains compared to the previous Cairngorms, that I could cross five Munros in five hours and that Roger could visit all the neighbouring tops in a day.

From the crossing of the Dee at Invercauld, it was a delight finding a way through the maze of tracks of the Ballochbuie Forest. This was a different style of navigation. Left at the next junction . . . cross two streams . . . right at the fork . . . and out of the dense trees onto the open heathery moors to the west of Lochnagar. I loved passing small isolated lochs under corries and scrambling onto hills via unconventional routes not mentioned in guidebooks. Finding a route and finding a way was a real joy of the journey. From the isolation of the rocky western spur, we met quite a crowd by the summit panorama stone of Lochnagar. Fast runnable country, up and down four more Munros and undulations only just topping 1000 feet, took us to Broad Cairn, and onto a good track to the roadhead at Spittal of Glenmuick.

We had hoped to park and camp for the night at the Spittal (meaning 'Hospice'), but 'No Overnight Parking' signs gave us second thoughts. The car park was full of orienteers fresh from their weekend's competition at the Scottish championships near Braemar. Coincidental meetings with friends were becoming regular. There, from our home club of Lakeland OC, we met friend and international orienteer, Jean Ramsden. Jean told us of a great little spot she had used for camping just three miles down the road. Readjusting the planned approach to Mount Keen, I put the road shoes on and jogged down the tarmac by the side of the River Muick.

Pauline's Diary, Monday 28 May
The petrol pump attendant in Ballater warned us that the road up Glen Muick is very long and narrow – he obviously hasn't been to Kinloch Hourn or up Arkaig!

Things are going well – Hugh is in high spirits and my voice is returning.

We have discovered this wonderful book by Prince Charles – The Old Man of Lochnagar. *Every sentence is action-packed and the children (and me) find it hilariously funny.*

Mount Keen – 'A hill ideally suited for a relaxed outing' – according to Irvine Butterfield's guide to *The High Mountains of Britain and Ireland (*a book which I found enormously helpful). This may be true if the mountain is approached by car from the north or south – but for an approach and departure on the western side, a far from relaxed outing was in prospect.

The first sound of frying chips for a week. The rain was heaving down on the roof as weather fronts were pushing in from the west. It was time for the maps, scissors and transpaseal again. As if to remind me that it was in the far east, I had to cut a tiny piece off the next OS sheet to fit Mount Keen onto my day's chart. The only piece of ground with any mountain rock was off the edge of the main map. All the rest was a great mass of peat bog, and with a cloud base at 2000 feet it was going to be fun finding a way through the hags and hollows.

The campsite was at the base of a track which took Roger, Les and I onto the top of the rounded hillock of Drum Cholzie. Unfortunately, the stony trod petered out after two miles and emptied us into a landscape of brown and green muck, and vegetation. Running in a straight line was impossible. Every few strides, a ditch would be in the way. We couldn't see anything of Mount Keen for the thick and heavy cloud, but I now knew that ground like this was going to make it a long and energy-sapping four miles; let alone the ten mile return bog trot to find a track to Glen Doll and the van.

In an attempt to guide us east, we picked up a tributary of the Burn of Lunkart. Our speed was trebled instantly as the hollow of the burn had no tangled heather to thrash through. We had found the answer to crossing this vast bog land – follow the lines of the water channels.

The visit to this far and isolated mountain was like a pilgrimage. However, there was no reason to stop for more than a minute on top, as the crown sat in a blanket of blowing mist. Descending from the summit's cone – 700 feet through boulders, we returned past reedbeds and random poles and cairns to the same tributary of the Lunkart. Enthused by the turn to the west, I ran and jumped mounds and tussocks with a light agility until I came to grief and fell headlong into a stinky brown pool of mud. Stripped from toe to waist, I rinsed the filthy clothes in a handy lochan.

In trying to follow more watercourses we stumbled upon a winding trough which took us two miles towards the indistinct hill of Fasheilach. It seemed that the local inhabitants had also grown wise to using these hollows to ease their movement. Animal prints abounded on the floors of these narrow peat clefts. Hundreds of deer and dozens of hares were our only sightings of other mammals in this whole sortie. I doubt whether many people choose to climb Mount Keen from this direction. Had all the routes between hills been like this, then I wouldn't have entertained the idea of the run for long. It was interesting and different for a day, but I was now beginning to yearn for a return to the sharp mountains and ridges of the west.

Twisting and turning inside the recess, it was hard to maintain a bearing. Roger Boswell occasionally climbed out onto the open moor to see if he could identify any distant features. We would run on, watching the compass deviate 50 degrees each side of the desired bearing. We just hoped that the eventual average would be about right.

By mid-afternoon we crossed a watershed, and the ground became grassier by the Burn of Mohamed (I had to look at the map twice to check this name, which I could pronounce for a change). Most of the streams and tributaries that feed the Glens of Mark and Muick have been christened. We passed burns, grains, allts and stripes all with names of people who must have claimed them in early stalking days. Nearing the top of the small watercourse of Shiel Stripe we turned to look for Mount Keen for the last time,

Returning from Mount Keen. (Les Stephenson)

before dropping down through the forests to Glen Doll. There, seven miles away as the grouse flies, the curtain of cloud had lifted from the hill that had given us a reason for being in this desolate land between Mark and Muick.

I had toyed with the idea of running the twin peaks of Driesh and Mayar on an evening circuit from our camp near the Glen Doll Youth hostel. However, the day had left me weary and I was only too happy to get the mud off my legs and have a thoroughly good shower, courtesy of the SYHA. Roger was travelling light as usual. He carried a beer mat which he used for cleaning his petrol stove, wiping his feet and drying his face. He took it to the youth hostel in the hope that he might also be able to wangle a much-needed shower. The warden wasn't too happy that I had brought an entourage. However he warmed to Les and Roger, and they had a long conversation about the previous travellers Hamish Brown and Craig Caldwell, who had passed this way on their long walks. When it was Roger's turn for a shower, the warden noticed him disappear with the grubby green beer mat. 'Come back! What's that?' he called. 'It's a towel,' replied Roger. 'You must be joking! You're not going in my shower with that! Come here.' Reaching into the cupboards of the laundry room, the warden found a pure white towel and handed it to Roger. Bucket washes in the van or scrub downs in the burns worked well, but a hot shower once a fortnight was a great luxury.

Pauline's Diary, Tuesday 29 May

Hugh is pretty tired tonight – spirits not quite so high as they have been – too many late nights he says. He has that characteristic zonked look upon lying down in bed – not very exciting!

This is an excellent parking spot for 30p per day – there aren't any 'no overnight parking' signs here.

Roger and Les are camped next to the van. Roger is cooking on a weird looking petrol stove which requires lighting in the same way as a primus. He primes it with petrol, i.e. he puts a match to naked petrol! The stove and all his cooking vessels are coated in soot which has been inevitably transferred to his eating receptacle – Banjo's dog bowl (What does Banjo think of this I wonder?) Only the dog's bowl is large enough to hold sufficient nourishment to keep Roger going (Perhaps I should get one for Hugh?) Roger must see a parallel between the mountain runner and the animal kingdom. Tonight he inquired about Hugh, 'Have you finished feeding the beast tonight? – I haven't heard him roaring lately.'

Changing the plan to add Driesh and Mayar to tomorrow's Munros, gave me time to think ahead and look at more maps that evening. Mount Keen had been a turning point, and the realisation that I was now eight days ahead of the original schedule made me begin to think of altering my target for the run.

Chapter 12   RETURN TO GLEN NEVIS

May 30 – June 6

My dream had been simply to run all the mountains. The one hundred day schedule was an appendage for the media to grab hold of. I was now forty-two days into the run and eight days ahead of schedule. Either my planning was hopeless or I was running faster than expected. It was a bit of both. The plan had taken into account times of weakness forcing rest days for recovery. Perhaps I would need some of these eight days in the future. With several million more strides to take, there was still a high risk of accident, injury or illness. Up till now I had considered the days ahead of schedule as an insurance policy for getting to Snowdon on time on 27 July. However, as the last hundred Munros loomed up on the horizon, I began to entertain the idea of setting a 'good time' for the Munro traverse. 83 days had been the Ben Hope to Ben Lomond plan, but this could be trimmed to 75. Although this was at the back of my mind, still the most important consideration was the day-to-day planning, and, 'to think about the mountain I was on.' I didn't want the run to become a race, but at the same time if I did happen to set a record, it would be a bonus if it was one which was hard to break.

The steep climb up Driesh took us past a great vantage point for looking at the classic glaciated valley of Glen Clova. The River South Esk sparkled and meandered in the wide flat bottom of the glen. We could see the van going down the valley. As was often the case, Pauline would be travelling further than me today. It was three times as far to the Devil's Elbow by road as it was over the hills.

Pauline's Diary, Wednesday 30 May

My Mum and Dad have come to spend a few days with us. The children decided to travel in Grandad's car on the journey to Devil's Elbow – an unfortunate arrangement in one way. In the absence of my navigator (Andrew) we became tangled in a maze of minor roads outside Kirriemuir (the first time we have been lost). My father then decided to lead the way, and with his usual air of confidence was certain of solving the puzzle. I couldn't help remembering the countless childhood journeys into the countryside which terminated in farmyards!

We encountered the first 'real' supermarket of the journey in Kirriemuir. So far we have mainly shopped in the local 'Spar' grocers which serve most of the Highlands. It was mind-boggling to be confronted by aisles of consumer goods. Such choice! Such variety! We went mad.

Today's eight Munros took less time than the previous day's one. It was a joy to be on running terrain again. Every now and again, a sudden thud would break our rhythmical

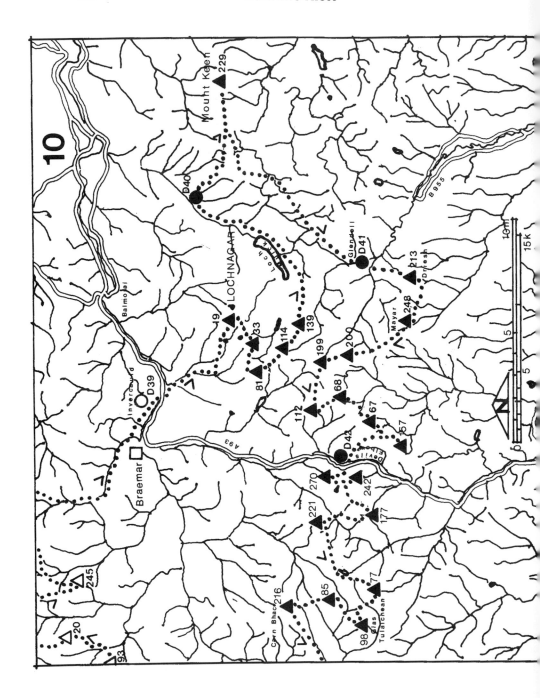

stride. Les had fallen over again. He would regularly hit the deck about three times a day, tripping on a stone or quartz block. He was lucky never to hurt himself. Roger and I would stop and turn round to see the tall sprawling body of Les picking himself up with a smile on his face.

Between Tom Buidhe and Tolmount, we saw something sparkling in the distance. It was a mystery. Running closer, we still couldn't make out what it was until we were on top of it. There was a gala gas balloon, caught by its string in the long grass. One face was silvery and the other depicted the red face of Mickey Mouse. Roger tied it to the back of his rucksack and gave a new dimension to the meaning of 'taking the Mickey'.

Dropping down to the high pass by The Cairnwell, we returned to ski country and the litter of fences, car parks, restaurants and ski tows. Places like this may look pretty in the snows of winter, but on a day like today, beneath a heavy sky, there is no beauty. Our resting spot in the car park was only for convenience.

Overnight, the mist had lowered to the 2200 foot level of the pass. It posed a threat to my big push through over the eight scattered Munros to Glen Tilt. With twenty metre visibility, it was slow feeling our way over the scarred mountains of Carn Aosda and The Cairnwell. Checking the directions of lines of cables offered a different style of navigation. Fortunately the mess doesn't spread far west away from the road, and I was back to the old regime of counting paces and running from lochan to lochan on compass bearings. Roger would occasionally break my concentration with an inquisition.

'What kind of teacher are you Hugh?'

'Maths, Roger.'

'You surprise me. I would have thought if you had added all this up beforehand, you would never have started.'

On the broad and rounded summit dome of Carn a'Gheòidh (hill of the goose), I

---

10   THE EASTERN GRAMPIANS

Munro Number	Munro	Running Order
19	Lochnagar-Cac Carn Beag	158
33	White Mounth-Carn a'Coire	159
81	Carn an t-Sagairt Mór	160
114	Cairn Bannoch	161
139	Broad Cairn	162
229	Mount Keen	163
213	Driesh	164
248	Mayar	165
200	Tom Buidhe	166
199	Tolmount	167
112	Carn an Tuirc	168
68	Cairn of Claise	169
67	Glas Maol	170
157	Creag Leacach	171
270	Carn Aosda	172
242	The Cairnwell	173
177	Carn a'Gheòidh	174
221	An Socach-West Summit	175
77	Glas Tulaichean	176
98	Carn an Righ	177
85	Beinn Iutharn Mhór	178
216	Carn Bhac	179

feared that we might miss the summit cairn. Roger, Les and I spread out in a line hoping that one of us would hit the top.

'Why don't we separate a little more,' I suggested.

'If we spread out enough we will never see each other again today,' Roger replied.

Les found the summit stones and gave a shout for us to zoom in. Bingo!

The mist began to thin on our approach to An Socach. The partial visibility created a confusion of sight. Roger stared and pointed into the distance.

'Is that lochan on your map Hugh?'

'Don't be silly – that lochan is a snow patch. Snow patches aren't usually marked on maps unless they are ice caps.'

However, we did pass lochans. One was big enough to be on the map but wasn't, even on the 1:25 000 scale. Another – Loch Nan Eun – was entertaining hundreds of gulls on its two tiny islands. Occasionally we disturbed a grouse. With a sudden beat of the wings they would take off, giving a rapid and raucous screech which would fade as they glided away. The shock of the noise is frightening and something that I have never got used to, even though it happens regularly on my local training ground of Baugh Fell near Sedbergh. Today, this happened before the climb of Glas Tulaichean. The bird left eleven eggs in a nest. I just missed running over them. I hoped the bird would soon return to warm the eggs.

The day improved over the rolling heathery wastes of the last three Munros. From the western summit of Carn Bhac, the Cairngorms stood on the horizon across the higher reaches of the Dee. Again they looked smooth, and the gentle slopes hid their true inner grandeur.

Having climbed 6500 feet and travelled 17 miles, we now had a ten mile downhill run to meet the van somewhere in Glen Tilt. The route took us through the tidy settlement of small pink buildings at Fealar Lodge. At 1800 feet it is the highest permanent habitation in Britain and, with twelve miles of winding track separating it from the main road to Pitlochry, it is one of the most remote. No wonder they choose to grow vegetables. But why such tremendous fertility so high up? I had hoped to get an answer this Thursday afternoon, but all was quiet except the gentle humming of a diesel generator in an outbuilding.

Crossing the Tarf on the Bedford Memorial Bridge, a solid Victorian suspension structure, we joined the narrow and straight Glen Tilt – a solid track making light work of the last five miles to the van at Forest Lodge.

Pauline's Diary, Thursday 31 May

Our sortie up Glen Tilt required a permit from the estate office in Blair Atholl. Sitting at a large desk, a very pleasant gentleman meticulously filled in the form – in slow motion – and charged us £5 for the privilege. Being a little curious about the state of the track and our ability to negotiate it, I made a point of informing him that we did have a large vehicle, not suited to rough stuff. He assured me that we would be fine so long as we did not travel at 90mph.!

It took an hour to twist and bump our way up nine miles of stony track, hemmed in by over-hanging trees in the lower Glen and pock-marked with pot holes throughout. My mother must be the world's most dramatic passenger (the children went with Grandad again) and she kept up a steady monologue of exclamations. The rough wooden bridge over the Tilt looked on the verge of collapse. An inspection was not reassuring but we crossed our fingers and went for it.

We reached Forest Lodge, much to the surprise of Mrs McGregor the stalker's wife, who exclaimed, 'Who wrote out a permit for that vehicle?' She was not pleased to see such a large van up the Glen, as a vehicle becoming stuck on the road would be a real nuisance to other users of the track. Fortunately she allowed us to camp. Later on Hugh took on the task of appeasing Mr McGregor who was unhappy about not being informed about us beforehand and none too happy about visitors up the Glen in general. It was easy to see his point when he explained the problems caused by careless walkers. A gate thoughtlessly left open can produce hours or days of hard work for farmers gathering up stray animals. The question of access is a hotly debated issue. I strongly believe in our right to roam, but the livelihood of the farmers must be respected. I can appreciate antipathy resulting from contact with inconsiderate and lazy trippers. Mr McGregor warmed considerably once Hugh had taken the trouble to explain our cause.

Parked next to the van was a small car with dozens of orange and white orienteering kites (checkpoint markers) on the back seat. I couldn't believe it – here was the third consecutive weekend that I had bumped into a competition. There was something mystical about the 19 April start date. Later in the evening, Andy Curtis (friend and runner from Livingston Athletic Club), returned from an afternoon's work on the neighbouring hills. He had been depositing kites for the Scottish Mountain Trial – a two day mountain navigation event. Mountain navigation competitions are so rare in Scotland (or England and Wales come to that), that the likelihood of bumping into one would be less likely than winning a Cornflakes packet competition and the probability of meeting three consecutive weekend events is as unlikely as meeting a Brazilian man and a Greek woman in a remote Scottish bothy.

Friday 1 June
A new month and perhaps the one in which I could complete the Munros. Finishing on 30 June would make it a 72 day traverse. I was beginning to get the bit between my teeth. However, that didn't stop me having a lie-in and a leisurely morning at our peaceful camp by the enchanting Tilt. The compact set of three Munros of Beinn a'Ghlo to the south-east provided a good excuse for a short day after the previous day's nine hour excursion.

Pauline's Diary, Friday 1 June
A wet day at first so we did some school work. We have decided that Gaelic can be a part of our travelling school curriculum. The names of the mountains cover an extensive vocabulary, and every day we look at the names of the mountains on Hugh's itinerary. Today he climbs Braigh Coire Chruinn-bhalgain which means 'the peak of the corrie of the little round bag'. The children are highly amused by this strange title.

The portable telephone worked erratically from this camp. Standing on the roof of the van with the phone often boosted the signal, subject to the possibility of being cut off without warning. Roger borrowed the phone one evening and commented, 'You usually go in phone boxes, not on them.' Knowing that there was some sort of reception, I put the phone in the rucksack for the run over Carn Liath, Braigh Coire Chruinn-bhalgain and Carn nan Gabhar – the three Munros of Beinn a'Ghlo. It was a good opportunity to talk to Richard Crane and Ann Parratt back in Cumbria. Until now, thoughts of

continuing the run to Ireland had been a distant dream. But now that the Scottish dream
was becoming a reality, I was beginning to think further. I gave hints of my thoughts to
both Richard and Ann, but was very shy to do so and asked them to keep it quiet. I was
reluctant to talk to friends about it. Occasionally, one would say to me,

'Have you thought of Ireland?'

'Well yes, but not seriously,' I would reply. I didn't want to commit myself to it. After
all, there were still 95 Munros, over a hundred miles to the Lakes, more to Wales and 15
Welsh mountains to Snowdon. Anything could happen! I was strong, healthy and
enjoying the run now, on 1 June, but it could be a different story next week or next
month.

Before leaving the wide ridges and steep walled corries of the Beinn a'Ghlo massif, I
couldn't resist the temptation of one more phone call. The twelve hour time difference
was right for a call to Australia and to fell-running friend Jon Broxap. The reception was
as clear as a bell. It seemed incredible to be on a mountain in Scotland and talking to
someone on the opposite side of the world. It turned out that one of Jon's first Munros
had been Beinn a'Ghlo. It was the first time that I had talked to Jon since his '28 Munros
in 24 hours round' – it was wonderful to be able to congratulate him from a mountain,
courtesy of Motorola and Cellnet.

Returning to Glen Tilt, Roger decided that after his five consecutive days on
mountains he was quite fit and ready for the Scottish Mountain trial. He couldn't turn
down the opportunity of competition with it being so near at hand. Finishing second in
the 16 mile B course adds evidence to running in the mountains not being an
exhausting activity!

The short outing and return to Glen Tilt allowed time for more planning and eating. I
spent hours force-feeding myself with cakes, sandwiches, christmas pudding and meals
of rice and pasta.

To the north-west of Glen Tilt lie four rounded and remote Munros known as the
Ring of Tarf. The problem was not so much how to do them, but where to go afterwards.
The logistics of arranging hills for a good line of attack was like a game of chess. Future
days had to be taken into account, and for the Ring of Tarf it was necessary to think as
far ahead as Drumochter Pass, Loch Ericht and Ben Alder. The previous winter we had

11   GLEN TILT TO DRUMOCHTER

Munro Number	Munro	Running Order
175	Beinn-a'-Ghlo-Carn Liath	180
63	Braigh Coire Chruinn-bhalgain	181
29	Beinn a'Ghlo-Carn nan Gabhar	182
188	Carn a'Chlamain	183
124	An Sgarsoch	184
145	Carn an Fhidhleir or Carn Ealar	185
121	Beinn Dearg	186
209	Meall Chuaich	187
226	Carn na Caim	188
235	A'Bhuidheanach Bheag	189
151	Sgairneach Mhór	190
119	Beinn Udlamain	191
178	A'Mharconaich	192
272	Geal Charn	193

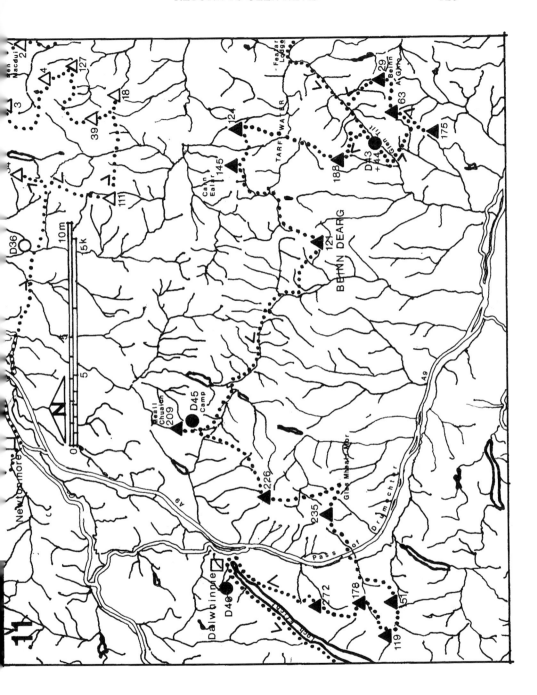

written to seek van access to Gaick Lodge, south of Kingussie, for an overnight staging point. Permission was refused, and I can understand the landowners wanting to maintain their splendid isolation. Their rejection caused another shortcut and reduction of a day from the schedule. Seeing no sensible place for the van, I accepted Dave Wells' offer of placing a high camp for me, sometime while I was not far from his home at Tomatin, south of Inverness. I had managed the Cairngorms without a camp, but now seemed the perfect opportunity, particularly as it was a weekend and Dave wouldn't have to take time off work. Dave drove into Glen Tilt to meet me on the Friday evening. We pinpointed a potential flat spot for a tent in a saddle and at a spot height of 614 metres, six miles east of Dalwhinnie. Just tucked nicely underneath the Munro of Meall Chuaich, it would be a long trek from the Ring of Tarf, but it would facilitate a new plan to climb the three Munros east of Drumochter on Sunday morning and the four to the west on Sunday afternoon.

The Tarf Hotel. (Mark Rigby)

Saturday, 2 June

Having given Dave the final food rations and bits of kit for the overnight camp, I departed for Carn a'Chlamain, the south-easternmost Munro of the Ring of Tarf. The weekend had brought about another change of company. Dave had brought Mark Rigby in for a five day voyage through to Glen Nevis and he took Les Stephenson out, to his long awaited pint of beer. Les had accompanied me over 35 Munros and had shown a visible increase in fitness during the week. Many pacers claimed a positive training effect, particularly Hélène Diamantides who went on to win both the Lakes classic of Wasdale and a race in Malaysia, and Mark Rigby who won Wasdale and Ben Nevis.

Running the Ring of Tarf anti-clockwise, Mark and I passed 'the Tarf Hotel' and stepped inside for a quick sandwich. The bothy had an 'AA' sign on the outside but offered comforts far from one star standards. Jumping a tributary of the Tarf Water, I slipped and banged a knee and ankle against rocks. The pain was sharp for several minutes. I feared that I had done damage to tendons and ligaments, and reminded myself that I must take care not to become over-confident.

The rounded hills of An Sgarsoch and Carn Ealar didn't excite me but I enjoyed the tranquil meandering watercourses that guided our route towards the broad stony summit of Beinn Dearg. The skies were clear but the isolation of the hills gives them unexciting views to the distant horizon.

The real pleasure of the day came in the twelve mile transit from Beinn Dearg to the high camp. Expecting this to be a long and arduous tramp through thick heather, I was surprised by the steep and narrow tributaries that cut into the high plateaux. I had trimmed and stuck together five 1:25 000 sheets for the weekend's eleven Munros. The resulting plastic map was five feet wide and ungainly to handle. Concentrating on a small area at a time by multiple folding, the map revealed footpaths on the sides of two tributaries. We climbed out of Bruar Water on one such narrow path. Half a mile of 2000 foot high bogland marked the watershed between the river systems leading to the Moray Firth and the Firth of Tay. We searched and found a tiny trod near the source of the Allt Gharbh Ghaig. This led up into a secret world that I felt only the deer knew. Ten miles from the nearest road and well away from any normal mountain routes, I rarely felt as isolated as this. A narrow stony track hugged the edge of the steep and deep valley, high above its floor. The burn tumbled down through rocks and past patches of green, which lay a hundred feet below us. Deer were grazing on small patches of grass in the narrow bottom. Protected and separated from us by steeply sloping banks of scree and heather, the deer didn't make the usual hurried escape.

Two miles further downstream, the valley broadened to the wide and flat plain above Gaick Lodge. Enjoying the serenity of the previous secret valley so much, we chose to climb out and return to the plateau via another narrow cleft – the Coire Bhrodainn. Forced out of the stream bed by huge blocks, we pulled our way up nearly a thousand feet on all fours. Clutching the heather of the forty-five degree slope with tight fists, we made a rapid and excited ascent to return to the open moor and a two mile trot towards Meall Chuaich.

Dave Wells' bright orange tent was easily spotted in the brown and green landscape of peat hags. He had found a good spongy piece of ground which provided a soft bed for the night.

Not wanting to miss an opportunity, Chris Bradley and Matt Dickinson of Zanzibar Films joined us to film the proceedings. Did people really want to watch me eating vast quantities of powdered spud cooked on a primus? Matt told me to expect a microlight to fly over me in the next two days. Pinpointing the proposed route to Ben Alder and beyond, Matt made plans to take a camera up and shoot some aerial film giving scale to the photography. Like all good film directors, Matt had a way of making things work. He happened to have a friend, Richard Meredith-Hardy, who was highly skilled at flying microlights. The excuse to fly over Highland landscape was good enough for Richard to drive his wings and engine up from Hertfordshire.

The camp couldn't have been better placed for a pre-breakfast bid for the broad, uninteresting mass of a Munro – Meall Chuaich. Nineteen minutes up and eight down was an ideal appetizer for Dave's mess-tin full of porridge.

Mark and I left Dave to decamp, and departed for the sprawling undulations leading to the Drumochter Pass. In clear visibility, we rounded the top of Choire Chais and reached Carn na Caim. Looking vaguely south, we saw our third Munro of the day and made a run for it across the tops of tributaries. Climbing the last few hundred metres, I looked closely at the map and realised that the gradient was steeper than shown. I looked around at neighbouring hills and began to doubt our position. There was only one hill in the vicinity which had a trig point on it, so the top would confirm whether we were on the right mountain or not. I had been lazy about navigation, this Sunday morning, and I wasn't surprised when the top didn't reveal a concrete trig point. Mark and I had run too far east. We were on Glas Mheall Mór. At 928 metres it is a Munro top, but eight metres lower than its neighbouring A'Bhuideanach Bheag, it is not the main Munro summit. It was frustrating but I could see the funny side of my mistake. A mile away to the north-west, we corrected ourselves to visit the less interesting higher mountain. Meanwhile we could see the microlight searching for us – so much for my pinpointed route.

It was the only occasion on which I visited the wrong peak, and ironically, I had arranged to meet the public relations manager for Ordnance Survey at Drumochter Pass. I was consequently half an hour late for my midday appointment. Had it been misty, I would have concentrated harder and used positive landmarks such as old fence posts. In the clear visibility we had run on a vague bearing to the hill on the horizon which looked most outstanding.

Part of my reasoning for combining east and west of Drumochter into one day was to avoid spending a night at the bleak pass. The fast, dense traffic was not conducive to relaxation, particularly with the children wanting to run around in the lay-by. Drumochter was a busier place than usual this Sunday lunchtime. Ordnance Survey staff arrived to meet me and photograph the van with its advertisement for Pathfinder (1:25 000) maps. Dr Bev Holt came to check me over, Zanzibar films continued to follow my moves and Richard landed his microlight by the roadside. Bev's scales recorded a half stone increase in weight in seven and a half weeks. The eating was working.

Plans were made to look out for the microlight on Geal Charn, the seventh and final Munro of the day. However, the weather had collapsed. Cold driving rain was heaving in from the west and flying conditions looked poor.

Mark and I crossed the railway line and set off for Sgairneach Mhór and Beinn Udlamain. I was now west of the A9. I had been ten days east of the Grampian trunk road – four days shorter than the estimated fortnight. The afternoon's peaks were scheduled for June 13th and it was June 3rd. Completing the Munros within the month of June now seemed a real possibility. A major stumbling block could be Mull. I had made no firm arrangements to borrow a yacht, but with Ben More on Mull being just twenty-eight Munros away, my thoughts were beginning to turn to my time of arrival on the west coast. I didn't want to waste time waiting for a boat. I discussed potential timings of mountains with Mark as we forced our way through high winds and hail. Whilst climbing the penultimate peak of the day – A'Mharconaich, we heard the drone of the microlight below us and to the west. The clouds cleared, and Richard swooped in from Loch Ericht and circled us as we climbed the last mountain. He saw a flat spot on the side of the hill and landed. As World Champion microlight pilot you would expect Richard to be skilled, but to land on a stony slope with gusting winds seemed pure madness. He made light of it saying, 'It's fine as long as a stone doesn't get thrown up and hit the propeller.'

I was tired enough to want a lift down the mountain to Dalwhinnie, but flying was against my rules. The four miles to the van on the far side of Loch Ericht was hard work even though downhill. I had covered nearly sixty miles and climbed 15 000 feet in the weekend and tomorrow's long run west to Corrour station could hardly be described as a recovery day.

Pauline's Diary, Sunday 3 June

The road to the meeting point on the Ben Alder track appeared to be blocked by the railway. Andrew pointed out that we could drive over the line. It looked possible but silly until we noticed the sign,

STOP

Before crossing, use the telephone provided to contact the station.
1) Open gate before crossing with vehicles or animals.
2) Cross quickly.
3) Close and secure gates after use.

We found a perfect site next to the loch beyond the dam. There are many who use the space of these wild places and yet seem compelled to leave their mark. The shore of Loch Ericht was strewn with the remnants of a party – aluminium cans, cigarette papers, bottles and crisp bags. We collected the lot and built a monument to the litter louts – a work of art constructed from the trash.

The 24 mile run over four Munros had to be paced to catch the 7:32 pm train to Tulloch. West of Loch Ericht there is no road until Glen Nevis – 2 days away. However, the vast wastes north of Rannoch Moor and the Blackwater Reservoir are cut by the main railway line to Fort William. To avoid spending a night away from the family, I planned to take a train ten miles from Corrour to Tulloch, where Pauline would park the van. I would return by train to Corrour the following day to continue the run from the same position.

Mark and I left camp at 10:30 to allow plenty of time for navigational errors, and for further filming from the microlight if Richard could find us amongst the mountains and rocks. Ten miles on good tracks alongside Loch Ericht provided a gentle start to the day. Beinn Bheòil with its head in the clouds approached slowly as we passed masses of bright yellow broom on our right and the waters of the long shoestring loch on our left.

Climbing into the clouds in deteriorating weather, we traversed the summit ridge and descended to Bealach Breabag occasionally capturing hints of the scale of Ben Alder, when breaks in the cloud exposed the huge bowl of Garbh Choire. The high and massive summit plateau of Ben Alder was still gripped in winter. Broken escarpments leading to the summit held large quantities of snow. Thirteen days after my previous visit to mountains in this great central wilderness, I was again robbed of views. At this height, above 3700 feet, there wasn't even a hint of a clearing to the Aonach Beag ridge. However, sights within the thick veil of mist were striking. Partially melted cornices hung onto the edge of the corrie in huge rolling coils of snow. Turning a corner for the last few hundred metres to the summit cairn, we passed the frozen and snow-covered Lochan a'Garbh Choire – perhaps the highest lochan in the Highlands. Making a beeline to escape the freezing wind, we plunged 2300 feet on the steep south-west face of the mountain to cross the Alder Burn. Crossing a peaty waste, we stumbled upon a lone cross dated October 1979. Without a name or any other evidence, the wooden remnant remained a mystery on the moor.

Hearing a distant buzzing sound, we stopped to listen more carefully. The microlight

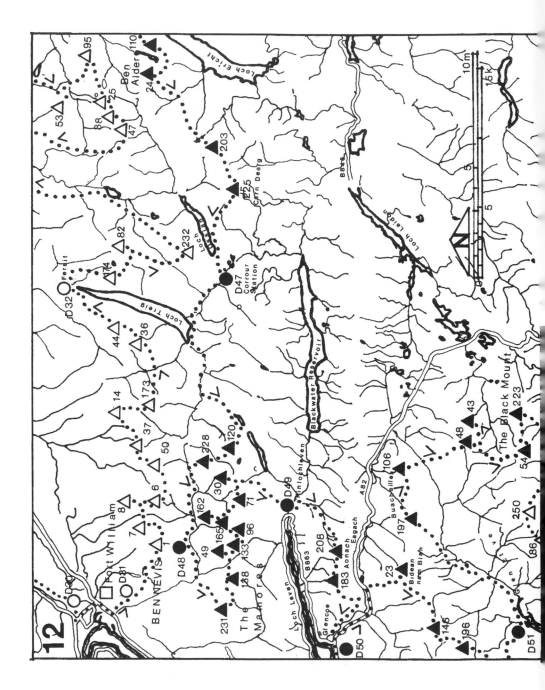

came into sight, a mile away to the west and very high in the sky. We waved our brightest clothing frantically but it vanished before seeing us. From our isolated position by Lochan a'Bhealaich, we didn't stand much chance of being seen. We climbed the steep eastern face of Sgòr Gaibhre, close to a long line of buttresses. A broad green ridge led us to the twin peak of Carn Dearg. Hearing the microlight again, we sprinted to the top, thinking that we would stand out more on a summit. Spotted at last! Chris Bradley was hanging over the edge of the cockpit pointing his film camera towards the ridge. I had previously been instructed to try to run on a skyline. Running down towards Loch Ossian whilst being swooped closely and repetitively made for an unusual descent of the mountain. I moved in fits and starts, posing for the camera with a strong stride when I knew it was close. Richard landed his tiny aircraft on the stony track between Loch Ossian and Corrour Station. He off-loaded Chris with his camera, before flying back to his car at Blair Atholl, navigating his way between mountains with a Bartholomew's map strapped to his knees. I strolled slowly towards Corrour Station with an hour to spare before catching the train to Tulloch.

Pauline's Diary, Monday 4 June
We used the multipurpose shop in Dalwhinnie to replenish bread and milk supplies

---

12 BEN ALDER TO THE BLACK MOUNT

Munro Number	Munro	Running Order
110	Beinn Bheòil	194
24	Ben Alder	195
203	Sgòr Gaibhre	196
225	Carn Dearg (Loch Ossian)	197
120	Sgurr Eilde Mór	198
228	Binnein Beag	199
231	Mullach nan Coirean	200
138	Stob Bàn	201
49	Sgurr a'Mhàim	202
133	Sgor an Iubhair	203
96	Am Bodach	204
165	Stob Coire a'Chairn	205
162	An Gearanach	206
71	Na Gruagaichean	207
30	Binnein Mór	208
208	Meall Dearg (Aonach Eagach)	209
183	Aonach Eagach-Sgor nam Fiannaidh	210
104	Sgorr Dhearg-Beinn a'Bheithir (see Map 14)	211
132	Beinn a'Bheithir-Sgorr Dhonuill (see Map 14)	212
23	Bidean nam Bian	213
146	Sgor na h-Ulaidh	214
196	Beinn Fhionnlaidh	215
233	Beinn Sgulaird (see Map 14)	216
197	Buachaille Etive Beag-Stob Dubh	217
106	Buachaille Etive Mór-Stob Dearg	218
48	Creise	219
43	Meall a'Bhuiridh	220
54	Stob Ghabhar	221
223	Stob a'Choire Odhair	222

and post some films. Not a very inspiring place, despite its claim to be the highest village in Scotland!

Just outside the village we bumped into Richard with his incredible flying machine. He was parked in a lay-by where we were able to satisfy our curiosity with a close inspection. It's pretty much like a hang glider with an engine – runs on 4 star petrol. Richard has been known to simply drop into a petrol station for a fill-up. 'The funny thing is,' he said, 'they don't bat an eyelid.' Probably too stunned. The propeller is made out of maple wood. There is no hi-tech improvement on this natural material. We watched him take off on the Glen Truim road.

The return train to Corrour was at 12:36 pm the following day. I could have had a lie-in but I had promised Steve Barber of Radio Cumbria that I would call him at 7:45 am for a live interview. The radio telephone didn't work away from the Cellnet stations on the A9 unless I took it up the mountains. This morning I walked half a mile to a phone box on the main road. It was jammed and out of action. I imagined Steve Barber giving commentary between records on the morning chat show. 'And now we go over to the Highlands to see how Hugh Symonds is getting on . . . Oh . . . He seems to have vanished!' In mad frustration, I raced back to the station and the Tulloch Mountain Centre which was next door. Explaining my situation to the staff at the centre, they took me inside to a phone, but it was too late – it was 8 o'clock and Radio Cumbria was into its news programme. What a start to the day when I could have been in bed asleep!

The rest of the morning was spent counting mountains to Mull and trying to predict the day on which I wanted to sail to the island. It was one thing forecasting my arrival time at a station at the end of one day on the hills, but to predict my passage over several days of Munros was mind boggling – particularly as the mountains of Glen Coe, Glen Etive and the Black Mount didn't offer a natural route. After a lot of puzzling over maps, I was prepared to commit myself to Monday 11 June. The plan was to leave the head of Glen Etive and traverse the outlying Munro of Beinn Sgulaird and then road run to Dunstaffnage Bay near Oban.

Long distance fell-running friend, Martin Stone, had been involved with British sailing and mountain races for many years. Having lots of connections in the yachting world, he had offered to try to find someone willing to give me a return trip to Mull. He had made a public announcement at the Scottish Islands Peaks Race in May, asking for offers of help. A phone call was made to Martin, telling him of my Mull on Monday plan. He was now going to follow up the contacts made earlier and I would phone back the following evening, hopefully to gain confirmation of a sailing.

Mark and I returned to Corrour on the train. It had been an easy morning physically, if not mentally. At least I felt I had improved the logistics of the next week. Mull was an obstacle to me. Now that I was beginning to see a Munro target of seventy days, as a possibility, I didn't want Mull to take any longer than necessary. I certainly didn't want to have to wait a day or more. The problem was now in Martin's hands and I felt confident that he could find a friend with a yacht somewhere near Oban.

Off-loaded at the bleak station on the moor, Mark and I followed a path below the railway line and ran to the south shore of Loch Treig. Good tracks continued to the east end of the chain of eleven Munros making the Mamores. By doing the two easternmost peaks of Sgurr Eilde Mór and Binnein Beag on the run across to Glen Nevis, I would make the following day easier with just nine Mamores.

Pauline's Diary, Tuesday 5 June

Whilst Hugh was busy with administration, we took advantage of the station timetable to do some arithmetic. The waiting room became our classroom for the morning. Using the times given in 24 hour format, Andrew and Joseph worked out how long it would take the train to travel from Tulloch to Tyndrum, or Fort William to Loch Awe, etc. When I later browsed through their school mathematics book, I was gratified to discover that the examples given there were not nearly so complicated as ours taken from the real world.

Having seen Hugh off on the train, we headed straight for Fort William and Roger's house, to pick up the next set of provisions. Roger insisted on doing our washing and before I could blink he had filled the washing machine with water which was soon overflowing all over the kitchen carpet. We left him to it and made for the Fort William swimming pool complete with waterslide. We all enjoyed a swim and came out of the showers clean – at least in body. The state of our clothes was a bit embarrassing!

The weather deteriorated as the afternoon progressed. I was glad not to be high for long. We descended the rocky summit cone of Binnein Beag and dropped into a flooded Glen Nevis. The three mile run to the van was a long splash through raging torrents and deep puddles. On both sides of the glen, waterfalls were full, powerful and roaring.

Pauline's Diary, Tuesday 5 June

We arrived at Glen Nevis at the allotted time – three hours before Hugh turned up. This happens too often to be worrying. In the event of an accident he would have to wait a long time before I called out the rescue!

Glen Nevis is spectacular – very Alpine. We walked a little way up the Glen, admiring the waterfalls and as usual collecting pretty rocks. The boot is weighed down by our collection!

The midges have made their first full-scale attack. I braved excessive torture in procuring tents from the boot for the pacers. They then cleared off to the youth hostel! I spent the rest of the evening coughing (they stick in the throat) and scratching.

Not being bothered to move, we ignored the 'no overnight parking' signs in the car park and settled for the night.

It had been two weeks since I had the company of more than two friends to run with. It was now party time again for the celebration of the two hundreth Munro – Mullach nan Coirean, the westernmost Mamore.

After an easy two mile jog down the Glen Nevis tarmac, I changed into fell shoes and met Tony Cresswell, Ruth Pickvance, Mark Rigby, Roger Boswell and his dog Banjo.

The summit celebration was brief in the rotten weather. Tony Cresswell, gentleman as ever, produced a litre of pure orange juice from his sack and after quick slurps all round we ran east along the ridges of the Mamores. The cloud had thickened and the wind had strengthened. This was no day to hang around on the summits. Rarely dipping below 2500 feet, we were exposed to violent gusts which whipped round the mountains and threw rain and sleet into our faces.

Roger returned to Glen Nevis from Sgurr a'Mhàim. The weather was too wild to take Banjo any further. Jogging along the narrow arête of the Devil's Ridge, Tony spotted something colourful a few metres below us amongst boulders. Not wanting to waste precious energy in clambering down for it, he allowed Mark the pleasure of the discovery. A jovial shouting match now broke the roaring wind.

'If it's anything valuable, then it's mine,' said Tony.

'Oh no. If I'm going to the trouble of this risky business of climbing off the Devil's Ridge, then I'm going to have it,' replied Mark.

For a few worrying moments, I hoped that Mark would only find a piece of debris, and not a body. There were still patches of snow around. It wouldn't be difficult for someone to go missing falling off this ridge and to be buried in snow not to be found for weeks. Mark picked up an ice-axe and a friendly argument immediately raged about who it belonged to. In trying to restore sanity and order on the ridge, I declared it belonged to Intermediate Technology and that it would be sold by auction with the proceeds going to I.T. 'Who will give me £1 . . ., £2.00, £2.50, £3.00?' In a three way challenge between Ruth, Mark and Tony, Tony eventually picked up a bargain for £5.75.

Returning to more runnable terrain, we pushed on over more peaks and ridges. In the saddle before An Gearanach, Ruth and Mark left us to return to their car in Glen Nevis. In the company of Tony, I completed the last three mountains to Binnein Mór in frequent blizzards. Tony began to think that his new axe might come in handy in this first week of June. I wasn't sorry to descend 3700 feet to Kinlochleven where the blowing snow had turned to torrential rain.

Pauline

On leaving Glen Nevis we went straight to Roger's to pick up the washing. It was caught in a giant web of line strung out across the beams of the attic. The attic has a floor in parts. Retrieving the dry clothes involved an unprotected mountaineering feat. Wouldn't it have been ironic if a careless move amongst the rafters had jeopardised the whole expedition? The last dry sock was retrieved without mishap and we headed off in the direction of Kinlochleven.

Arriving with a little time to spare in torrential rain, we decided to visit the Heritage Centre – a fascinating exhibition on the history of the Blackwater Dam and the Aluminium smelting works. The water from the dam drives Pelton wheels in order to produce electricity for the smelting. Kinlochleven was chosen for this industry because of its high rainfall, averaging 80 ins per year. The very same 'Pelton wheels' are incorporated into Intermediate Technology's designs for small-scale Hydro Power. Plants to be built on the many fast-flowing mountain streams of Nepal. Money raised from our 'Help from the Howgills' venture in 1989 was used to fund courses for Nepalese technicians, instructing them in the manufacture and installation of Pelton wheels. This project was consistent with I.T.'s policy of offering the gift of knowledge so that many might profit. Through the provision of electricity, the people of remote villages will be able to process their own agricultural products, thus stimulating the local economy. Value is added to their wares and the resulting produce is usually much easier to transport than the raw material.

Not happy to spend the night in the middle of a housing estate, we motored to a site on the shore of Loch Leven. The van was buffetted by gales blowing in from the sea, and holiday makers were marooned in their tents. My current companions couldn't face dealing with tents after the rough day on the mountains, so Ruth, Mark and Tony

A bite to eat on the Mamores. (Tony Cresswell)

escaped to the soft environment of the youth hostel in Glen Coe. As there wasn't a phone on the campsite Tony volunteered to contact Martin Stone from the Hostel, and let me know of the sailing plans the following morning.

The evening hours passed by dealing with administration, eating and looking at the next day's routes. At 10:15, I was almost ready for bed when there was a knocking at the van door. I stirred from my slumber on the back seat, and opened the door to an unusually anxious looking Tony Cresswell. He knew that he brought unwelcome news, but he felt that it was better to tell me as soon as possible, giving me more time to think about it. Consequently, Tony had taken the trouble to drive eight miles from the youth hostel to let me know the sailing details for Mull. Martin had provisionally arranged two crossings. I had to make the choice within the next day and confirm one and cancel the other. Neither of them suited my destined time of arrival on the west coast. One was too early – Sunday 10 June, and the other was too late – Saturday 16 June.

I was tired from a series of late nights and now I was faced with another. The easy option would have been to catch a ferry – but I really didn't want to do that. The traverse had to be self-propelled. (I couldn't blow into sails, but at least there was no fuel or engine involved in sailing.) There seemed to be no sensible way of going for Sunday's boat. The road running and retracking to missed mountains would be excessive. I was developing a sore throat and headache, probably caused through mental tension. At least if I opted for the following weekend, it would allow me flexibility if I needed a day off through illness.

I stared at maps until midnight and juggled mountain orders around like dice. I began to think that I could use the spare days before the following weekend but I was concerned about committing myself to a date ten days in advance. I went to bed confused and concerned. I was in a state that I hadn't been in for over fifty days and I sensed that I was developing a bug. All I knew was that I had to make a decision tomorrow, and that tomorrow the forecast was bad when I had planned to be on the notorious Aonach Eagach Ridge.

Chapter 13   MOVING MOUNTAINS FOR MULL

June 7 – 15

Sleeping didn't solve my problem. A day on the hills did! The weather was still stormy in the morning. Weather reports stated that two inches of rain had fallen in Aviemore and it was still raining in the west. Fresh snow decorated the eastern Mamores.

With a ten thirty appointment to meet Scottish TV on Sròn Gharbh, to the south of Kinlochleven, I had little time before breakfast to consider moving mountains for Mull. All I knew was that tomorrow I would be somewhere south of Glen Coe and that today I wanted to traverse the two Munros of the Aonach Eagach and climb the twin peaks of Beinn a'Bheithir to the south-west of Ballachulish.

The wide track of the West Highland Way led Tony Cresswell and I past the aluminium works and out of Kinlochleven. Leaving the popular Fort William to Glasgow walkers' route, we headed south and west into the rain-drenched valley of the Allt Coire Mhorair. What would normally pass for a wee Scottish burn was a raging, dangerous torrent. We searched for over ten minutes to find a crossing point to enable us to go onto the shoulder of today's first hill. We eventually found a section which was only knee deep. On occasions like this, goretex socks were incapable of keeping my feet dry. They filled from the top and then oozed water out in squelches. However, they did act as a kind of wet suit which trapped the warmth and stopped my toes from becoming too cold.

On the hills again, we stomped up 2000 feet to meet Alan Thomson and his son Malcolm perched on top of the non-Munro summit of Sròn Gharbh. Alan Thomson is a rare kind of freelance journalist: he gets his story from where it happens. Alan wanted to get his story on the mountain, not by telephone or on the pavements. Carrying a heavy Betacam video recorder and tripod, Alan and Malcolm followed me for the first section of the Aonach Eagach Ridge. Stopping and starting for action and replay was a long and tiresome business. The camera became temperamental in the cold wet air and caused constant frustration with poor battery connections.

Eric Whitehead had also arranged to meet me on the Ridge. He was taking photographs for *The Sunday Correspondent*, when Malcolm spotted something large and red, two hundred yards away below crags. Both Alan and Malcolm are members of the Glencoe Mountain Rescue team. They feared that someone might have fallen off the ridge – not a rare occurrence. Eric said that he had seen a car in the car park below. It had been there both last night and that morning – apparently unmoved. Fearing the worst, Tony and Malcolm scrambled round the crags and found a large red, empty exposure bag trapped amongst rocks.

What should have been a three hour crossing from Kinlochleven to Glen Coe turned into almost double that. I just hoped that the eventual ten minute film shown on Scottish TV would help to raise funds for I.T.

The Aonach Eagach is one of the finest mountain ridges on mainland Britain. Compared to the Cuillin of Skye, the exposure is only slight. However, today, even the large and chunky hand and footholds were disconcerting in their wet and greasy state. Our route was guided by the usual polished rock and crampon scratch-marks. In the thick mist, we could rarely see more than fifty metres ahead. Just occasionaly an opening below us gave an unusual sense of scale, with the tiny dots of cars motoring along the thin string of tarmac half a mile below in Glen Coe.

Emerging out of the clouds, we descended the scarred scree slopes to the west of the Clachaig Gully. After a seemingly endlesss drop, we met Pauline by the Clachaig Inn on the old Glen Coe road. By the time I had lunched, looked at maps, been interviewed again by Scottish TV, and run three miles of road to Ballachulish, it was five o'clock. Tired and in need of rest and time to consider the Mull options, I was tempted to call it a day. However, I knew that I would regret it if I allowed media time to cause me a day's setback.

Pauline's Diary, Thursday 7 June

Not the sort of day I enjoy really – too much hanging around in situations where it is impossible to do anything constructive – the kids messing about with nothing in particular to do. We can't go on a walk because we have too many visitors – runners, TV reporters (Alan and Kay). We can't leave them and just amble up the track to meet Hugh because his descent route is ridiculously steep and rocky. We can't do any work in the van because it is full of people, food and cups of coffee.

It is certainly interesting being involved in TV filming and interviews, although I always find it difficult to give the right impression – I feel that I always end up making silly comments and expressing myself badly. Alan Thomson goes about his job in a very professional manner, and is always very understanding of the commitment which reporting demands from the reported. It is time-consuming and tiring but of course all very worthwhile in the cause of raising money for I.T.

After the difficult afternoon it was bliss to be so well looked after at the home of David and Kshema Cooper in Ballachulish. They were really helpful – two loads in the washer, help with Hugh's route planning, loan of the kitchen, and baths for all. It was a strange feeling to be in a house – a building that you can actually walk around in. This is only the second time that we have met the Coopers, but they have already become good friends (they were introduced to us by Peter Yorke, a teaching colleague of Hugh's).

Tony and I left the village of Ballachulish for the wet, misty and darkening Munros of Beinn a'Bheithir. In no way did Tony try to put me off the evening outing. Only when we were halfway up the first climb did he let on that he hadn't expected me to pursue the two hills on the same day. I was glad I did go on. I needed a psychological boost to help me make the decision about the boat to Mull.

For the traverse of the peaks I was in a semi-coma. I was going through the motions while my mind was working out a new plan. I had an idea to move east to Schiehallion and Ben Lawers before returning to the west coast for Mull. That way I could usefully spend the next week running up mountains rather than dangling my toes in the sea waiting for a boat.

Meanwhile we were being buffetted by gusts of wind. Fortunately the navigation wasn't difficult, for my mind wasn't really switched on to it that evening. Only the final stony descent by waterfalls called for care. Gently graded tracks through forests returned us to Ballachulish and David Cooper's house. It was nine o'clock. At last I had stopped moving for the day, but it was now time for decisions and phone calls. Having the freedom of David's house for a bath, telephone and the spreading out of maps was perfect for getting myself ready to make the final choice of sailing time for Mull.

A circuit of 37 Munros in eight days would take me over the Southern Highlands between the Lochs of Rannoch and Tay. It would be a commitment with minimal flexibility for returning to the west. Having phoned Martin Stone, I contacted Fearghas McKay to comfirm the arrangements for sailing. It was a matter of trust. Fearghas and I didn't know each other. He was sitting examinations early in the week and was looking forward to having a purpose to sail the family yacht the following weekend. I explained my difficulty with getting to a phone and arranged to meet him on Friday evening 15 June unless he heard otherwise.

There were 65 Munros to go. The reordering of the southern Highlands had moved 54 of these to different positions on the original list. It wasn't just a question of changing a Munro number to fit a new day. Route possibilities had to be verified from maps and guidebooks. This was not a problem with the rounded grassy hills of the east. However, the western mountains are often steep and heavily cragged. Powerful and prolonged dissection by glaciers has made these mountains more dramatic than those of the east, but they are also more difficult to negotiate.

Having been active and busy until after midnight, it was a slow start to the day. I left David's house at 10:30 and ran on the right hand side of the fast Glen Coe road. Precipices and ridges may be dangerous but the first four miles of this day were more perilous than most. Twice, I was forced to jump off the side of the tarmac. Running on the right is usually safe because approaching vehicles can be seen and avoided. The theory doesn't work when overtaking cars approach from behind on the same side as the runner. In the flat section before the twisting climb at the top of Glen Coe, cars compete for a front position so as not to be held back by slow traffic. In over three months of running on mountains and roads, I came far closer to being a victim of fast-moving metal than I ever did to fast-moving rocks.

Pauline

These fast two lane roads, with little room each side for a quick escape, worried me far more than the crags and ridges. Following Hugh up the road, I would often stop before the arranged meeting place, just to reassure myself that he was still moving. If ever an ambulance or police car went by, my heart would stop. Hugh always reassured me that he was quite safe and always ready to leap into the hedge if necessary.

The majestic enclave of Glen Coe was given to the National Trust for Scotland in 1937, predominantly through the efforts of Percy Unna, then president of the Scottish Mountaineering Club. Unna laid down conditions, which have since become known as 'The Unna Rules' designed to ensure 'that the land be maintained in its primitive condition for all time' – a haven for mountaineers with unrestricted access for those prepared to travel on foot and enjoy the landscape on its own terms. Paths were not to be extended or improved, no bridges were to be built, no signs, cairns or paintmarks to be placed and no facilities introduced to aid the tourist.

Driving up the modern, fast two lane highway, itself a scar on the soul of Glen Coe,

I couldn't help but feel an empathy with the spirit of Unna. It was hypocritical of me, I know, to resent this aid to fast travel, but the mere presence of a main through route dampened the atmosphere of this, perhaps the most inspiring of all Highland glens. How wonderful it would have been to step back in time, to the days before the road led to the wide expanse of Rannoch Moor, when the Macdonalds farmed a fertile and wooded valley and up to a thousand head of cattle roamed the valley floor. Now one can park in one of many lay-bys, safely cross the River Coe on a sturdy wooden bridge and follow signposted paths leading up to secret hanging valleys. The mystery is eroded. But for his dependence on the vehicle, Hugh's journey was true to the challenge of the landscape – finding his own way from summit to summit, often off the beaten track, wading through rivers and paying little heed to the dictates of weather. For this I envied him.

In the Glen Coe visitor centre, a place much regretted by the disciples of Unna but nevertheless enjoyed by the children, we learned of the bloody massacre for which the glen is famous. A story much changed in the telling, and despite evidence to the contrary, proclaimed as the direst of all Highland bloodsheds. MacIain, chief of the Macdonalds had supposedly failed to 'swear fealty' to the King by the given deadline. Troops led by a Campbell and sent into the glen under orders from King William, enjoyed the hospitality of the Macdonalds for nearly two weeks before turning on their hosts at 5 am on 13 February 1692. Many died, and many fled, perhaps only to perish in the vile weather on Rannoch Moor.

It was a relief to leave the highway for Glen Coe's highest mountain, Bidean nam Bian. A trail of depressions had been rolling in from the Atlantic all week. At last there was a break, and the cloud base lifted above the summits. Bidean's commanding position offered superb views in all directions. The top thousand feet of Ben Nevis was white in a fresh coating of June snow. To the south and out to sea lay the mountains of the isles of Mull and Jura. Clear visibility was an advantage for the descent round steep rock slabs and gullies to the south. The four Munros of Bidean nam Bian, Sgor na h-Ulaidh (peak of the treasure), Beinn Fhionnlaidh (pronounced yoolah according to the postman in Glen Etive) and Beinn Sgulaird lie in a straight line, but the run between them was far from that. These knobbly ridged mountains required a careful approach. Separated by deep *bealachs* and rough open ground, the single traverse of these mountains is an arduous task involving 10 000 feet of ascent. It was tempting to leave Beinn Sgulaird for another day. The long flog to the summit via the eastern corrie was rewarded by an expansive view of glistening reflections across the sea to the Isle of Lismore. Tony and I crossed four miles of tussocks and bogs to our camp by Loch Etive.

The evening air was thick with midges. Two seconds was too long to stand still by the loch. Never had I seen a tent erected so quickly. Tony vanished inside not to be seen until the morning. The family cursed me for opening the door of the van. It was impossible to get in without taking a thousand of the horrible little biting things inside. A burning coil gradually killed them off but the air was stifling without open windows and the itchiness of bites lasted into my sleep.

The coil had merely anaesthetised many of the midges. They seemed to come alive again in the early hours of the morning. I woke up with an itchy skin, a sore throat, a pain in my head and a generally weary feeling. I felt concerned that I might be incapable of the big day ahead.

The day was split into three stages. If it did prove impossible to go on, then I could opt out at one of the two meeting points with the van. However, if I failed to climb the

Lismore and Mull from Beinn Sgulaird. (Tony Cresswell)

two Buachaille and the four Black Mount Munros then it would be a setback in the plan
to meet Fearghas and his yacht the following Friday.

Tony's night in the tent had been horrendous. The midges had found a way in. He
had still been awake and suffering at four in the morning. He looked more dreadful than
usual at breakfast. These tiny insects penetrate more than just your body with their
needle-like injections. They inject a tension into the brain that makes normal rational
thinking impossible. Tony said that if he had had a knife, he would have slashed his
wrists.

The six mile road run up Glen Etive was a therapy for the throat and head. The sky
cleared and the morning air became warm. In the previous week's stormy weather, I
had forgotten what a delight it can be to exist in the hills unencumbered by thermals and
waterproofs. Summer had returned and it was back to tee shirts and shorts. The change
revitalised me, and I enthused about the surrounding mountains during the transit of
the Buachaille summits of Stob Dubh and Stob Dearg. The second Stob was a popular
spot this Saturday morning. It is a most striking mountain viewed from the road at the
top of Glen Coe. Its steep crags make it appear tall and fearsome. Treading carefully over
the loose rocks of scree, we descended south towards Glen Etive. Occasionally a stone
was dislodged and set rolling and falling down the mountain. We could see the sparks
and smell the burning as a large one smashed against boulders. Fortunately we were off
the beaten track. Few people venture this side of the mountain and sheep and deer
couldn't graze on these desolate slopes of stone.

Pauline had parked the van at a perfect picnic spot by the River Etive. Basking in the
sunshine on deck chairs was bliss. However, there was no hesitation about going on.
The challenge and the mountains combined to push me forward and upwards again,
adding another couple of thousand to the day's total of 11 000 feet. We climbed
through what seemed like an endless and vertical line of crags to the summit ridge of

Creise – the first of the Black Mount Hills. Rounding the steep and deep corrie to the north, we crossed onto the rocky rib that joins the main ridge to the outlying Munro of Meall a'Bhuiridh. Turning round to return to the ridge, we avoided seeing the ski tows and slopes to the north. The only hint of our being in a ski area was a pole that had been implanted in the summit cairn.

The high traverse south was broken by the steep drop to Bealach Fuar-chathaidh. Deep shades of green and oddly shaped snow patches decorated this inland landscape of the Black Mount, whilst wide views across Rannoch Moor exposed a bumpy horizon of distant peaks.

From Stob Ghabhar, another Aonach Eagach (notched ridge) led us east towards the lowest Munro of the four – Stob a'Choire Odhair. Descending the last peak, Tony and I both saw a motionless man in an old grey coat. We stopped still to watch, but the man did not move. Feeling chilled with fear of this strange being, we walked slowly towards it until close enough to see a couple of stones on a boulder. Our tired eyes were playing tricks. Relieved with laughter, we jogged down to a path and the dirt road to Forest Lodge.

Pauline

We had obtained permission to take the van up the rough track beyond Forest Lodge, as far as the Glasgow University Hut. After a short distance a basic, narrow, wooden bridge crossed a small burn. The supporting metal girders looked strong enough but some of the planks had cracked. I didn't fancy it. The alternative ford was even less appealing, the exit being soft and sandy. We decided to retreat to the Inveroran Hotel – hoping for a drink later! The children busily set to the task of designing an artistic, informative and eye-catching note for Hugh, which we placed at a strategic point by the old bridge.

Pauline wasn't at the arranged meeting point, but a colourful message written and painted by the children instructed us to run on another mile to the overnight camp by the Inveroran Hotel.

Another marathon, and another long day. Arriving at camp at 8:30pm was too late for me to spend the evening relaxing. Certainly, it was impossible to sit outside in the warmth, as the midges had turned out in full force again. There was only time to eat and to sleep. The wisdom of my commitment to Friday's appointment for Mull was very questionable. Although my body was surviving, mentally I was deteriorating and becoming nervous and edgy. I desperately needed a short day, but not knowing any of the hills to the east, I had little idea of the times involved, and couldn't be sure that getting to Mull wouldn't be one long slog.

Pauline's Diary, Saturday 9 June

Hugh is rather low tonight. He has a throat problem – could be the same infection that I had some time back. It could be making him feel worse than he'll admit! He says his foot hurts on the top – probably nothing much. He could just be tired and suffering from mental overload – the strain of reorganising the hills around the sail to Mull. The midges do take some of the fun out of life – the children can't enjoy running around outside, making family life much more stressful. Doesn't look like I'll get my drink in the pub tonight.

Sunday, 10 June

The fine anticylonic weather soon burnt off the morning mist and the midges. Two and a half flat road miles eased me into the day before the direct ascent of Beinn Dorain from Bridge of Orchy Station. An unrelenting straight grass slope just asked to be climbed quickly. A fifty-five minute dash took Tony and I to the southern summit cairn. The ground was easy and fast to move on. Delighted at the speed at which we traversed the peaks of Beinn an Dòthaidh, Beinn Achaladair and Beinn a'Chreachain, I began to think that a short day was on the cards. But for the descent before the fifth Munro, the undulations between peaks stayed well above the 2000 foot contour. The summit of Beinn Mhanach was the last I shared with Tony Cresswell until the Lake District. His five day trip over 28 Munros had come to an end. Tony had seen me through a difficult section of the run. Knowing that I was in need of rest and an early night, he had made a special effort to speed me through this day. Stopping for a minute on this final summit cairn of the day, Tony shook my hand and wished me well for the days and weeks to come. He returned west to his car at Bridge of Orchy whilst I ran east to Loch Lyon.

Pauline's Diary, Sunday 10 June

Our route to Glen Lyon took the road past Lochan na Lairige and the Ben Lawers visitor centre. A sign at the junction read, 'Road suitable for cars and small vans only after 4 miles'. 'Can it really be any worse than any of the roads we have already been on?' I asked myself. 'Am I getting too confident?' I thought, 'Maybe it really means what it says!' We drove the 2½ miles up to the visitor centre, where we inquired about the condition of the road. The receptionist reckoned that we would manage, as long as we took care and could reverse (I had now learnt to do this without slipping the clutch!). The road came into the 'exciting but not horrendous' category. We even managed to pass another van! A very attractive route which I couldn't fully appreciate due to the necessity of keeping my eyes on the road.

By five o'clock, I had run two miles of road east of Loch Lyon and had met the family at a peaccful riverside camp under the first of the following day's peaks. The early finish allowed me time to relax with the family, and time to eat and recuperate. The more time I had to eat, the more food I consumed. It was through a nervousness of wasting away that I spent evening hours digesting more and more piles of pasta, cakes and puddings.

The consequences of eating so much caused me to make a rapid exit of the van at seven in the morning, and to run to some soft ground with a trowel.

Monday mornings were always a reminder to me that running over mountains was a luxury, and that normally at this time of year I would be preparing pupils for examinations. This particular Monday was unusual in that I was on mountains, but I had a lot of contact with the family during the day. The three Munros of Meall Ghaordie, Stuchd an Lochain and Meall Buidhe did not fit sensibly into any other day's plan. As isolated hills they required separate trips from road positions which were easily accessible for the van.

Mike Anderson, Paul Williams and Robert Gardner drove round from their homes in Glencoe and joined me for this day of four separate outings. The first was a rapid one hour forty-five minute out and back visit to Meall Ghaordie from our camp position by Cashlie in Glen Lyon. After a half hour coffee break, demolishing a huge, delicious chocolate cake which Mike had brought, we ran north to Stuchd an Lochain, whose summit revealed the steep northern corrie which guards the small circular blue waters of Lochan nan Cat. Rounding the top of the corrie, we descended to the road by Loch an Daimh, after the second hour-and-three-quarter outing of the day. A cooked lunch of bacon and eggs was a rare treat which fuelled me well for the hour and a half return trip to Meall Buidhe. Early afternoon tea sat outside in the warmth preceded the last run of the day – a gentle six mile jog along the road to the small settlement of Innerwick.

Camping by picnic tables and public toilets was a rare opportunity to not have to go digging with the trowel.

Pauline's Diary, Monday 11 June

It seems that the Tuson family is reaching the limit of its patience with Paul's frequent forays up North. This time the whole family has come. In many ways it is the families left at home who are making sacrifices in order to help our venture – the women left behind looking after the children while the men spend a few days enjoying themselves on the mountains. I think that it is important to recognise this hidden contribution. It is unusual for women to have either the opportunity or the ability to run along with Hugh – three notable exceptions being, Hélène Diamantides who is single and a phenomenal mountain runner, Ruth Pickvance, the Women's British Fell Running Champion, and Sue Parkin, who took an equal share in pacing with her husband, Mike.

The challenge of visiting the four Munros on the ridge to the north of Glen Lyon was not so much in doing them, but in tying them together with the fifth Munro of Schiehallion further to the north.

The broad featureless ridge connecting Carn Gorm, Meall Garbh and Carn Mairg,

---

13   LOCH LYON AND LOCH TAY

Munro Number	Munro	Running Order
62	Beinn Dorain	223
130	Beinn an Dòthaidh	224
91	Beinn Achaladair	225
59	Beinn a'Chreachain	226
205	Beinn Mhanach	227
90	Meall Ghaordie	228
194	Stuchd an Lochain	229
244	Meall Buidhe	230
100	Carn Gorm	231
182	Meall Garbh	232
88	Carn Mairg	233
57	Schiehallion	234
167	Creag Mhór	235
134	Meall Greigh	236
35	Meall Garbh	237
9	Ben Lawers	238
45	Beinn Ghlas	239
65	Meall Corranaich	240
257	Meall a'Choire Léith	241
87	Meall nan Tarmachan	242
61	Beinn Heasgarnich	243
80	Creag Mhór	244

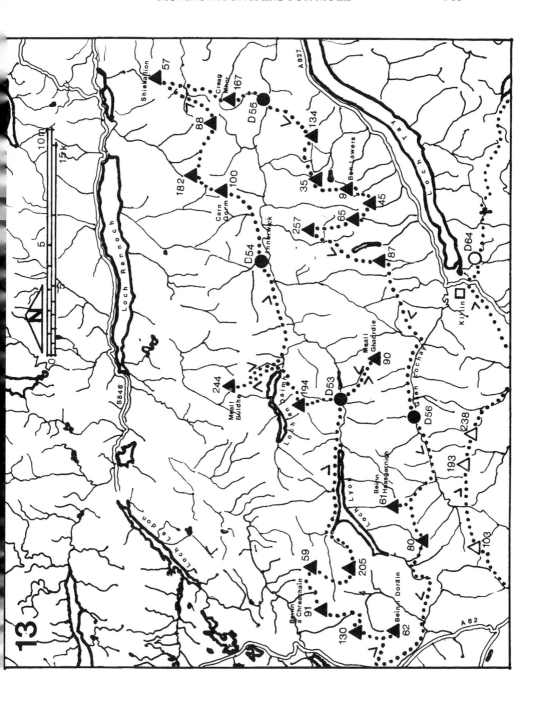

The meeting on Schiehallion. (P.S.)

provided the perfect environment for communication by telephone. Contact was made with Ann Parratt. Press interest was hotting up and it was becoming apparent that if fundraising potential was to be maximised, it would be essential to predict dates for Ben Lomond, Glasgow, the English Lakes and Snowdon. I wasn't prepared to commit myself then, but I promised to do my best to give a date for the Munro finish as soon as I returned to the mainland after Mull. Reaching Mull by Friday couldn't be a certainty and even if I did, the length of time it would take to sail there, run Ben More (Mull's only Munro) and sail back would depend on the wind conditions. Ann also informed us that the police were anxious to get in touch with us in connection with the 'bullet hole case'. Knowing that Alan Thomson had been trying to contact me, Ann followed our conversation with a call to him to say that the phone was working.

Paul and I ran in a straight line across the higher reaches of Gleann Mór for a direct ascent of the final 1800 feet of Schiehallion. The steep, heathery slopes turned into a mass of mixed boulders halfway to the top. Scrambling and dodging round large quartzite blocks, it was impossible to see the summit cairn until the last few metres. Suddenly our heads peeped over the crest and we surprised Pauline and the children who hadn't seen us coming.

Pauline

I seized any chance available to take the children up the mountains, but opportunities were remarkably few, as we seldom had the time to make much progress at four-year-old pace. I was delighted when Angela Tuson offered to look after Amy (keeping her youngest daughter Emily company), and to meet Paul and Hugh at the end of the day. I was able to take the bigger children, Daniel Tuson (8), Ann Tuson (6), Andrew and Joseph up Schiehallion (the fairy hill of the Caledonians). This mountain was an excellent candidate for a young person's assault, being easily accessible from a high point on the road. We had a rough idea of Paul and Hugh's timetable and aimed to meet them on the top.

We had only been on the summit for five minutes, searching the landscape for two fast-moving figures, when two heads appeared above a mass of quartzite boulders on the steepest side of the mountain. Who but Paul and Hugh would be ascending this way?

The 'mountain as a telephone box' came into its own once more as Hugh took the opportunity to contact the police. Quite a surprise for our local policeman Kevin Shires. Our case was progressing as forensic evidence had linked up the lead shot found in our van with the gun of the accused.

Turning south, we picked our way down through the boulders and returned to cross Gleann Mór again. Cutting through a col to the east of Carn Mairg, we looked up to see brown dots moving around on a snow slope. Coming closer, the dots grew bigger and we realised that they were deer. In the heat of the afternoon they had found a cool spot to relax in, but not graze.

As we left the last summit of Creag Mhór, the telephone rang inside the rucksack. Alan phoned in to arrange a meeting on Ben Lawers at twelve the following day.

We returned to Glen Lyon, choosing the shortest route convenient for the first of the following day's hills. Unfortunately, the best line was through private land and we were spotted. A stern-looking man walked towards us stiffly as his dogs ran at us. Paul and I stopped running and slowed to a gentle walk, carefully passing round the outside of a meadow field. We knew that we were in the wrong and were ready to take the consequences of a sharp rebuff, but we were not ready for the stunning piece of news that he was unwittingly about to let loose. Approaching us face to face, he opened the conversation:

'I do believe we have met before, haven't we? You're from the Nature Conservancy Council aren't you?'

Not being particularly good at lying, I denied the connection.

'This is a protected area, don't you know? You should approach the land owners first, otherwise you might get shot next time. At a different time of year there could be deer culling going on. The area can't handle a lot of people you know. Too many people want to go onto these hills. We even had a request from the Karrimor International Mountain Marathon organisers to hold a large competition here in October. Fortunately it's going to be a little further east than here.'

Paul's and my eyes met, and glimmered a tiny smile. We could hardly believe what he had just said. The 'Karrimor' is a major two day mountain navigation event, held in a different place every year. The precise location is usually only released to runners in the preceding fortnight. As keen competitors in the event, it was a strange coincidence to find out about the 1990 location in this way.

The crossing point of Glen Lyon was not suitable for an overnight stop. Angela was waiting to transport us to a nearby campsite and the luxury of showers.

Pauline's Diary, Tuesday 12 June

We are staying on a campsite remarkable for its collection of animals – ducks, geese, a peacock, a fox, lots of deer, a rabbit and hens. The ducks hang around the van and nibble at the dirty dinner plates, until the children chase them away.

Had a disaster with the van loo – spilt half the contents all over the bathroom floor. Luckily there is a hole in the plastic floor, where the shower water drains – I dread to think of the effect on the grass below. It nearly made me sick. We try to avoid using the portaloo, but it is a saviour in awkward situations – in bad weather and in civilised areas. The children are quite adept at digging holes with the trowel and burning the loo paper.

Hugh is brightening up – seems to have come out of a mentally low patch. There have been no problems with the running but he's been mentally rather dull.

The journey continued the following morning from the point just a hundred metres from where we had met the angry landowner. The glen is rich and dense in woodlands at this eastern end. I was hopeful that we wouldn't be seen as we climbed around a locked gate to a shaky suspension bridge, and crossed to the south side of the river. My pulse raced with nerves for fear of being caught trespassing and being called back. Paul and I hurried upwards amongst streams and onto the open ground of the free mountains where hundreds of deer were grazing. The air chilled drastically as we climbed to the windy summit of Meall Greigh. We raced on over the rocky top of An Stuc to arrive on Ben Lawers on time for the appointment with Alan Thomson. It was even colder on top of Britain's ninth highest Munro at just under 4000 feet, and I felt reluctant to stop for photos and filming. Alan's videorecorder had spent three days in his airing cupboard since our last meeting in Glen Coe. It now worked reliably and filming for Scottish TV was finished within an hour. Photo sessions offered the opportunity of a rest for pacers, but for me, hundreds of extra metres were run in posing for the camera. Rather than being tiring, I found these meetings with the media injected me with adrenalin which spurred me on, particularly if the photographer was well-organised and purposeful like Alan Thomson. The publicity delivered would all hopefully be worthwhile for Intermediate Technology. Alan's skill with the camera and written word combined to tell a true and accurate story, unlike some journalists who prefer imagination to reality.

After another half hour's taking of photos for *The Observer* and *Climber and Hill Walker*, Paul and I ran on along the broad scarred path to Beinn Ghlas. Turning to the north, we completed the high chain of the six Munros of Ben Lawers and descended to cross the high road pass above Lochan na Lairige.

The seventh and last Munro of the day came as an interesting and welcome surprise, contrasting sharply with the previous six peaks. Having climbed to the cairn of Meall nan Tarmachan, we followed its high grassy ridge two miles west over numerous knolls and hummocks and past the occasional tiny lochan. The intricate fine detail of small bumps would have called for care in poor visibility but in the fine weather of the warm afternoon, it was a pleasure just to run without the map and follow the line of the ridge.

It was now that the modified route before Mull made least sense. Ideally, the route would have dropped south to Killin, round Loch Tay and on to Ben Chonzie. The most isolated peak of the southern Highlands would now wait until after Mull. The extra ten or twenty miles covered by moving east, then west to Mull and then east again, were compensated by flat and easy road running in the Glens of Lochay and Dochart.

The mountain route descended to the farm of Duncroisk on the quiet no through road of Glen Lochay. Pauline and Andrew's provision of a pit stop was spot on as usual.

Pauline

Andrew had developed into a competent and trustworthy navigator. It was a great help to me, as there was no need to stop the van in order to survey the map. We usually used the 1:50 000 version as Hugh carried the 1:25 000 pathfinder series. Linking the symbols on the map with the features (both man-made and natural) on the ground, Andrew would follow our progress meticulously. If I asked him how far we still had to go, he would usually reply, 'Oh no! We must have missed the turning.' He was very fond of teasing.

After tea, cakes and a change into road shoes, the children joined me for a mile or so of gentle running. They loved these short runs. Pauline would drive ahead half a mile at a time ready to pick up tired little athletes. Amy usually managed three quarters of a mile with her short, quick and energetic stride. Joseph could run up to two miles in his own meandering relaxed style and Andrew occasionally ran up to five miles. With three miles to go to our planned overnight stop at Kenknock, I was on my own again.

Drifting into my usual semi-comatose state of lonely road running, sudden shouting from behind startled me into life. Turning to see what the commotion was, I saw Alan and Joy Evans catching me rapidly on bicycles. Not expecting to see the Evanses until the Lake District and their home town of Ambleside, this came as a great surprise. Alan had been a key figure in influencing me to run from north to south. In the twenty minutes we had together to the end of the tarmac road, Alan asked me enough questions to get a good idea of how the run had been going. In his usual energetic way, Alan created and shared enthusiasm with a dynamism unusual for a fifty year old.

Chris Bradley and Jeremy West arrived at our camp in the early hours of the morning and returned for another few days of filming. Jeremy quizzed me in his usual skilful manner and taped the following:

Jeremy's sound track
'So now, Thursday 14 June, I'm looking westward again, looking towards Dunstaffnage Bay and tomorrow evening's liaison with the yacht. Between now and then, I'm crossing seven more Munros, over towards Glen Etive, Ben Starav and then a long track run through to Taynuilt and the west coast.

'Looking back to April, the major challenge was to run the mountains of Britain, and to do that in any amount of time at all would be very satisfying for me. But as the journey has gone on and I've become more physically fit, and more at one with the mountains, and the navigation, I feel more of an urgency now to do it within a certain amount of time. Looking at the last 50 peaks, and breaking them down into day schedules, I could see the possibility of getting to Ben Lomond on Joseph's birthday, 25 June. This would really be a satisfying first point in the journey, the finish of the Scottish section – the Munros.

'Throughout the journey so far there have been minor points to aim for, like Skye and now Mull, but the first major one now is Ben Lomond. I guess I've put pressure on myself by saying I'd like to be there for 25 June, when really it doesn't matter. But having set the target I want to do it. If I can make it for then, before midday, then this would mean I will have traversed the Munros without motorised transport in 67 days, something that I would be very pleased with. So why do I put myself under pressure, when really I'm just here, happy to enjoy the mountains? I'm not sure. I ask myself this when I'm on the mountains. Why am I trying to race through it, when I could just be enjoying them forever? Perhaps it's a bit like the four minute mile. There is demand on the human spirit to see what is possible, what can be done. Can you reduce the time by this much? Looking at the southern Highlands which I'm not familiar with, some days the ground is very easy, and very runnable; very different to the rugged mountains of the far north west, where running at times was just dangerous and very slow.

'So the challenge I guess is to see how quickly these mountains can be run. But why?'

Going beyond a locked gate at the end of the tarmac, Paul and I ran two more miles west to the cottage at Badour before turning north towards Beinn Heasgarnich. A 3000 foot climb up a long grassy slope took us to the top of the big whaleback mountain. A steep descent and ascent and we were on the summit of Creag Mhór, just two and a half miles from Ben Challum – a Munro in a chain of three to be saved until after Mull.

From the second and final Munro of the day, we dropped sharply to the west and followed streams through to the railway line and the West Highland Way. We followed the major walking route for six miles and returned to the Inveroran Hotel for a second night's camp. Hardly had I stopped running when Jeremy had a microphone in front of me:

Jeremy: 'How was it Hugh?'
Hugh: 'That was very enjoyable. It was a short day, that's five and a half hours we've been out, very important because tomorrow is quite long. Over 30 miles, five Munros to push through to Dunstaffnage Bay, for the boat to Mull. I find it quite important physically and psychologically to have a relatively easy day before a long one. Conditions on the tops are just perfect at the moment, there's just a gentle breeze, and the sunshine isn't fierce. The ground is bone dry, so I'm getting good traction.

'After eight weeks I can now see most of the Southern Highlands, the last 30 or so Munros lying before me. And there's again the sense of sadness that the journey, the Scottish journey, is coming to an end. But there's also a sense of urgency in that I ought to be putting dates on places. Places such as Glasgow and the Lake District, where I know that my team back at home, my team of fundraisers are working hard to make money for Intermediate Technology, to raise funds for development in the Third World. I know that this is very important, but at the same time it's a cause of anxiety in putting a date on a place. I can hazard a guess and work to a similar schedule I've been doing so far, but it's always in the hope that my body can keep going at the some rate, and just because it has done for eight weeks I don't really know that it's going to keep doing it for the next two, three, four weeks.

'If I set a time which gives me leeway, than I could be frustrated by going a little bit

---

14   GLEN ETIVE AND BEN CRUACHAN

Munro Number	Munro	Running Order
250	Meall nan Eun	245
86	Stob Coir'an Albannaich	246
142	Glas Bheinn Mhór	247
60	Ben Starav	248
192	Beinn nan Aighenan	249
185	Ben Móre-Mull (see Map 15)	250
31	Ben Cruachan	251
141	Stob Diamh	252
168	Beinn a'Chochuill	253
152	Beinn Eunaich	254

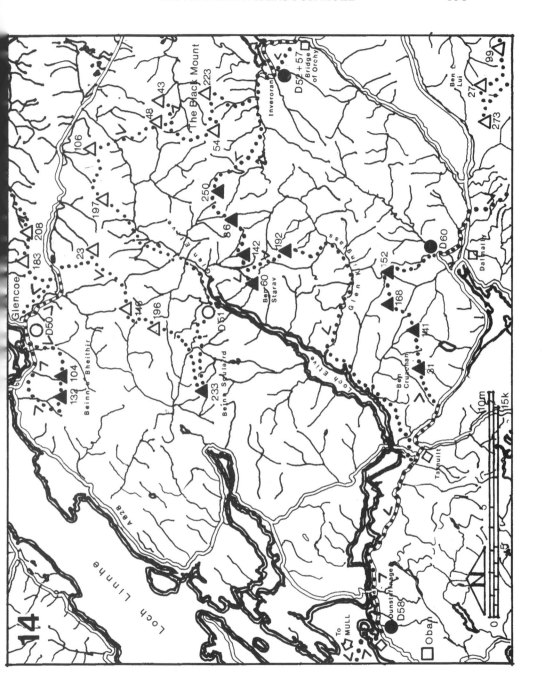

slower than I need to. If I set a challenging time which I could respond to, it could be dangerous, because I might just go beyond the knife edge and cause myself damage that could set me back several days. So it's very awkward setting a date for places. I've taken the radio phone on the hill today, and made two contacts. One press contact, one liaison contact, and I know that people want to know when I'm going through Kendal, back to the home town.'

Paul returned home with his family. Company wasn't expected until Friday evening, so I planned the long day ahead on my own. Looking roughly at the map, I expected an 18 mile run on tracks and roads to follow the 18 miles over five Munros. Normally a day such as this would be split into two separate days, but with the knowledge of having to meet Fearghas on Friday evening at Dunstaffnage Bay, there was no choice but to run it in one. After demolishing a whole Christmas pudding, I retired for an early night.

Pauline's Diary, Thursday 14 June
Hugh is again in good spirits – contemplating the hard day ahead with relish – the dash for the boat. Extra running for the film crew doesn't seem to worry him at all.
At last – managed to get a drink in the pub!

Up early with the midges the following morning, I opened the van curtains to see a twitching bivvy sack outside the van door. A large envelope had heavy red felt pen scrawled on it: *'Here lies the body of Dermot McGonigle. Please disturb'*.

Dermot had phoned Paul just before midnight, when Paul had only been home for half an hour. Having found out that the following day was the only day of Munros without planned company, Dermot, friend and rival fell racer, had zoomed up in his car. Unfortunately he was caught speeding close to his home in Glasgow, in the early hours of the morning.

We left the Inveroran Hotel camp at 8:00, Dermot taking the load of food and spare road shoes that I had expected to carry on my own.

Pauline's Diary, Friday 15 June
An early start for Hugh meant that we could escape this midge-infested site as quickly as possible. It is impossible for campers. Jeremy is eating his muesli out of a large tin mug (his equivalent of Roger's dog bowl) whilst pacing up and down the road. This movement, along with the large towel wrapped round his head, helps to fend off the worst of the little fiends.
We arrived at Loch Awe just in time for the 11:15 tour of the Loch by paddle steamer. This immaculately kept boat, built in 1927 on Lake Windermere, was powered by burning peat. The owner of the boat, a maker of surgical intruments, passed the whole of the journey polishing the brass whistle. He reckons that coca cola is the best polish for this job. I dread to think of the effects of this fizzy drink on the lining of the stomach!

Five Munros lie between Glen Etive and Glen Kinglass. They were one of the few groups of hills that I had previously traversed. In the clear and warm conditions of the morning, a map was unnecessary. It was a pleasure to be able to concentrate on the ground and the scenery. Once we had climbed the steep southern face of Meall nan Eun, it was easy to run and chat, as we followed the undulating line of Munros to Ben Starav. It had been a late decision to change the day's fifth Munro to Beinn nan Aighenan from Ben Starav. It meant that the good track in Glen Kinglass could be used and that the fine eastern ridge of Starav would be enjoyed twice. In terms of distance, there was little difference between descending to Loch Etive from either Starav or Aighenan. The six hours to the fifth Munro appeared to vanish. The arrival of a new pacer always brought about fresh conversation, and with it, a timelessness of transit over mountains. Suddenly I was on my own again. Dermot returned to his car at the Inveroran Hotel, taking with him a plastic covered OS map of the area and an exposure bag, both of which we had found whilst climbing the last peak. What happened to the owner?

The silence and isolation came as a sharp contrast. I felt weary on the descent to Glen Kinglass and feared for the eighteen miles still to be run to the coast. Although I frequently felt tired during the whole run, having company and conversation reduced my awareness of fatigue. The last mile downhill to the dirt track in the glen was taken at a walk. It was hot in the depths of the glen. I stopped to drink, eat glucose tablets and change into comfortable road shoes before the long afternoon run.

After an hour's slow running, Chris Bradley and Jeremy West intercepted me for some filming by Loch Etive.

Jeremy's sound recording

'I've always planned a big day's run to the coast before sailing to Mull. Thoughts of this one have been with me for over a week. It's such a long day that I guess I have fears of causing physical damage. It's a marathon as the crow flies and far more than that on foot. I've got odd little bits of cramp coming in, which are going to arise because of the heat. Really is quite fierce today. I'm losing salts rapidly. It's important to drink frequently. All the time as I go on towards the end of the journey through the Scottish section, I'm thinking, 'Can I still keep going tomorrow?' Particularly the case today with it being so long, but I should have time to relax on the boat and Ben More should be an easy climb.

'For many of the long flat sections from the north of Scotland I have been on my own, but on the mountains I've had company for all but two of them. The mountain company is good for safety, but it's also a great help to me, to carry gear. Today I've gambled a bit on the weather; the forecast is very safe. There's a big high pressure area over Scotland, so I've got minimal kit. There's a waterproof, some thermal gear, gloves, hat and exposure bag. But, today because of the long road run, I've got an extra pair of shoes. So the load is probably six or seven pounds.

'Quite often on the hill, when I've got company, I'm not carrying anything, and this is a tremendous help for me. I think the essence of this trip is speed and lightweight motion in the hills.'

The brief stop for the interview was welcome, particularly as Chris had carried in a can of coke which vanished in seconds. Continuing along the winding track above Loch Etive, I met Pauline an hour later, just one mile east of Taynuilt and the main road to Oban. In wanting to avoid traffic for as long as possible, a route was devised to cross fields and the River Awe on a pedestrian bridge. Not wanting to dirty my best road shoes for this potentially mucky section, arrangements were made for another pit stop for a shoe change, one mile west of Taynuilt.

Having drunk pints of water, I departed for the third main outing of the day. The fields and footbridge near Inverawe House were negotiated with ease, but the streets of a housing estate in Brochroy were confusing and I took a wrong turning. Time and distance were wasted and the meeting with Pauline was missed. Thoughts of the long road sections south to Wales began to worry me. Planning and executing rendezvous points in suburbia was going to be a far harder task than meeting in the wild glens of the Highlands. Pauline found me grinding my way along the tarmac two miles west of Taynuilt. This was no place to park the van, with fast traffic whizzing by. After a quick shoe change, I sent Pauline on to Dunstaffnage, to hopefully meet Fearghas and to tell him that I was on my way. The last ten miles were uninspiring. Tin cans and newspapers littered the sides of the road and fast overtaking cars threatened to take my left elbow with them. The only thing that kept me going was the appointment with Fearghas. I just hoped that he would be there. It was now eight days since we had made the arrangement to meet. I had been unable to contact him since. He could have easily found something better to do than to sail a sweaty runner across the sea to Mull.

Chapter 14   ANCHORS AWAY
June 16 – 17

Pauline

A mixture of excitement and anticipation coloured my feelings as we parked the van by the Marina in Dunstaffnage Bay. For a short while we were to exchange our world of lofty wilderness for the bustle of the seafarers' base.

We couldn't hope to find Fearghas as having never set eyes on him, we had no idea what he looked like. I was confident of him finding us, however, as 'Ben' (our name for the van), was fairly conspicuous. The large white van wore a decorative collection of stickers proclaiming both our cause and our sponsors. In no time at all a dark, smiling young man flanked by two young women could be seen striding purposefully towards us. Their red 'Scottish Islands Peaks Yacht Race' fleecy tops gave them away. Fearghas and his crew, Gill and Janet, introduced themselves to us, and to the film crew, Jeremy and Chris.

Our van was once more becoming a hive of activity. Chris and Jeremy set themselves up to catch Hugh as he ran into the Marina. Matt Dickinson (the film director) zoomed in with his usual mega-enthusiasm.

Hugh ran in looking remarkably normal. No one would have guessed that he had just run nearly 40 miles (it was further than he thought). How did he do it? I had this theory that he worked just like an engine – so long as the fuel was fed in he would keep running.

Late in the evening Dave Bayliss and Ian Rooke arrived. Plans had to be worked out involving not only Hugh's sail and run, but support for Hugh on the island and transport of the film crew. The resulting arrangement gave me a free 24 hours as Dave and Ian were to take their car onto Mull, saving the expense of transporting the large van.

Hugh planned to sail at 8 am. It was 11 am before the Pavane of Lorne *floated noiselessly out of the bay, with her sailing crew, film crew and manic mountain runner on board. Andrew, securely dressed in a life-jacket, had been allowed to join them. He was absolutely thrilled. This 31 foot Nicholson was the only vessel in the harbour forsaking all use of engine power. The wind was slight and we had only a vague idea of when they would return.*

Why the delay? Matt was keen to capture this epic moment on film. He commented on the difference it makes when a runner with his own schedule has to be taken into account – they were working quickly! Hugh showed no signs of anxiety. I was constantly looking at my watch and wondering if Hugh would have time to climb the mountain on Mull today, as planned. Hugh seemed to have a faith that everything would work out.

The afternoon was so strange after the activity of the morning – suddenly everyone was gone – just Joseph, Amy and myself left. I had a slight feeling of missing out on the real fun. Lucky Andrew! We headed for the Sea Life Centre – a very stimulating display for the children and they were fascinated.

An update on the phone to Ann Parratt resulted in a shower of messages, mainly covering media contacts – press, TV and radio. It seemed that life would be busy later on!

Jeremy's sound recording on board *Pavane*

Hugh: 'It's Saturday morning, 16 June, and this is the first time in four weeks that I've not been running first thing in the morning. Getting out of Dunstaffnage Bay was very exciting 'cos we couldn't use the engine for the boat. That would be against my rules of self-propulsion. We dodged 20 or so boats in harbour, and had to tack several times. It was very hectic with pulling in the ropes, and steering and dodging buoys and dodging boats. But finally we cleared the harbour and we're now bobbing up and down on the waves, sailing at about four knots towards Mull.

'It's very relaxing, particularly after yesterday's long hard day. It was 38 miles, and I could feel last night that there's quite a lot of stiffness in the legs. I'd perhaps overdone it. But Pauline had learnt some massage before the trip from a physiotherapist friend, and for the fourth time in the trip she applied this to my legs for about ten minutes. I've responded and this morning I feel quite reasonable. I'm looking forward to running when we land on the island.

'Ben More will be a new mountain for me. There will be a seven mile road run from Salen followed by five miles on the hill – a straight climb from sea level. Then seven miles back to Salen. Then we'll take the boat back. I'm not sure when we're going to set sail again. It will depend on timings. Perhaps we'll go overnight, it's up to Fearghas. I'm in his hands for this, but I would really like to be back on the mainland and running the Ben Cruachan ridge tomorrow afternoon.

'I've set my sights on a 67 day Munro traverse of Scotland. That would complete the trip on June 25th – Joseph's birthday. If we fail to return in sufficient time tomorrow to be on Ben Cruachan tomorrow afternoon, then it could add a day to the Munro traverse, making it 68 days; or I could attempt to combine two days sometime next week. Put two days together. That's always a bit risky. Perhaps it really doesn't matter, perhaps I should settle for 68? Well, even if we do return in 24 hours, it's by no means certain that I will complete it in 67 days. Other things could go wrong, I could hit some bad weather, I could make navigational mistakes, as always I could twist an ankle on some rocks. There have been several occasions in the last week where I've been pulling uphill on a rock, and it's pulled loose and come down. It's crushed one foot once, and crushed a shin on the other leg another time, and left me in pain for an hour or so. Fortunately it's not been more severe. But in doing 296 mountains, the risk is that at some stage something like a rockfall could cause damage. So the target is now 67 days for the Munros.

'Several people have completed the Munros in under a hundred days, using vehicles between the peaks. Being self-propelled and not using motorised transport or wheels between the mountains, that has not been done before. So, whatever I do is a record in its own right. The fastest the Munros have been done using a car is 66 days by Mark

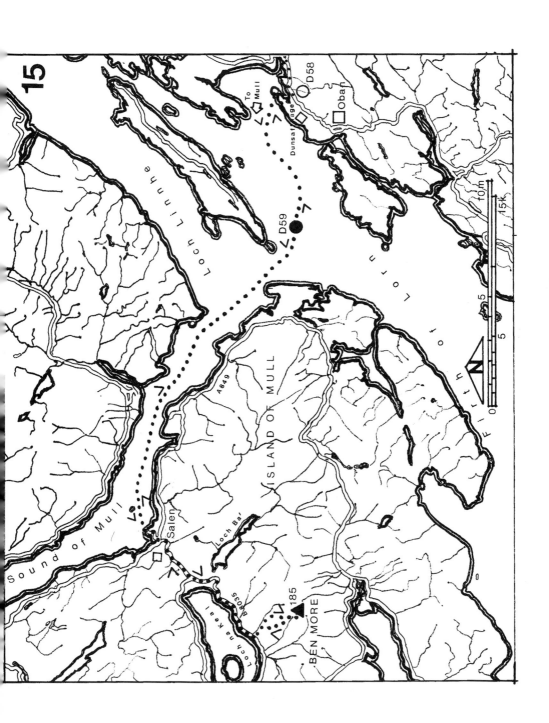

Midnight anchor. (Matt Dickinson)

Elsegood. Hamish Brown completed them in 112 using ferries and a bicycle. In my original schedule I planned on about 83 days, allowing 17 days to get from north of Glasgow through to Snowdon.

'Now, if I do it in 67, it gives me a lot of time left to get to Snowdon. Although I'm beginning to perhaps look further than Snowdon, change my targets, and I'm just wondering whether I can do something else in those hundred days.'

Matt: 'What would that be?'

Hugh: 'I'm keeping that to myself at the moment. It's a challenge which is very enticing, but because between Glasgow and North Wales, I and my family might become rather tired of suburbia we might change our minds. We might feel that we want to be back inside four walls and under a roof. On the other hand the ideas that we are playing with would return us to the magic of the Highlands and it might be that we are enticed to return to that.

'I really don't want to tell anybody what we're thinking of doing because we want to leave our options open.'

The twenty-five mile sail through the Sound of Mull took six hours. The moorings at Salen had been wrecked by stormy seas long ago. We dropped the anchor in the bay and rowed the rubber dinghy across a hundred metres of calm sea-weedy water to land on a stony beach. It was 5.30pm and fortunately one of the longest days of the year. I would need most of the remaining daylight hours to run to and from Ben More before darkness set in.

Dave Bayliss and Ian Rooke were patiently waiting by the beach. Dave and I ran for an hour along the quiet road to the north of Ben More. Meanwhile, Ian drove the film crew to the base of the mountain so that they could get to the top first. After a rapid drink and shoe change based by Ian's car, Dave and I departed for the direct climb to the summit of Ben More – the 250th Munro of the run. The fine ridges leading away from the summit looked interesting and enticing. Unfortunately these were not on the route plan. This evening, they were just admired from above along with the shimmering red glows in the sea across to the Isle of Ulva. Following a chilly forty minute film and interview session, the route back retraced the outward steps and we returned to Salen at 10:30. The evening twenty mile jaunt had seemed short compared to the previous day's mammoth excursion.

Before returning to the yacht, there was just time for a rare Saturday night drink in a pub. It was tempting to stay in the bar, but 27 mainland Munros beckoned, and to stay on the new schedule I wanted to be back at Dunstaffnage for breakfast.

I drew the anchor up in the darkness of midnight, and a gentle breeze blew us out of the bay. Fearghas, Gill and Janet took the controls of *Pavane* through the night whilst the rest of us tried to sleep. Andrew and I shared the small V-shaped cabin at the front. I had a restless night. I wasn't used to beer in the blood, the sound of water splashing all around, and rolling from side to side. Every now and again, I was aware of tacking. There were shouts from Fearghas to get the ropes in. Suddenly the boat would be thrown over to the opposite side and the sound of rapidly winding capstans would disturb my half sleep. At one point there was a shout of, 'Dolphins!' Andrew and I untied the ropes holding us into bed and pulled our way out of our sleeping bags. By the time we appeared on deck, the dolphins had disappeared. It was six o'clock and the speed gauge had dropped to zero knots. We were becalmed somewhere between Lismore and Mull. Fearghas said it could be hours or even a day before a breeze would blow us back to the mainland. I climbed back into bed for another attempt to sleep.

Suddenly there was a call from Fearghas for me to drop the anchor. Four hours had vanished and we had arrived in Dunstaffnage Bay. Feeling slightly groggy and wobbly-legged, I gingerly stepped onto deck and hauled out the chain to lower the anchor to the sea bed.

Pauline's Diary, Sunday 17 June

Just beyond the marina a yacht glided peacefully over the water, tacking from side to side. It had to be Pavane. *All other boats were using motors to get in and out of harbour. The relative solitude of the last 24 hours was soon shattered and replaced by frantic activity. Hugh launched straight into the plans for the day. I struggled to communicate Ann's messages to Hugh, and Amy made an almighty fuss about where to eat her breakfast. It was impossible to conduct a rational discussion. I lost my temper with Amy and had to leave the van to cool off. I never really understood Hugh's reluctance to spend even one night away from the family. In a situation in which it isn't always easy for him to either relax or make plans I would have expected him to enjoy the odd calm interlude.*

The sailors looked very much the worse for wear. Matt begged for Paracetamol as he had developed a terrible headache and had missed his plane to London (even worse, he had missed his prearranged motor bike driving test!). Jeremy was starving as he had struggled to eat on the boat. Fearghas looked half asleep as he had been up all night sailing Pavane.

Andrew was too excited to be sleepy – he had obviously had the time of his life. Hugh wasted no time – he was impatient to get going again.

Andrew's Diary

I got up early because I was excited about going to Mull. Fearghas, the man who was sailing Dad and me to Mull, came with my life jacket. With a bit of trouble we made it fit. Then Fearghas rowed me to the yacht (called Pavane*). I waited for about half an hour, while the film crew filmed Dad rowing out of the harbour. When Dad got on board we put the sails up and sailed out of the harbour, dodging the other yachts. We had to go about half a mile out to sea and then turn around and go back, so that the film crew could film us. We got about halfway to Mull when a ferry came by and we waited until it had gone past. As soon as it went by we undid the rowing boat from the back of the yacht, and the film crew got in with their film camera and microphone. We sailed a little way away from them and they filmed us. When they had finished filming us they got back in the yacht and we sailed the rest of the way to Mull.*

As soon as we got to Mull, Dad and the film crew got off the yacht and started up Ben More (the only Munro on Mull). Janet and Gill are two people who came to Mull with us. Gill took me on to Mull to buy some food, and I bought some sweets. When we got back on the yacht we had some tea. About half an hour later Dad and the film crew got back. We set off back to Dunstaffnage Bay.

At midnight we had a tin of beans each. Then I went to bed. In the middle of the night Fearghas saw some dolphins. I woke up the next morning to the sound of Fearghas telling Dad to put the anchor down. We rowed back into the harbour and we had our breakfast in the campervan.

Ten o'clock was later than I had hoped to return to the mainland. After another short row in the dinghy and after a good breakfast, I put road shoes on and headed east again. The section of road past Connel and Taynuilt was one of the least stimulating, and to have to run it for the second time in three days was unpleasant. At least being a Sunday morning, there was little traffic. Concentrating hard to keep a rhythm, I clocked up the twelve miles in an hour and a half. On route to the meeting point close to the Bridge of Awe, I passed a body by the side of the road. A tramp was asleep with his head on a rucksack – I hoped that Pauline wouldn't see him whilst driving by and think that I had collapsed or been knocked down.

Pauline
'There's a body by the side of the road,' Andrew called out.
'Are you sure?' I replied.
'There's definitely a body. It's lying on a rucksack.'
'It can't be Daddy then, he hasn't got a rucksack with him.'
All the same it was a relief to meet Hugh before he left for the hills.

It was a great relief to leave the fast road and set off into the hills again. The sharp undulating ridge of the two Ben Cruachan Munros had looked inviting several times in the previous fortnight. Dave Bayliss accompanied me for the afternoon clamber along the rocky arête. The weather had turned wild and I was glad not to be at sea. Even

Ben Cruachan from Beinn Eunaich. (Dave Bayliss)

though it had been a relatively calm couple of crossings, my legs were still bouncing with the memories of the motion of the boat. Strong gales and cloud made us run a speedy traverse of the ridge and the two Munros of Beinn a'Chochuill and Beinn Eunaich to the north. Unfortunately there were no distant vistas, just occasional sightings of steep gullies and nearby glens.

Pauline

The wild weather was of no consequence to us, deep in the heart of Ben Cruachan. As Hugh climbed the windswept summit, we joined a tour into the vast cavern underneath the very same mountain. Here an underground power station had been hollowed out of the rock – not a bad way to house a power station. The waters of Loch Awe are pumped up to a higher Loch during the night, using surplus power. During the day the water returns to Loch Awe, through turbines, creating power at times of peak demand. This visit was our way of covering the science syllabus!

We descended the southern shoulder of Beinn Eunaich to the overnight camp in Glen Strae. Another weekend had passed. Dave and Ian's help had been vital in supporting me both on and off Mull. It had been disappointing for Ian that due to a virus he had been unable to run. However, by providing the extra vehicle, the weekend logistics all fitted into place. Amazingly, the yacht beat Dave and Ian back from Mull due to the shortage of ferries to Oban on Sunday mornings. The provision of a support vehicle on Mull was not essential, but very helpful. It meant that when I returned to Dunstaffnage, I was able to meet Pauline, have breakfast and start running early enough to reach Ben Cruachan by the afternoon. Dave and Ian returned home. The next time we would run together would be between the mountains of England and Wales.

Hugh's Diary Sunday evening, 17 June

Sailing arrangements and the whims of the wind are now behind me. All that lies between me and a successful Munro traverse are one hundred and forty miles and 23 mountains. Provided I can keep going in the same way as the previous nine weeks, and avoid accident and injury, then the first major landmark – Ben Lomond – should be no more than a week away.

Chapter 15   SURVIVING THE MUNROS

June 18 – 25

There were 254 Munros behind me and 23 to go. My sense of self-preservation and caution in negotiating roads and mountains was stronger than ever. I was very aware that should I, for any reason, be forced to drop out in the following few days, then the mission would just be a long unfinished journey. At least if I was forced to drop out between Glasgow and North Wales there would be the satisfaction of having run the Munros, if not the Mountains of Britain.

After a healthy lie-in avoiding the morning midges, I departed Glen Strae for the isolated and unexciting hill of Beinn Bhuidhe. Mike Walford and Phil Clark had returned for their second session. The relatively civilised, suburban environs of Dalmally contrasted strongly with our previous meeting points on Skye and in Knoydart.

Running over wet grasslands and a mixed terrain of occasional rocks and knolls, we crossed seven miles of open land. Nearing the wet and misty summit, we startled a young fawn which was hidden behind a rock. It ran to escape but plunged into a pool almost as deep as itself. Mike pulled it out and it ran away in a flash. A few minutes later we were on the summit and suddenly blasted by southerly gales and rain. The noise of the wind was too loud for talk, but before racing away from the tumbled trig point, we found a packet of fruit pastilles and a good luck message from Kendal runner, Mick Fox. The postcard dated 30 May showed that the sweets had been there for nineteen days. Either this hill has few visitors or Munro climbers are honest people.

We ran across more wet undulating ground and descended through thick bracken to Glen Fyne.

The short outing allowed lots of time in the evening to think ahead. The time was getting closer to having to put dates on places.

Jeremy's sound recording
'Putting dates on places in the future is almost impossible. In the three years planning I've come up with a schedule and come up with places and dates and it hasn't worked. I'm now almost two weeks ahead of schedule, which has surprised me greatly. Being used to traversing Munros by now, I've got a reasonable idea of what I can handle – about 20 miles and 6000 feet of ascent each day.

'Beyond the Munros I'm into unknown territory. I'm onto the road, and I've been warned that the transition from the mountains to the roads can cause injuries like shin splints. So, I don't know beyond Glasgow whether I'm going to be able to do 20, 30, or perhaps 40 miles a day. The motivation to move on to the Lake District and further mountains is going to be enormous, so I'm going to have to be cautious not to do too

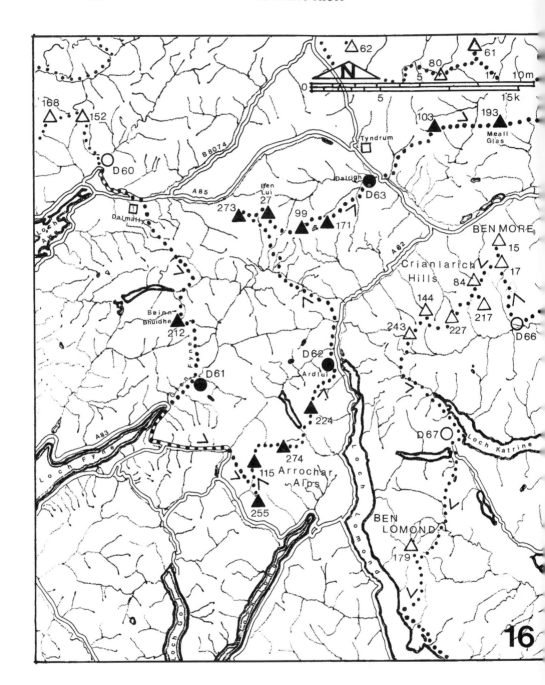

16

many miles and cause injury. I have to get it right. So after Glasgow I will have to feel my way again. It's going to be a new start for all of us. I think the places where we've camped in the last two months have been in most cases absolutely ideal, and the children have learnt lots of things about the outdoor life. Unfortunately I think south of Glasgow we're going to be in places where we're going to have to protect the children much more. Perhaps stay on campsites where we're enclosed and safer. Running along the roads is going to be more dangerous, perhaps more dangerous than running along some of the knife-edged ridges of Scotland. And the entertainment value of the trip will perhaps be lower, so we'll see. I might want to get it over with as quickly as possible – Glasgow to Carlisle, Kendal to North Wales.

'The niceties of pacing are manifold. There's the pace of the instant – if you go too fast then the heart and the lungs create oxygen debt which is uncomfortable and you go through your food resources very quickly.

'There's the pace of the whole day. How do you go if you're moving for five hours, eight hours, perhaps more? It was fifteen hours on Skye. You have to be eating and drinking sufficiently to regenerate the fuel resources at the same rate.

'There's the pace of the whole week, the month. Piecing it all together is quite complicated, and you have to listen to your own legs, body and mind as you run. But running is a therapy and it is a time when you can listen to yourself. When asked how long has it taken me to train for this event, the answer is 21 years. That is the learning of the pace. But even with that experience it's a new experience now because never before have I run for two months on mountains and then had a transition to hundreds of miles of roads.'

Although I could delay decisions until the last moment, I knew that it would make Ann Parratt's and Intermediate Technology's job of fundraising much more effective if as much advance warning was given as possible. I was now trying to get a rough idea of the number of days it would take me to run to Glasgow, through England and to Snowdon. For the first time since leaving home, maps of Glasgow, South West Scotland and the Lake District were brought out of the cupboard. Little time or thought had been given to planning routes south of the Munros. There was an element of superstition in not looking at maps of areas like Dumfries and Cheshire.

Mike and Phil joined us inside the van to discuss routes through the Lakes and to escape the abominable midges. Outside they were denser than ever. For half an hour

---

16 BEN LUI AND THE ARROCHAR ALPS

Munro Number	Munro	Running Order
212	Beinn Bhuidhe	255
255	Beinn Narnain	256
115	Beinn Ime	257
274	Ben Vane	258
224	Ben Vorlich (Loch Lomond)	259
273	Beinn a'Chleibh	260
27	Ben Lui	261
99	Ben Oss	262
171	Beinn Dubhchraig	263
103	Ben Challum	264
193	Meall Glas	265

Mike stepped into his Architect's role, and brought out the Barn plans in order to discuss final amendments. He could justify leaving the office for a few days as he was 'on business' visiting his clients! It felt strange to have our thoughts directed back to Sedbergh.

Hugh's Diary
'Tonight the midges are like a floating rain. I'd rather be soaked right through than threatened by a bite on every piece of bare flesh.'

They were still at it in the morning. Mike and Phil's tents and gear were packed away in the van's top box in an instant. They started running before I was ready. It was impossible to stand still without being eaten alive. After rapidly putting my road shoes on, I chased them up Glen Fyne faster than the midges could. Settling into a steady stride of eight minute miles, we ran in single file along the busy main road along the side of Loch Fyne, and into the straight V-shaped Glen Kinglas. Off the road within an hour, we headed into the hills from the bend in the road by Butterbridge. Ahead lay the four Munros of the Arrochar Alps.

The summer appeared to have collapsed again. Hail threw itself at us and thunder rolled in the distance. Mike left his sack full of my clothes and his near the Bealach a'Mhaim. As we climbed higher onto Beinn Narnain, I regretted leaving thermal bottoms behind as my legs were now numb from tingling hail. We quickly turned round on the rocky summit and raced back to Mike's sack. For an anxious few minutes we couldn't find it. The pollution-free sack, coloured in green, blended well with the grassy surroundings. We traversed Beinn Ime in wild wind and mist, and descended to a sheltered saddle for a brief lunch break before crossing Ben Vane to the Loch Sloy dam. From there the steep south-western face of Ben Vorlich worked our legs and lungs hard as we climbed two thousand feet in half a mile. Sunshine broke through the cloud in the afternoon. Across Loch Lomond, just seven miles away, stood the familiar hump of Ben Lomond. With most of the remaining eighteen mountains in sight, I felt happy to predict 25 June as the Munro completion date. However, having descended to the campsite at Ardlui and met Pauline, I was thrown into a mild panic, with the news that all dates through to Snowdon were needed as soon as possible.

Pauline's Diary, Tuesday 19 June
The style of the expedition is about to change. I spent a long time today talking to Ann on the phone, and it woke me up to what is going on back at home. Ann really has got the wheels turning with help from others. The new I.T. man in charge of fundraising is really getting things moving. I feel that our plans for Ireland are just a dream. It no longer seems possible to just slip away after Snowdon. The way things are going there will be a lot happening – a trip to London perhaps? When everyone – especially Ann, has worked so hard, we can't possibly desert the show at the end. Sounds like it could be very BIG and hopefully money for I.T. could come in in a big way too. We have to do all we can to make the biggest possible noise about what we have done, and who we are doing it for. It isn't just a low key jaunt round the mountains – we didn't set it up that way. There is now an incredible team behind us – a huge number of people involved in some way or other. We owe it to them to do all we can.

Hugh is doing his best to fix dates for the rest of the trip. He wasn't keen at first, but he now sees that it has to be done if events are being organised around us. Barring accidents, he should be able to stick to the schedule and reach Ben Lomond on Joseph's birthday.

I do have slight reservations about the aftermath, mainly about the prospect of Hugh being tied up with events whilst I am looking after the children. There is a limit to how long I can operate as virtually a single parent! The workload and support role extends far beyond the actual journey. A phenomenal amount of time has been devoted to this project before the traverse of the mountains and it seems likely that there will be much to do afterwards. After the run, it would be so therapeutic just to enjoy some time together as a family.

The eight days of mountains between Glencoe and Mull had accustomised me to running to a timetable. Although it had been a commitment, it had stopped the run from becoming an out an out race – something which I never wanted. I didn't like the pressure of forecasting for three weeks ahead but I didn't see a way of avoiding it without causing complications for the fundraisers. The Ardlui campsite provided a good environment to plan and communicate. The children played happily by Loch Lomond, giving me a peaceful time in the van, and the neighbouring hotel had a telephone – something which wasn't usually available at our evening camps. Our Motorola phone would only function sporadically in the Highlands. Spreading out more and more maps and looking for the possibility of good places to spend nights, I estimated being able to run 25 to 35 miles each day. This meant running between Glasgow and the Lake District in four days and between Kendal and Snowdonia in five. Scribbling notes into a diary, I eventually came up with a schedule of dates through to Snowdon, which was fixed for 11 July. I phoned Ann Parratt and relayed the timetable for Ben Lomond, Glasgow, the Lake District, Kendal and Snowdon. Her obvious delight eased my concern for having made the commitment and I returned to the camp with a strong feeling of relief that I had got rid of one problem even though I knew that I might have been causing another.

Leaving the comforts of the campsite, Mike, Phil and I ploughed our way through thick green bracken to the railway line running parallel to the road. For the two miles we had to move north, it was safer to run on the stones and sleepers of the railway than the tarmac of the fast and narrow road. Turning every few seconds to watch out for trains, it was difficult to admire the surroundings until we struck north-west for a hydro track which led us to the hills. Again, the summery air of the glens was exchanged for the wintry chill of the tops.

From Beinn a'Chleibh, a view north to the Black Mount was sneaked before climbing 700 feet higher into the dense clouds and onto the summit of Ben Lui. With no real joy to be gained from the hills this day, we raced over Ben Oss and Beinn Dubhchraig in cold and heavy rain. Cutting through new plantations and climbing over the occasional high deer fence, we descended to the overnight camp at Dalrigh after a shortish day of six hours.

Pauline's Diary, Wednesday 20 June

Hugh is pretty flaked out tonight. Is it because we have run out of Christmas Puds? He looked weary enough for Amy to feel sorry for him. 'Poor Daddy, he has to run all those mountains,' she murmured whilst gently hugging him.

The real problem of the moment is, what to do when we get back? We don't want to get back. Despite the drawbacks of this trip, I have to admit that returning home is

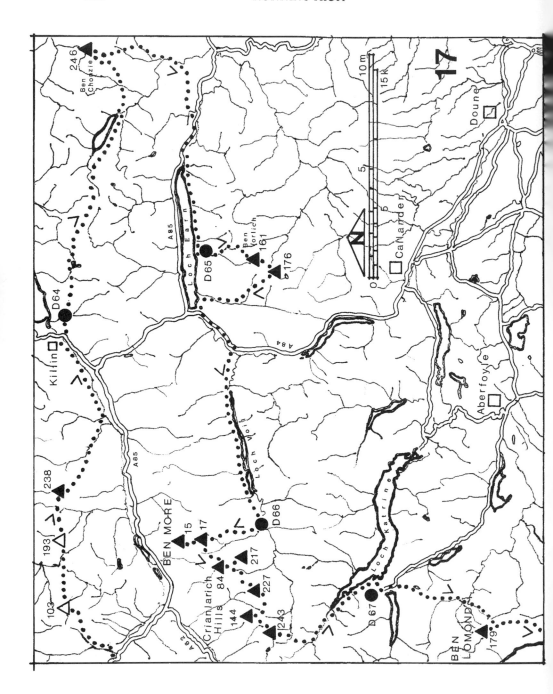

a comparatively dull proposition. The imminent end of the Munros generates the feeling that the journey is coming to an end. Including Ireland would prolong the agony and the ecstasy, but this extension to the dream now seems to be unrealistic.

A similar day in terms of distance and height followed. Sixteen miles and 6000 feet over the three mountains to the south-west of Glen Lochay saw a return to Loch Tay and the east. Dave Wells made the last of his surprise Munro interceptions on the third peak of Sgiath Chuil. It was a luxury to drink herbal tea and eat chocolate cake whilst admiring the high bastions of Ben More and Stob Binnein to the south. A five mile jog along the quiet lane by the River Dochart completed the running for the day and helped build an appetite for the evening wedding anniversary celebrations of Chianti and steak *au poivre*.

The following morning, our camp by Loch Tay became a hive of activity as the number of pacers grew to six. Dave Richardson returned to join me until Ben Lomond, having finished summer examinations at Lancaster University. Martin Stone, Adrian Belton and Hélène Diamantides had all just completed the Three Peaks Yacht Race at Fort William. Having run up Snowdon, Scafell Pike and Ben Nevis, sailing between the peaks, they were returning south by car and called in to join me for the run to the lonely Munro of Ben Chonzie. A twenty-eight mile day was required to visit this uninteresting solitary peak. Finding a good route east along tracks, by pipelines and across moors of heather and peat, was a challenge in itself. We found a way through to the stony shore of Loch Lednock where the dam produced an unusual obstacle to the route. Concrete ramparts and short sections of fixed metal ladders provided an alternative terrain for hands and feet. Ben Chonzie was an easy afternoon's outing from Lednock. Running across lush and boggy grasslands, the shortest route was taken to a wide and stony track which climbs to the broad southern spur. A large area near the rounded summit was littered with old fences and cairns. Piles of stones stood randomly in places which can't pretend to be subtops. Four miles further south, we waded the Lednock and joined the road for a tea break near Kingarth farm. Footpaths guided us via a shortcut above Comrie and led us through the grounds of the Whitehouse of Dunira – a well-kept estate of brightly painted houses. Six miles of road led to the overnight camp by Loch Earn.

The children had gone to bed, and Pauline and I were about to fold down the table and make our bed when an old orange VW camper drew up alongside us. Two fit

17 LOCH EARN TO BEN LOMOND

Munro Number	Munro	Running Order
238	Sgiath Chuil	266
246	Ben Chonzie (Ben-y-Hone)	267
161	Ben Vorlich (Loch Earn)	268
176	Stùc a'Chroin	269
17	Stob Binnein	270
15	Ben More (Crianlarich)	271
84	Cruach Ardrain	272
217	Beinn Tulaichean	273
227	Beinn a'Chroin	274
144	An Caisteal	275
243	Beinn Chabhair	276
179	Ben Lomond	277

looking people walked purposefully towards the van. I hadn't met them before, but I soon recognised Mike Cudahy and Inken Blunk from pictures in their book. The previous winter, I had asked Mike if he could join me whilst in the Highlands. In 1984, Mike Cudahy became the first person to run the 270 miles of the Pennine Way in under three days. His experience of ultra-distance mountain running is beautifully described in *Wild Trails to Far Horizons*. I looked forward to chatting to Mike about running and writing, during tomorrow's outing. A saying from the book stood in my memory and was in my thoughts several times during the run: 'When I stand at the beginning of 100 miles of moor, mountain, valley and meadow I am standing on the threshold of a dream.' I had not been able to sense this on Ben Hope, as the dream was too far away. But now, just three days running from Ben Lomond, it was a curious coincidence that Mike should join me by surprise and see me on the threshold of *my* dream.

We climbed together onto the summit of Ben Vorlich and followed the steep stony ridge to the adjoining peak of Stùc a'Chroin. The thick forests of Strathyre prevented a direct line west, so a detour was made north via Glen Ample and the Falls of Edinample. Road running is an anathema to Mike, so he left Dave Richardson and I to jog the remaining ten miles of road alongside Loch Voil and Loch Doine. There was now a strong sense of nearing the end of the Munros, but at the same time a tension grew within me. I saw the following day's seven mountains, 20 miles and 11,000 feet of climbing as a threat. Now that I was working to a fixed timetable, and I was due to meet the press at midday Monday on the summit of Ben Lomond, I couldn't afford anything to go wrong on the penultimate day.

Pauline's Diary, Saturday 23 June
We eventually bumped into Hugh's parents at the end of the no-through road terminating at Inverlochlarig. All day yesterday they had been hunting for us. They brought presents for the children, delicious cakes and, best of all, a casserole for our dinner.

It was our first meeting since leaving home. The children were delighted to see their Taid and Nain (Welsh for grandfather and grandmother) but they can't have found me too sociable. If I wasn't eating, then I was busily transpasealing and cutting maps. After their visit of one hour, they disappeared to a hotel. The family would see them the following day, but I wouldn't meet my parents again until Kendal. I felt bad for hardly saying more than a few words to them. My single-mindedness kept me on the right track, always thinking about tomorrow, but I must have appeared strange and distant to them that evening.

The Sunday morning was warm and midgy even at the early hour of seven. The farmers' forecast had warned of gales and rain but not until late in the day. I made two unforgettable mistakes between Ben Hope and Ben Lomond. One had been running out of food on the first of the big days in the Cairngorms and now, on the penultimate day, after 270 Munros I went into the mountains with insufficient clothing for the day ahead. It was 24 June, dry and balmy in the glen and just turning cloudy on the tops.

Dave Richardson, Martin Stone, Mike Cudahy, Inken Blunk and I left our camp in the car park at eight. Even dressed in tee shirts we sweated buckets as we climbed the first thousand feet of Stob Binnein. Never before, in the preceding 65 days, had the contrast between glen and summit been so marked. Another 2000 feet higher and we were on the first of the day's seven peaks. A strong westerly gale blew us off balance as

Mike Cudahy, Dave Richardson, Martin Stone and Inken Blunk weathering the storm on Cruach Ardrain. (H.S.)

we ran ahead to the higher twin of Ben More. By the time we reached the trig point at 3843 feet, the gales had brought an icy driving rain which was penetrating my light-weight waterproof. My body was beginning to chill as we returned to the *bealach* between the two peaks. Now heading directly into the onslaught, my thin leggings were soaking up the rain like blotting paper. I felt foolish for not having my overtrousers and good waterproof. Running towards the third Munro, I grew colder and began to seriously doubt my ability to survive the day. The doubts played on my mind and interrupted my concentration on the navigation. Thick cloud reduced the visibility to a few metres. Sounds of the howling wind and rushing water distracted my attention and confused my thoughts. The ground between the mountains was awkward. With deep corries, steep glens and craggy tops, careful use of the map was imperative to find the next five summits. In an attempt to reduce my inner tension, I picked a black slimy slug from the sodden ground and offered it to Mike, pretending it was food. He replied, 'No thanks, I've just had some chocolate.' We sheltered behind crags before climbing onto the exposed summit of Cruach Ardrain. The brief rest was an opportunity to discuss my problem. Mike and Inken had already decided that they would return to their van after the fourth peak of Beinn Tulaichean. I don't know what Martin's intentions had been, but when he heard of my plight, he gave me his overtrousers and an extra layer of warm clothing. Martin returned to Inverlochlarig with Mike and Inken, leaving Dave and I to plough on through the mountains and the sustained downpour.

With the extra kit, I was still wet through, but at least I felt a little warmer. We carefully contoured under the crags of Stob Glas before climbing the fifth Munro of Beinn a'Chroin – 'The Mountain of Harm or Danger'. My confidence was returning and we ran west past tiny lochans before descending to the Beallach Buidhe. The cloud was so low and dense that it prevented any views between the peaks, even at this lower level. An easy shoulder led us to the top of An Caisteal. A direct line to the seventh Munro, Beinn Chabhair, took us by steep crags and grassy slopes which were pouring water in hundreds of fast-running streams and miniature waterfalls. On Beinn Chabhair, I punched my fist in the air, celebrating the day's seven peaks and my attainment of Munroist stature. Having previously been to the summit of Ben Lomond, I had now visited all 277 Munros, although the complete Munro traverse still had thirteen miles to be run.

Pauline's Diary, Sunday 24 June
I just managed to reach Ann on the Motorola phone. The news on Glasgow is bad! Calor Gas, having taken on the responsibility of organising publicity in the city, do not seem to have achieved anything. Plans for us to meet the Lord Provost of Glasgow seem to have fallen through! The Lord Provost is on holiday until tomorrow and is therefore not contactable. We plan to reach Glasgow on 27 June, the day of another big charity event in the city!

Our night spot here on the pier overlooking the vast waters of Loch Katrine, has been achieved through negotiation with the Water Board officials. They seem to own all the land around here and do not normally allow campervans to park for the night. I have now become quite accustomed to explaining our cause to custodians of the land and generally they have been very helpful. Dave Richardson will be delighted to know that the vast luxury of the Ladies' Cloakroom is all his for the night. I don't imagine that he will have many visitors!

The day had been a trial, but at last I could see little stopping me from reaching Ben Lomond at noon the following day. Running south, we crossed the higher reaches of the River Larig and climbed through a saddle to pick up a track under pylons in Glen Gyle. After four miles of track and tarmac, we found Pauline at the unusual camp position of Stronachlachar pier.

Pauline's Diary, evening, Sunday 24 June
Hugh is pretty zonked. Is it mental or is it physical? On this extremely taxing day in abysmal weather he misjudged his kit badly. Martin Stone feels that Hugh's nervousness about this crucial watershed of the journey could explain his error.

Sacks were packed more carefully for the final Munro morning. Expecting a summit party and a series of live radio interviews on the portable telephone, lots of clothes, a tent, a stove and a kettle were amongst the extras placed on our backs. Dave and I left the pier by Loch Katrine at 8:45, allowing plenty of time to run the final six miles of the Munro traverse. After a mile of road, we cut across three miles of rough open country to the farm at Comer, nestled underneath the steep northern ridges of Ben Lomond. Sunday's Atlantic fronts had blown east and the summits were now clear of cloud. The final Munro stood tall and inviting from this pathless northern side. My eyes locked onto the mountain and my legs pumped the last Scottish 3000 foot climb. Joining the main summit ridge for the final few hundred metres, suddenly the calm of the northern face was swept away by southerly gales. We could see friends walking up the main wide track, but not stopping to chat yet, we raced on to the summit, blown along by the wind.

It was eleven o'clock on a Monday morning – a good time for a private celebration on a peak. Expecting to stop for at least an hour, I pitched the tent next to the trig point

With Bev Holt, Dave Richardson and Paul Tuson on the last Munro – Ben Lomond. (Chris Bradley)

and crawled inside to make coffees and answer the frequently ringing phone. Between live chats with Radio Cumbria and Radio Manchester, I popped outside to see friends. Bev Holt, Paul Tuson and Dave Richardson had been on Ben Hope, and now, 67 days later, we were together again. Our meeting emphasised the transition of distance and time over the past couple of months. Tomorrow, I would be looking to avoid roads and there would be no more mountains for a week. To the north lay the Munros I had grown to love and respect – the Munros that had given the reason for the journey. There was no real sense of victory, just a hint of sadness that there was no more wilderness to the south.

Chapter 16   GOODBYE TO THE WILDERNESS

June 25 – July 1

By 1:30, after two and a half hours on the summit, I was ready to start running south. The wide, eroded track led down to the shores of Loch Lomond by Rowardennan. The day had been planned to be short and easy, just thirteen miles, allowing time for celebrations and time to rest before the long, hard road that lay ahead.

On the way to Glasgow with Janet Bell. (P.S.)

Pauline's Diary, Monday 25 June

A day for a double celebration – the completion of the Munros and Joseph's seventh birthday. We have a delectable-looking chocolate birthday cake, made by Hugh's mother. Joseph insisted on inviting everybody to see the candles lit, sing happy birthday and share the cake. The cake vanished in the blink of an eye as a large group has assembled here to welcome Hugh on his last Munro.

Janet Bell, from the I.T. Press Office, has made a special visit in order to salvage something from the tumbling plans for Glasgow.

Running friends disappeared after Ben Lomond. I had had company every day since leaving Ben Hope, but now things would change. Between Loch Lomond and Snowdon there were four days in the fortnight when I ran the roads alone. Perhaps, in the Highlands, I had been a good excuse for my fell-running friends to go north and bag Munros.

The first four miles towards Glasgow were a joy, running by Loch Lomond, by thick forests and alongside the gently whirring wheels of Janet Bell's mountain bike. Dressed in a bright white 'Intermediate Technology' sweat shirt, Janet was an escort for this initiation to the roads south. We parted ways at the first campsite by the Loch. Janet vanished to Glasgow to organise publicity and I disappeared under a long hot shower,

before going to the Rowardennan Hotel with the family. In appreciation of my achievement, we were all offered drinks and delicious puddings on the house.

The morning of the first non-Munro day was like a holiday. There was nothing in particular to do, just relax and enjoy the peaceful setting by the Loch. Twenty flat and easy miles whiled away a few afternoon hours and saw me along the West Highland Way to Mugdock Reservoir on the north side of Glasgow. Just seven miles from the city centre, we were on the edge of housing estates and parked by a popular spot for dog owners to take their beasts for poos.

I didn't want to run through Glasgow. I feared the traffic, losing Pauline or even worse – being mugged. Fortunately, I didn't have to navigate. Three Glasgow residents and hill runners – Mark Rigby, Peter Baxter and Eddie Dealtry – arrived at 9 am to escort me through the concrete and cars. The air was different, even on the edge of town. A constant hum of traffic had replaced the sounds of nature that we had grown used to. The sky was dulled but for an orange glow towards the southern horizon of rooftops. We left in torrential rain and I crossed my fingers that I would see the van in an hour or two's time in the centre of town.

Past smoky bus shelters and hundreds of number plates, through brightly painted subways, we turned left, then right and right again, down alleyways, through parks, by rivers, across flyovers and into the centre of the city. Glass-fronted shops, bin men and buses were novelties which thrilled and humoured me. Suddenly, out of the wilderness, I had arrived in this maze of humanity with fire engines and police cars, racing and ringing for all they were worth. Dodging the points of a thousand umbrellas and jogging from left to right avoiding pedestrians, I came to George Square via a labyrinth of shopping precincts.

Pauline

Having guided Hugh safely across the sea to Mull, Fearghas now offered his services through Glasgow to the support crew. Using his intimate knowledge of the fast-flowing currents of moving traffic, he kept us securely on course, until roadworks forced us through a narrow backwater. Fearghas, in his much narrower vehicle, slipped through easily. We became trapped between a fence and a car boot hanging out of a repair shop. Luckily the mechanics were able to move the protruding vehicle, and we continued our voyage to a safe mooring in George Square. Andrew was very upset by this appropriation of his role as navigator.

Publicity-wise, Glasgow was a great non-event. Janet had done her best. The arrangements had been confused by 'Calor Gas'. They had supplied all our gas for the trip and had offered to organise the publicity in Glasgow. Hugh had run over all the 3000 foot mountains of Scotland, but Glasgow was oblivious to the event apart from the one reporter from the Glasgow Herald. However, we must be thankful for this as his article prompted a generous donation of £1 000 from an interested reader.

Life in the city centre was novel and exciting, until the children became restless. Hugh was obviously very ill-at-ease and couldn't wait to leave.

A *Glasgow Herald* photographer took me to a park bench and asked me to jump it for the camera. I refused, telling him that it wasn't on my route. A more natural pose was arranged just running across some grass, but now I was told – 'You're making my easy job difficult. Can't you run slower please?'

After a couple of hours parked outside the City Chambers, I was glad to run south and head out of town. But not before I had crossed the Clyde and passed a hundred high-rise flats and billboards. Eddie's carefully prepared route had been nurtured through a winter of long training runs. Knowing where the vicious rottweilers and alsatians paraded, his route guided me via station platforms, cemeteries and golf courses and out to the edge of civilisation at Carmunnock and East Kilbride.

The city's walls of claustrophobic streets had been left behind. Horizons had opened and quiet lanes splattered with cow muck led me south to an overnight camp by some woods, west of Strathaven.

The next unavoidable city en route would be Carlisle – a hundred miles to the south. Three days in which to avoid the A74 – the M6 extension to Scotland. The lorry-laden dual carriageway had frightened me enough in the past in a car, and there was no way I would be tempted to set foot on it in running shoes.

Thursday 28 June – an unusual day – for all I had to do was just run a marathon. There were no appointments and there was no fixed route. Without mountains as checkpoints, I could please myself where to go as long as it was south. The entertainment was now in finding an interesting way which was economical on distance but away from main roads.

Lanes, footpaths and fields took me to the gates of a prison at Dungavel. Pauline had pulled off the road by the entrance and was given a lot of hard stares by prison staff who must have been on a midday shift change. My planned coffee and cake break was abruptly shortened when we were asked to move on. Maybe they thought we were planning an escape for some of the inmates.

With a 'Walkman' in my bumbag, and headphones on my ears, I ran on to the small town of Muirkirk to the rhythmical tune of Latin American pipe music. Eight miles of tarmac vanished with the musical scene of the accompanying hills rolling by.

Sixty miles of hard surfaces since Ben Lomond and my legs were beginning to stiffen.

Unlike mountains, which provide an ever-changing pattern of movement, the roads offer no variety – just a constant pace which eventually shortens and tightens the hamstrings. Stopping every couple of miles to touch my toes eased the tension a little, but there was no better therapy than the afternoon trip across-country. Ten miles of soft tracks round the west side of the 2000 foot Cairn Table led to a night's stop on a no-through road above Sanquhar.

Pauline's Diary, Thursday 28 June

It made a pleasant change to be on our own as a family. A relaxing drive through rolling hills culminated in a 10 mile climb up a valley very reminiscent of our home country – the Yorkshire Dales.

However, our evening peace has been shattered. The Motorola phone works and hasn't stopped ringing. It was impossible to get through the children's evening story. Ann has been having a hard time with a sponsor who has asked her to persuade Hugh to hold back for ten days, so that arrangements can be made to meet a dignitary and the press on Helvellyn. Their organisation cannot keep up with Hugh's running speed! Ann has politely, or not so politely, said 'no'.

It was a Thursday evening and I wasn't expecting company until the weekend. I was enjoying the solitude and was looking forward to another thirty mile day on my own, when Dave Richardson arrived, late in the evening. It was a shock to see him as we hadn't told anyone our position. Dave had hitch-hiked from Kendal to Sanquhar and had asked a few people in the town whether they had seen a large white van with stickers. Nobody had, but one lady pointed north, up the hill towards Fingland and told Dave that the tiny dot of a white object three miles away wasn't usually there. Pauline, the children and I were just getting used to a new routine of meeting each other several times a day. Although the children continued to have their usual ugly quarrels over toys, the rare experience of being just the five of us gave us a privacy and togetherness which we hadn't enjoyed for over two months.

Dave blended into the landscape with his tent and wasn't seen until the morning. Things were tense after breakfast. The children had reached a peak in their battle over the choice lego pieces. Had I been on my own for the day, I might have stayed in the van a little longer, to wait for the atmosphere to cool down. I didn't like to leave the family in such a fraught state. Having Dave with me, I felt that we ought to be on the road and running south. I was embarrassed by the noise coming from the van. The departure from the Highlands had instilled a tension. The beauty had gone and the natural places for children to play had been left behind. Contradictions were playing on my mind. I liked the company of running friends, but I wanted to be on my own with the family. I wanted the run to go beyond Snowdon and on to Ireland, but I didn't know whether we could sustain living in the four walls of the van, or if my legs could maintain the constant pounding of thirty miles a day.

Dave and I jogged down the hill to Sanquhar and passed morning shoppers on the streets. Beyond, on the main road to Dumfries, we were splashed by lorries in heavy rain before running onto a parallel quiet lane along Nithsdale. We ran through the grounds of the splendid Drumlanrig Castle, past Poet's Corner – a farm by the road where a sign read: 'DANGER – FREE RANGE CHILDREN'. Seeing what I thought to be a footbridge marked on the map, we headed across fields towards the River Nith. With no bridge in sight, I read the map more carefully and saw the word 'ford', but even this didn't seem apparent under the dark peaty waters. Asking a man where the ford was, he replied, 'Oh – there used to be stepping stones there many years ago.' We waded across the gentle flow and pulled ourselves out through deep reeds. Roads, lanes, a golf course and stony tracks took us to, and then through the vast forest of Ae. After a short tea break in the village of Ae, we ran another ten miles of lanes to Lochmaben, to take the day's total to 33.

Another 33 miles away in a straight line stood the 278th mountain, Skiddaw, the first of the Lake District hills. On foot, the journey was over 50 miles. For a long time I had hoped to wade or row across the Solway Firth south of Annan, hence saving over fifteen miles and adding adventure to a tedious part of the run. However, concrete knowledge of the Solway had been hard to come by; there were just rumours of fast currents and quicksands.

I couldn't accept the idea of a long day on roads. Searching the map for any opportunity to use tracks and fields I found what seemed like a good route north of the village of Brydekirk. The previous day's crossing of the Nith had given me a taste for river crossings and this route offered the challenge of the Annan. The weather had been a typical summer mixture of sunshine and heavy showers, with enough rain to swell the river into fast flow. I had been joined for the weekend by previous mountain companions – Chris Davies, Frank Thomas and Ian Rooke. They looked in disbelief as Dave and I plunged into the river. The current was forceful and we were swept sideways a few feet. Bracing ourselves with a tight grip of each other's hand, we edged slowly to the far bank with the river washing above our shorts. Behind us, the trio did a circular dance and at one stage looked like they would float away. Frank tripped on a moving rock and suffered a complete dousing. The river was a massage for my legs and therapy for the brain – just what was needed before joining an unavoidable stretch of the A74, near the English border just south of Gretna.

For two miles, we were deafened by the roar of traffic racing up and down the dual carriageway. Running in single file, we hugged the edge of the hard shoulder until the first minor road junction led us onto tiny lanes to Carlisle. My legs were now tightening badly, and it was becoming more difficult to run with my usual long stride. The cold rain of a sudden and violent thunderstorm didn't help, and the last four miles to the campsite at Dalston Hall seemed long and slow. Even after a good hot shower, my legs felt sore. I worried for the morning, for the long days through Lancashire and Cheshire, and wondered how Kelvin Bowers and Bruce Tulloh had ever managed their epic long-distance road runs. Both these men had been an inspiration to me – Bowers in running 10 000 miles across the World, from Stoke to Sydney, and Tulloh in running across the States, averaging 44 miles a day.

A shorter day of just 20 miles was the menu through to the north of Skiddaw. I woke up sore, but not incapacitated, at least not as incapacitated as some of the pacers who had been to a local pub for Saturday night drinks. Fortunately, a gentle pace was ensured for the last flat run through to the English hills. The Cumbria Way cuts through the heart of the Lake District on its 70 mile route from Ulverston to Carlisle. A 10 mile section along the banks of the Caldew provided a natural break from roads, and a charming route through rich agricultural land to the village of Caldbeck. Quiet lanes and tracks, skirting the northern edge of the Uldale Fells, led to the overnight camp, a mile east of Bassenthwaite village.

The five day total of 140 miles had left me tired and jaded. I was in need of rest and I hoped the following day's return to mountains would provide the necessary therapy.

Chapter 17   THROUGH THE LAKES AND BEYOND

July 2 – 8

Between the two little hills of Cockup and Great Cockup, flows the stream of Dash Beck which tumbles down from Skiddaw via the waterfalls of Whitewater Dash.

A short day of thirteen miles was ideal to ease my fatigue, to give time to meet friends and time for the media to interview me. Skiddaw turned out to be the busiest mountain of the run. Hardly had we had breakfast when the BBC rolled into our camp by Dash Beck. Filming delayed my departure by over an hour, but I hoped that even five minutes on 'North West Tonight' would help raise the profile of Intermediate Technology. With the phone in my sack ready for a BBC World Service interview on the summit at midday, I ran off towards the long-awaited mountain, exactly seven days to the hour since I had been on Ben Lomond. Stopped in my stride by a ringing telephone, I answered the call of Border TV who booked in for the south side of the mountain. Now delayed even more, I rushed towards the top hoping not to miss friends who were expecting me at twelve. The World Service caught me on the way up in a rare session of heavy breathing. Whilst answering questions on I.T. and running mountains, I pushed on over flat slaty stones towards a large group of seemingly frozen statues. There, waiting by the North Top of Skiddaw, were friends from Kendal Athletic Club, Simon Madge – running captain from Sedbergh School, and a group from William Hulme's Grammar School in Manchester. I had taught at WHGS before moving to Sedbergh. Boys and staff were there to wish me well and to hand over a cheque to I.T. After a quick series of handshakes, in descending cloud and heavy hail, I ran south over the main summit and down for the next appointment between Jenkin Hill and Latrigg.

Sound extract from TV recording

'On arriving in the English hills, you're immediately aware of the fact that they're used so much more than the Scottish mountains. The whole countryside is used. It's a very delicate balance between the interests of the farmers, the tourist industry and the National Trust. It's quite a difficult job for the National Park wardens to keep on top of it all, but possibly the last thing they want to do is put closed gates on the outside of the Lake District and count the number of people who go in and out. But from here it is beauty, sheer beauty, looking across Derwent Water and looking to tomorrow's hills – Helvellyn, Scafell Pike and Scafell. It's great to be back on the hills after a week's road running. South of Glasgow I enjoyed it for a day or two, finding quiet lanes and river banks to run on, but after four days of 30 miles a day my legs were beginning to feel like reinforced concrete. They've been loosened off by Skiddaw and I'm feeling enthusiastic about the run again. Unfortunately the Lake District isn't large enough for many days

18 THE LAKE DISTRICT

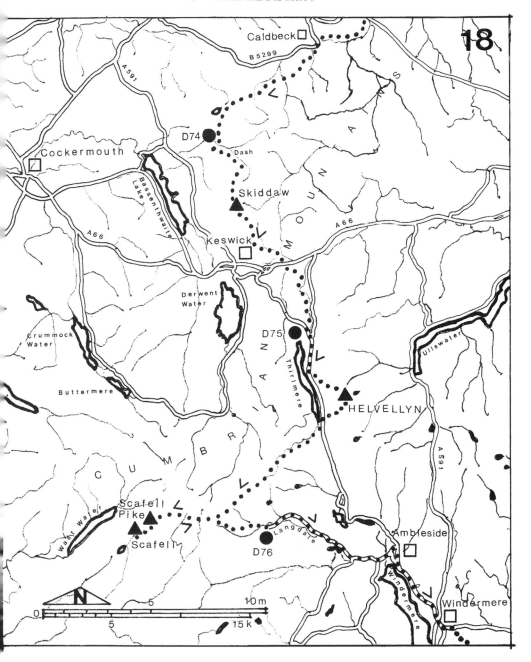

On Helvellyn (*Eric Whitehead*)

running, so I'll be out again on Wednesday through Ambleside and Kendal which I'm sure'll be very pleasant. But then my route goes south through St. Helens, Runcorn and into Snowdonia, so it'll be a trial of patience through the industrial North West before I reach the mountains of North Wales.'

I had visited all four of the English 3000 foot peaks many times before, but in the transit from Caldbeck to Kendal, there was new ground to be covered and there were several pleasant surprises. Whitewater Dash had been the first, and now, in the afternoon of the same day, I tracked down new pastures in following footpaths through the picturesque St. John's in the Vale, a peaceful crag-rimmed valley, south of the village of Threlkeld.

The day's short run through to Thirlspot allowed me to recover from the wear and tear of the previous week. Throughout the run, the mixture of long and short days seemed to work in maintaining my health, fitness and enjoyment of the journey.

After the previous day's cold and heavy showers, it was a pleasure to pass through the heart of the Lake District in bright, summery weather with clear distant views. Many friends joined me for the 20 mile run through to Langdale. A wide stony track led us up the 2500 foot climb to the summit of Helvellyn, where a group from home were waiting to greet me. Richard Meredith-Hardy landed his microlight on the summit stones, his right wing missing the trig point by an alarmingly narrow margin. He picked up Chris Bradley plus film camera and planned to track me through the day.

Running south west in a direct line towards England's highest mountain, we passed the south end of Thirlmere and approached the Central Fells via a muddy track by the side of Wyth Burn. Rounding the north of High Raise, the route crossed open country until we joined a broad track at Angle Tarn. The well-trodden and familiar path took us to the popular summit of Scafell Pike, where dozens of people were resting and admiring the scenery. Just forty-four feet lower and less than a mile away, Scafell contrasted dramatically with its deserted summit cairn. Separated by the narrow col of Mickledore, the route between Scafell Pike and Scafell is made tricky by the awkward stepped blocks of Broad Stand. For twenty feet, outward-facing, smooth and slippery slabs provide delicate manoeuvres which force the scrambler away from any firm handholds. Such exposure, even though brief, was intimidating and something that I hadn't experienced since Glen Coe. Our steps from Scafell were retraced to Angle Tarn, beyond which we met the film crew, without microlight, at the top of Rossett Gill.

Before this final three miles to the overnight stay in Langdale, Zanzibar stopped me for a few minutes and taped the following interview:

Jeremy's sound track, Tuesday 3 July
'The comparison in size between the ranges of mountains in Scotland and those of England has been emphasised now that I'm finishing the English mountains after just over 24 hours. I'm dropping into Langdale now and going to pass by one of the most dangerous things I'm going to have to cope with, and that's the Old Dungeon Ghyll Hotel, where they serve a dozen real ales. So it's going to be very tempting tonight, but I'm going to have to keep the clampers on.

'I can see in the distance and on the skyline, my own training fells, the Howgills. It's two and a half months now since I've had a run over those and I'm not tempted to go across; I'm not tempted to go home. I've got used to the nomadic life and I'd be quite happy to stay out running over mountains for longer.'

Chris Bradley and Jeremy West – above Langdale. (Martin Stone)

Pauline's Diary, Tuesday 3 July

As our van dawdled along the confined lane towards the legendary Old Dungeon Ghyll Hotel, a familiar sound whirred overhead. Richard, enjoying the freedom of the skies on his flying motorbike, was seeking a suitable landing patch. A small, but level field next to the hotel, enclosed by the usual dry stone wall, offered a suitable clear site. The microlight touched the grass and headed towards the wall at great speed. The plane came to a halt just short of the wall. The brake cable had snapped on landing. 'It's not disastrous,' Richard casually remarked. 'You can always stop by pushing the mudguard against the wheel with your foot.' (This was reminiscent of the way children stop bicycles with their feet.) From behind his dark, unruly mop of hair one could detect a twinkle in his eye as he made these deadpan comments. His incredible skill speaks for itself, and he has no need of flamboyancy in manner or dress. A dull pair of brown trousers and a sloppy brown sweater forms his standard ground uniform. From the exterior, Richard's apparent gamble with life and limb is difficult to detect. It is my belief that his intimate relationship with his machine and knowledge of its capabilities, coupled with perfect control ensures his safety and accounts for his calm demeanour.

Despite having entered the hills once more, the journey has lost that magical quality inherent in the remote Highland glens of Scotland. I have read the phrase, 'loved to death' used to describe this pretty garden of hills, and how true it is. Richard has seen from the air the vast net of ever-widening paths and tracks laid over the land. Even greater numbers ply the tarmac. How different was the road to Altnaharra where the lack of passing places caused no problems as we met so few travellers. As I look through the road atlas the Gaelic names of the Highland mountains catch my eye and I feel homesick for the north. I long to go back and climb the mountains. These days supporting running on the road do not inspire me. I could not enjoy following an ultra-long road run as I have enjoyed this mountain epic. We hope for more inspiration at the end of our journey.

Pauline's Diary, Wednesday 4 July

A real treat last night – a meal out in the Old Dungeon Ghyll. Surrounded by a large number of good friends, we had an hilarious time – I haven't laughed so much in ages.

Dozens of pints into the evening, a tall, fair and fit-looking young man entered the climbers' bar. Hugh, eyeing the person with interest, couldn't resist sharing his thoughts. A startling realisation had come upon him, 'It must be Dave Clarke!' This comment soon sorted out the knowledgeable from the ignorant. Jeremy, the sound man and Chris, the camera man, looked at each other, 'Who's Dave Clarke?' The very same thought shot through my head. Luckily, Martin Stone, thoroughly amazed by Hugh's perceptiveness, was there to share the astonishment. Hugh corrected our ignorance. 'Dave Clarke is the most consistent British cross-country runner of all time and winner of more than one National Cross-Country championship,' he informed us.

Bev Holt, our doctor, had prescribed a half of 'Marston's Pedigree' for Hugh. Late in the evening Hugh retired, having consumed far in excess of the recommended dose! He will probably suffer for it today. Our turn to be filmed this morning – driving the van at speed through a huge puddle, the result of a few hours of monsoon-like downpour.

Jeremy's sound recording of Hugh

'The British summer has collapsed and my feet are becoming more and more webbed. I think I'm going to have to wade through to Ambleside. Running on a day like today you get cold legs, cold hands and just want to sit in a hot bath. But I haven't had one of those for over two months, until Neil Walmsley, landlord of the Old Dungeon Ghyll, kindly offered me one last night, and it was luxury.'

The rain teemed down for most of the day. Fed up with being soaked by traffic splashing through deep puddles, I left the road after 14 miles and headed across-country. It was better to plough through deep fields of mud rather than grind the fast tarmac of the Windermere to Kendal highway.

A timely break in the clouds cleared the rain for the 4 o'clock meeting with the Mayor. Running through Kendal with dozens of young athletes and supporters, I felt more like a pied piper than a long distance runner. It didn't quite seem real running through the town where I had shopped for final items just two and a half months previously.

I was on view and in a dream whilst running through the streets of Kendal, but my real dream was still a week away. I wasn't just running now, I was publicity for much of the day. Radio Sussex before breakfast, *The Independent* following me to the Mayor, *The Westmorland Gazette* in the evening and Radio Cumbria early the following morning. The adrenalin flowed and kept me talking, but I was very aware of the long days to North Wales. The hills had eased my legs after Carlisle but the next section south was to be a day longer than the traverse of South West Scotland.

Kendal. The Mayor and Keith Helsby (Manager of Yorkshire Bank). (P.S.)

Whilst being entertained at our friends' house, I felt on the fringe of the party. The wanting to let loose and enjoy myself was held back by the knowledge of being so near and yet so far from Snowdon.

Pauline's Diary, Wednesday 4 July
Our first night spent outside the van, much to the disapproval of my mother-in-law who believed that a soft bed would be our undoing! Old friends, Andy and Barbara Clifford, offered us the freedom of their home in Kendal. I had forgotten how comfortable and convenient a large house can be. Living in the van loses some of its appeal when not parked up a remote Highland glen. Just 10 miles to the east lies our own home, but there is no temptation to go there.

At nine o'clock on the Thursday morning it was time to leave the home town and set off for the final stage south. I was glad of the company of friends to ease me into the first few of 140 miles towards Snowdonia.

Canal tow paths guided us and kept me off the roads for over half of the thirty-five mile day. One by one, friends returned to Kendal as I journeyed further south. By Carnforth, I had been joined by friend and teacher, Guy Woolnough who led me into the grounds of his High School where I was greeted by dozens of children who gave me drinks and donations of money to I.T.

By Lancaster, I was alone and the canal banks were of no use to me anymore. Before a long stretch of A6 pavement, I met Pauline in a supermarket car park and collected my 'Walkman' to help carry me south. Aided by a following wind and the music of Pink Floyd's 'Delicate Sound of Thunder', I ran effortlessly for miles without hearing the sounds of the traffic rushing by. I was almost in a state of oblivion. The music merged with the scenery and gave the effect of being submerged in a captivating film. Tears rushed to my eyes when I imagined my arrival on Snowdon. I was now higher on running than I had ever been before. I seemed to be almost levitating as I drifted along the road – not fast, but with a motion of apparent perpetuity and more akin to the gliding of a soaring bird than the running of a long distance athlete. I had always dreaded the long roads south, but now they seemed to act as an opportunity to savour what had passed behind me and to look forward to what was still to come.

On arriving in the town of Garstang, and seeing a travel agency, I couldn't resist the temptation to pop in to ask about ferries across the Irish Sea. We still didn't know whether we would go onward to Ireland, but at least we now had ferry brochures and a basic map showing Dublin and Cork. Five minutes further down the road, I found the van and we motored to Preston for the first of two overnight stops with Pauline's parents.

The following morning, my mother-in-law drove me back to Garstang. It seemed a long way, even by car, but I soon returned to the rhythm of running, a rhythm which carried me another thirty-six miles through rural and urban Lancashire. South of Preston, I left main roads and ran along attractive lanes and footpaths from village to village and from farm to farm. Through Eccleston, Appley Bridge, Up-Holland and Crank, I dodged between Skelmersdale and Wigan, avoiding big towns until the urban sprawl east of Liverpool. Past dozens of video shops, newsagents and pubs, I saw busy businessmen driving flash cars, scruffy children playing in car parks and a pig on the street between the Triplex glazing works and St Helens Rugby Club. No way did I want to spend the night in the van in suburbia, so I returned to Preston, first marking the overnight break point by touching the station sign at Thatto Heath.

It was the twelfth weekend of the run, and the third one for which Ian Rooke and Dave Bayliss joined me. Our meeting point couldn't have contrasted more sharply than with the previous Highland spots. From Thatto Heath we ran amongst hundreds of Saturday morning shoppers, then south a few miles to Widnes and the River Mersey. This one wasn't for wading or swimming. The stench from chemical works suggested poisonous waters. The view from the high Runcorn Bridge was colourful but not clear: the river and the Manchester Ship Canal being so polluted that they would probably melt running shoes.

South of Runcorn, we became confused by dual carriageways and housing estates. Tangled in a network of motorway slip roads, we escaped on a railway line before joining the main road to Frodsham. The challenge was now to cross the base of the Wirral peninsular avoiding fast roads. I eyed the map for ages before finding a line through the maze of lanes north of Chester. Intricate route-finding kept me entertained as we edged west, over fields, along a section of the Shropshire Union Canal, through the village of Saughall, and then, across the Dee and into Wales at Queensferry.

Pauline's Diary, Saturday 7 July

Over the last few days our style has completely changed. For the fourth consecutive night we are sleeping in a house and our evening meal is being cooked for us. Our washing is in the machine and the children have novel toys and new friends to play with. Andrew demonstrated his urban navigational ability, expertly guiding us from Shotton Station where the day's run ended, to the home of friends at Barston, near Birkenhead.

Our venture has come to resemble a job of work. We make our separate journeys – Hugh along footpaths and minor roads and myself along the more major routes – meeting at prearranged points every 5–15 miles for tea and cake breaks. For the last couple of days the children have enjoyed staying with Grandma, whilst Hugh and I have got on with the job of covering the mileage for the day. Not an inspiring occupation in itself, but our goal is within reach and draws us near. The tranquil atmosphere has been a novel experience – I have read the newspaper and listened to the radio. However, I have come to realise that the journey would be far less entertaining without the children – less of a challenge and probably a little dull. Perhaps I do enjoy their company after all!

Sunday was a slightly shorter day, just a marathon, taking the week's total to 180 miles. I had survived this second dose of long flat distance better than the first, before the Lakes. But for a few miles of shin soreness north of St Helens, I had been unhindered by stiffness or injury. Just as I had become accustomed to running Munros, my body seemed now to have become accustomed to continuous running on the level. Through Northop, the high village of Halkyn Mountain and the small city of St Asaph, Snowdon was getting closer by the mile and the dream was coming closer to reality.

Chapter 18   WALES.
IS THIS THE END?
July 9 – 11

Switched on to the gentle Celtic music of Enya playing on the Walkman, I glided away from the overnight staging point, two miles south of Abergele, and ran the last fifteen miles of road towards the Welsh hills. The sight of misty mountains across the Conwy Valley was tantalising. There lay my ambition. The Mountains of Britain were nearly complete, but somehow, it wasn't enough. Physically, I was fit to continue; emotionally I wasn't ready to finish. Having thought of the Irish Mountains and read of them in the final chapter of Butterfield's *The High Mountains of Britain and Ireland*, the journey would have seemed incomplete without continuing across the Irish Sea. There was now no doubt that both Pauline and I wanted to go beyond Snowdon. It was just a question of doing it.

Thoughts of Ireland vanished to the back of my mind when Pauline failed to make the rendezvous at Bwlch y Ddeufaen (the pass of the two standing stones). I had run 1700 miles and Pauline had driven 2600 from Ben Hope, and now, for the first time since Strathfarrar, we didn't meet. For an hour I waited in Chris Bradley's car at the end of the no-through road. As the minutes passed, I thought of more and more things that could have gone wrong. Eventually, I couldn't bear the waiting any longer, so Chris drove me back down the single track lane to the village of Roewen. But there was still no sign of the van. Assuming that the road had been too steep or narrow, we searched another steep lane to the south. Three roads led towards the planned overnight spot. They were all marked with arrows on the map but there was no way of telling how wide they were. It seemed bizarre that we had survived the Scottish glens and passes, and that now we had met a stumbling block on our first meeting with the Welsh mountains. After half an hour's searching, we gave up and returned towards the overnight spot.

Pauline's Diary, Monday 9 July

An exciting end to the day. We set off from Roewen on the shortest route – a narrow, overgrown lane rapidly ascending the hillside. The arrows on the map didn't particularly worry me as we had managed the steep climbs out of Kinloch Hourn and over the Ratagan without problems. As we climbed, the gradient steepened and the lane gradually closed in on us, giving the sides and roof of the van a good brushing down. The tarmac could only have been about 6 inches wider than the wheel width. A low-hanging branch forced us to stop so we took the opportunity to study the map. Had we by mistake taken the track marked in white on the map? Andrew and I agreed that we were probably on the right road, but it was difficult to be sure. If this was the right route, why hadn't Chris or Hugh come to let us know that it was impassable? The

19   NORTH WALES

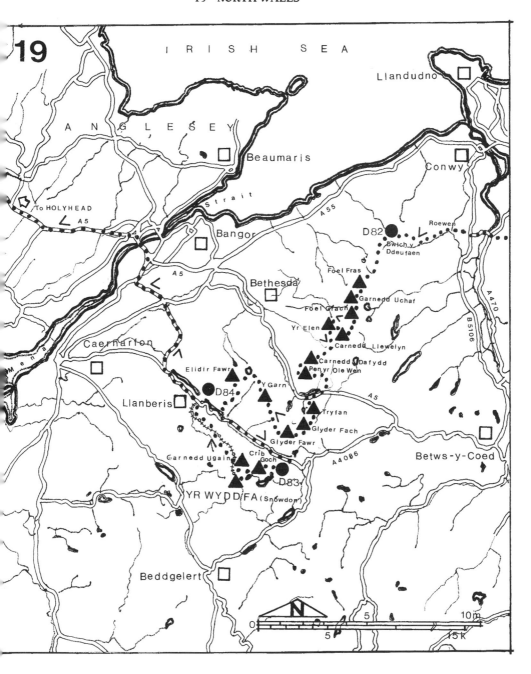

notice at the bottom had said, 'Unsuitable for caravans', but we had successfully negotiated many such roads in Scotland.

After breaking off the branch we carried on, feeling distinctly uneasy and hoping for a sudden opening of the landscape. We were finally defeated by a steep gritty section with insufficient grip for the front wheels to pull us up. It was impossible to manage a 'run up' and the road beyond looked even less promising. There was little option other than to abort the route and reverse down. Immediately we discovered that the roof vent had been left open and it was gobbling up the trees above. I stopped the van, taking extra care to leave it in gear as the hand brake wouldn't hold on the steep slope. I climbed onto the roof to free the trees so that we could close the vent. Giving the children strict instructions not to utter a sound, I inched back down, struggling to detect the road margins amongst a fringe of ferns and wild flowers. I kept calm, did my best and hoped for luck. After what seemed like an age, we made it to a narrow gateway where it was just possible to turn round.

It was a relief to be going forwards once more, although the route still demanded care. I reached the bottom feeling very hot with nervous energy. One slip and the wheels could have become firmly lodged in the ditch hidden by the vegetation.

I thought that I had seen it all in Scotland, but this minor Welsh road proved far more difficult. I was reminded of childhood holidays in Wales, our old family vehicles grinding to a halt on the steep tarmac. Our Hymer managed well so long as the surface was firm.

On reaching Roewen once more, I sought out someone who looked local and asked about the alternative routes. I was anxious to avoid a repeat performance. A friendly young gentleman confirmed the impossibility of the route we had tried – it narrowed to 6 feet further on. Our van was over 7 feet wide! He suggested an alternative which was steep but quite manageable. By now we were nearly two hours late for the rendezvous – there was little I could do. Fairly high up the road we struggled past a car. The occupants informed us that two men in a car were looking for a large van with stickers – surprise, surprise! I tried out the mobile phone and made contact with Angela Tuson. This was the agreed procedure in an event such as this. At that moment Chris and Hugh rolled up behind, relieved to see us and doubly relieved to see the van in one unblemished piece. 'I knew I could rely on you,' said Hugh. Did he mean it? I'm not sure. I bet he had visions of the van stuck in a ditch!

We had missed Pauline on the one road that we hadn't tried, and she had slowly but surely managed to drive the van up to our planned meeting point at 1500 feet.

All the high mountains of Wales lie close together in Snowdonia and it is not uncommon for them to be climbed in a single outing; the record of Colin Donnelly's currently standing at 4 hours 20 minutes. The plan of attack for the fifteen Welsh 3000 foot peaks was to run twelve of them through to Pen-y-Pass, leaving the final three for Wednesday morning.

The sport of fell running has become more popular in recent years, particularly around the mountains of North Wales. I was fortunate on this Tuesday morning to be joined by five local runners. Trefor Jones, Del Davies, Steve Jones, Emlyn Roberts and Gary Williams provided excellent company for the penultimate British mountain day. I had only previously known Del Davies, but before reaching the first mountain of Foel Fras, I seemed to have been swallowed up by a tremendous air of amicability. Friendship came across instantly in their manner and despite frequently talking to each

Bidean nam Bian from Buachaille Etive Beag – Stob Dubh. (Tony Cresswell)

Allt Gharbh Ghaig. (Mark Rigby)

Far left. Sock change and tea break in Glen Lednock. (P.S.)

Left. Scrambling up the north of Tryfan. (Del Davies)

Below. From left: Emlyn Roberts, Steve Jones, Trefor Jones and Del Davies. Tryfan behind. (H.S.)

Above. Radio interview on Snowdon. (Stefan Lepkowski)
Left. Brandon Peak from the eastern cwm. (H.S.)

Far right. County Tipperary. (P.S.)
Right. Approaching the summit of Ben Macdui.
(Matt Dickinson)
Below. After 2000 miles – Brandon Bay. (P.S.)

3
EATHARLACH
GLEN OF AHERLOW
BAILE AN LONDRAIGH
BALLYLANDERS
T50
ANGLESBOROUGH
3
GALLBHAILE
GALBALLY

Brandon summit. (Tom Fox)

On the Cannon above Llyn Ogwen. From left: Trefor Jones, Emlyn Roberts, Steve Jones. (Del Davies)

other in Welsh, their soft blending chatter conveyed calmness and companionship. It was hard to imagine these runners racing each other into the ground at weekends. In common with many fell runners, these Welshmen gave no hint of any fierce competitive spirit. The fell race is more a scene of each individual having their own combat with the mountain. Perhaps racing is an excuse to venture into the hills regularly, not so much to tune the body for fitness and competition, but more to appreciate the nature of mountains. Whilst running from Garnedd Uchaf to Foel Grach, we talked of recent races and we talked of my desire to continue to the Irish hills. I couldn't have hit a better springboard of enthusiasm.

In dark windblown mist, we traversed the desolate high level crest of the Carneddau, passing peaks studded with upturned spikes of flaky rock, appearing like delicate sculptures. By the seventh peak of Pen yr Ole-Wen, the sun had burnt through the mist. The temperature soared, suddenly reducing us from thermals to tee shirts and shorts. The setting was superb. Most of the remaining mountains opened up and revealed cliffs, cwms and arêtes, the like of which I hadn't seen since Scotland. My appetite for mountains was as strong as ever and Tryfan provided the perfect play area for an hour's scrambling after the lunch break by Llyn Ogwen. The fine wedge of Tryfan achieves Welsh Munro status by a mere metre, but in terms of rock sculpture and elegance it is one of the finest hills of all Britain and Ireland. In the warmth of the afternoon, it was a joy to place hands on rock and pull ourselves up the north ridge, stopping to clamber onto 'The Cannon' half way up. This protruding finger of rock is one of several impressive balanced stones to be found in this Glyder region of the heart of Snowdonia. The entertainment of the rocks made the 2000 foot climb seem effortless. On the summit boulder field stands the final challenge of the mountain. I couldn't resist the temptation of jumping the five foot gap between the rock monoliths of Adam and Eve.

The route now swooped over the Glyders, past the extraordinary collection of rock spikes which form Castell y Gwynt (Castle of the Winds), and on to the last peaks of Y Garn and Elidir Fawr. The portable telephone had been useful during the day, with more incoming calls than ever before. Radio interviews were arranged, Del Davies made contacts to attempt sponsorship for a sea crossing to Ireland, and now, Martin Stone rang in to try to convince me to sail the Irish Sea. It was hard for me to commit myself to any boat, but I was more than happy for Martin to make enquiries. If we were going beyond Snowdon then the continuation of the principle of self-propulsion would be preferable to accepting the mechanisation of a ferry. In the meantime, the run descended to the village of Nant Peris and after a short tea break and change to road shoes, I ran three miles up the Pass of Llanberis to the road summit at Pen-y-Pass.

Hugh's Tape
'Wednesday 11 July. The morning of the final day – or is it the final day? The mist is swirling round the hills, way under the height of Crib-goch. Friends and family have arrived, and little by little they have set off up the mountain for the midday celebrations on Snowdon. I am enjoying another cup of coffee in the van and waiting with Steve Jones, Del Davies, Gary Williams and Eric Whitehead before our departure at 9:30.'

Into wet condensing mist we climbed the summit cone of Crib-goch and beyond, onto the fine rocky knife-edge leading to the penultimate peak. The telephone rang as predicted at 10:40, and a live interview with Frank of Radio Wales was broadcast from an airy crest between pinnacles. Unfortunately, the cloud showed no signs of clearing, and we could only imagine the drops lying to the north and south. Frank's questions helped promote the cause of Intermediate Technology. When he turned to the physical aspects of mountain running, he accused me of being addicted to exercise. I was inclined to agree with him and didn't argue. It just added fuel to the need to continue west across the sea. I didn't let on that I might not be finishing today. I didn't want to let people down. So many people (at least 50) had come to Snowdon. Perhaps I was cheating them if I declared that it was simply another intermediate point like Ben Macdui, Ben Lomond or Scafell Pike. In a way, the finish wasn't exactly in our control. With not having made it well known that we were thinking of continuing to Ireland, there was the possibility that arrangements would have been made for post-event I.T. fundraising.

Ann Parratt had liaised with the Royal Navy to helicopter me and the family off Snowdon. The stunt was guaranteed to generate publicity and thrill the children but the day's thick hill fog made the flight unlikely. I had had a practice hover over Sedbergh the previous winter, and the flight crew of the Lynx from HMS *Hermione* had reconnoitred the Snowdon and Llanberis area. One mile from Snowdon, whilst still clambering along the Crib-goch ridge, the phone rang again. A message was relayed from the Royal Navy, saying that their helicopter had been diverted to other operations and was unable to come to Snowdon. I couldn't help but feel relief, as at least now my journey would continue on foot from the summit of Snowdon to Llanberis. Had the helicopter lifted me off the mountain, the run would have been broken, and if I was continuing to Ireland a second climb of Snowdon would have been needed to continue the journey between the peaks.

A few hundred metres on, the arête widened to the broad summit of Carnedd Ugain (also known as Crib-y-ddysgl). It was 11:30 and too early to run on to Snowdon for the midday appointment with family, friends and press. I waited in mist by the trig point. As if he knew that I would have spare time on my hands, Mike Walford phoned in to discuss how the application for detailed planning permission was progressing on our Dales Barn at Underwinder. This was bizarre. It was 11:45 and I was talking about

The summit of Snowdon (*Eric Whitehead*)

window openings and chimneys whilst waiting for Pauline to join me for the final few hundred metres to Snowdon. Apparently we were going to have to live in a dark box as the Yorkshire Dales planners were not going to let us knock holes in the walls. Normally, this would have upset me, but I just told Mike to appeal, put the phone back in the rucksack and returned to the moment. Pauline appeared out of the heavy cloud, her hair dangling wetness over her eyes and face. She had already climbed Snowdon and left the children in the company of grandparents. I wanted to share these last strides over the 'Mountains of Britain' with her. To reach the summit alone would have been false, for without Pauline, I wouldn't have stood a chance of the luxury of running all these mountains and more.

Across stony ground to the railway line, over the oily sleepers of the cog railway, and then, hand in hand, the final steps to the cairn, where dozens of friends cheered and applauded. For twenty minutes, I stood on top, opening champagne bottles, answering the phone and chatting to friends. Sizeable cheques were handed over to I.T. by Kendal friends Pete and Ann Bland and by sponsoring companies Berghaus and Calor Gas. Gradually, the cold wet air drove people into the summit cafe, the phone stopped ringing and I found time to put extra clothes on. I had achieved my target, but now there was more to think about. My direction became temporarily confused when John Mills, a friend of Martin Stone's, phoned in and offered me a sail from Pwllheli to Cork. Had I accepted, I would have run south off Snowdon to Beddgelert, but the seven mountains of Ireland are spread from East to West in a line from Wicklow to Dingle that passes well north of Cork. There was only one sensible place to start my traverse of Ireland and that was on the east coast, south of Dublin.

I had finished one journey and was now starting another. Grandparents took the children down the mountain on the train, while Pauline and I raced it to Llanberis. There we all met in a car park by the railway station and Pauline and I told our parents that we weren't going home.

Pauline

We had set our target so long ago – Ben Hope to Snowdon within a hundred days. Hugh had made this commitment a year in advance in order to give the fundraising machinery plenty of time to get going. It was a brave move at the time. We hoped that this challenge would stir people's imagination and in so doing draw attention to our cause. Intermediate Technology had placed their trust in us – a link with a failed expedition would do little for their public image – and so we felt that in times of low moral, the desire to succeed would be rekindled by the knowledge that so much depended on our success. We had succeeded – we had achieved our goal – the goal which so many had known about for so long. I.T. were thrilled with both funds raised and publicity achieved. Friends, helpers, runners and relations were all so happy for us. However, in reality the driving force had come from within Hugh. It was strong, lasting and its essence lay in the intoxicating combination of 'running' and 'mountains'. Now, an idea that had grown throughout our journey – a private idea known only to Hugh, myself, the children and a few others – had become our personal target. The force within tugged hard and the pull of the Irish summits could not be resisted.

The children had some idea of our plans. They had listened to many quiet conversations during the evenings in the van. They certainly wanted to go – a journey across the sea, a new country. Post-event plans had not materialised and were unlikely to pose a problem. In any case we were still within the original time limit.

I too was keen to carry on. I knew that Hugh would certainly regret turning for home now. On a more mundane level, what would be the sense in going home with the long summer holiday stretching out before us? Life on the move in such a luxury vehicle was to me a privilege which was unlikely to come my way again. I wanted to make the most of it. And of course we all wanted to see Ireland, known for peace, beauty and its haunting music which had kept our spirits high for so much of our journey.

Once the private target became public the reaction was interesting. Knowing nothing of our plans, Hugh's parents had been confused when asked to bring up a two week supply of food from our stores in Sedbergh. It was not an easy task for them as Hugh's father was due to go into hospital the following day, and carrying heavy food boxes was out of the question for him. They had been unselfishly considerate in not telling us about the hernia operation, as they didn't want us to worry.

My own mother was just as bemused. Watching me stow away the groceries in the van she inquired in a baffled tone, 'Why aren't you going for a good night out – a meal in a hotel – a celebration? Are you really just going to carry on as you are?' Hugh's parents may well have harboured similar thoughts but they kept them to themselves. Some of our friends shared this bewilderment. Only the runners really understood. The Irish peaks beckoned and the task would be incomplete if we chose not to include them. We were looking forward to a peaceful end to our journey, without the pressure of appointments and media.

Martin was determined to find me a yatch. His latest contact, Eoghan Llavelle, was possibly able to sail me from Holyhead to the Irish coast just south of Dublin. Eoghan was very keen to help, but pessimistic about the chances of crossing the sea without using the engine. His boat was old and heavy, and the winds were forecast to be light. The journey could take days. I arranged to phone him again in the morning. Contact with the ferry companies was proving impossible. The Motorola phone functioned erratically in the deep Welsh valley. The last cheap boat according to the brochure was at 2:45 the next day. Subsequent boats would cost almost double as the summer peak prices came into effect at midnight.

These last-minute negotiations posed a multitude of dilemmas. How important was it to maintain the idea of self-propulsion? If I sailed the Irish Sea would we have problems meeting on the other side? What if the ferry was full and Pauline became stranded in Holyhead when I had landed in Ireland? Should I try to run for the cheaper ferry or would the resulting rush risk injury or exhaustion?

Pauline and I discussed the problems without reaching any conclusions. However, whilst settling down to sleep my mind turned ideas over, and gradually I came to realise that I had to rise early, and run across Anglesey, in an attempt to reach Holyhead by midday.

Chapter 19   THE CELTIC CONNECTION

July 12 – 25

Pauline.

'I'm off,' said Hugh, before I had time to wake up. 'We're going for the 2:45 boat.' I was amazed by his motivation so early in the day. Thirty miles of fast road lay ahead of him – he reckoned he could do it in time.

I hurriedly packed up, muttered goodbye to Chris's tent (he had come up to film 'the Finish') and drove away from the campsite feeling muddled and uneasy. It felt incongruous to be still on the move after the public finish. Uncertainty lay ahead. There was no guarantee that we would reach the ferry terminal on time and no guarantee of a place on the boat. We just had to try.

There was no time to seek out pretty routes from the map. Into the morning traffic heading for Bangor and along a dual carriageway leading to the Menai Straits, I passed road signs forbidding pedestrian access. The Britannia Bridge was designed for carrying trains, cars and lorries across the water to Anglesey but evidently not walkers or runners. Fearing that I might be picked up by the police and deposited further along the road, I sprinted over the bridge hoping that my journey wouldn't be inadvertently broken.

The first break point, for a quick second breakfast and rest was at LLANFAIRP-WLLGWYNGYLLGOGERYCHWYRNDROBWLLLLANTYSILIOGOGOGOCH. The children spent the whole of the half hour stop copying the letters of the station sign onto endless pieces of paper and into their diaries – Amy's version was backwards! Pauline and I had a remarkably unhassled time until I finally made telephone contact with Sealink and was told that there was no space for high vehicles on any of their ferries to Ireland. They couldn't guarantee tickets for a week. Suddenly, our desire to go to Ireland seemed to have been quashed.

'Why did I get up so early and run a fast ten?' I asked myself. For five minutes, I was directionless. But somehow, I had already given the day momentum. I had set my mind on the thirty to Holyhead. I found it hard to believe that there would be no space on the next few ferries. Surely there would be some late cancellations or a lorry wouldn't turn up? With hope in mind, I continued the dash along the busy A5. My thoughts turned to planning alternatives if we were unable to cross the sea. Perhaps we should just enjoy a few days on the sandy beaches of Anglesey. However, if the journey was broken for a few days, I would find it hard to rebuild the momentum to run the 270 miles across Ireland. Maybe I should accept lifts between the peaks and just enjoy a leisurely holiday on the Emerald Isle?

The situation was out of our control. All I could do was to send Pauline on to queue at Holyhead while I ran the remaining miles as fast as possible. Looking behind me, the cloud had lifted on Snowdon and the mountains were becoming smaller on the horizon. With each mile I was growing thirstier in the increasing heat and I was glad of the occasional petrol station to refuel on coke. After four hours of running, I closed the paces on a large Sealink ship and found the van second in a reserve queue, parked behind a Mini. Our chances seemed good. However, two hours later, we watched the ship glide out of the harbour without us, or even the Mini. Appeals at the ticket office had failed and the chances of sailing on the next boat at three in the morning seemed slim. The Irishman in the Mini threatened to drive the three hundred miles to Stranraer where ferry space was available. At less than twenty miles per gallon and all petrol money coming out of our own pocket, we didn't even consider the Ulster option which would have also involved a long drive from Belfast to Dublin. (There are no 3000 foot peaks in Northern Ireland.)

Pauline
Despite the comforts of our mobile home, the children were becoming bored and irritable with the long wait in the queue. Hugh and I were no doubt tense as a result of the uncertain delay. The line of vehicles behind us grew. It was a surprise to find that most of the occupants had tickets for the ferry which had just left, but had missed the boat. Funny that there had not even been room for an extra Mini? There was no telling how long we would have to wait – it could be days. Hugh decided that it was time to take action.

Remembering the name of the Sealink man Del Davies had phoned from the Carneddau on Tuesday, I decided to do a crawling act and approach the people in charge at the Sealink offices half a mile away. I told my story of a record-breaking attempt and its dependence on sailing soon. Magically, I found tickets in my hands at a cut price rate for the next overnight boat.

With a few hours to spare, we shopped (losing Amy for five minutes in Kwik Save), exchanged money and then parked ourselves by a sandy beach at Trearddur Bay. While the children played happily with sand and shells, Pauline and I reorganised the van and prepared ourselves for Ireland. Secretly, hidden away in a far corner of the van, I had two maps which had been given to me eight years previously when I was editor of *The Fell Runner*. Douglas Barry, the chairman of the Irish Hill Runners' Association had sent me maps of Dublin and Wicklow with an open invitation to visit and compete in a local race. These, which would be sufficient for the first two days in Ireland, and the sketch map in Butterfield's book, were all I had to guide me. Shortly after digging out the maps the phone rang. Whilst recovering in hospital from a kidney operation, Ken Jones, organiser of the annual Snowdon Race, and influential man in Welsh and International mountain racing, had heard me on Radio Wales in my chat from Crib-goch. He had also heard from Del Davies that I was on my way to Ireland. Wanting to help in my trip to foreign lands, he had contacted Douglas Barry and told him of my exploits. Ken Jones gave me Douglas Barry's phone number. That this circuit of friends were able to provide help for this last stage of my journey, through a series of chance connections, seemed too amazing for a mere coincidence. Also by chance, Douglas's home was en route to the first Irish mountain and he was now expecting me to call by in the morning, at his home town of Bray.

After a restless few hours in the bowels of the *St. Columba*, cramped into stiff upright chairs amongst sleeping bags and pillows, we off-loaded ourselves at Dun Laoghaire – Dublin's ferry port, conveniently placed on the south side of the city.

Throughout the journey over Britain's mountains, duplicate maps either purchased or sponsored by Ordnance Survey, had enabled Pauline and I to find each other at predestined spots, marked each day with crosses on both our maps. With only one map between us for the eight mile route south to Bray, I made brief notes before leaving Pauline with the map and running my first miles in Ireland.

Tired from the previous day's run from Llanberis and from the poor night on the boat, I was happy to settle for a short outing and to spend the remainder of the day discussing my route across Ireland with Douglas Barry. Douglas's enthusiasm was unstoppable. Between inspections of maps and guides, he was phoning newspapers and radio stations. Had we given him more warning that we were coming, he may have been able to convert his dynamism into more funds for Intermediate Technology. We watched in amazement as he tried to do in 24 hours what it had taken us eighteen months to do. Douglas was keen to work out an itinerary for me but I was reluctant to have another timetable to work to. I guessed that it would take between 10 and 14 days to run the 260 miles to the Atlantic and I promised to phone Douglas as soon as I knew the date that I would finish the coast to coast run across all of Ireland's seven 3000 foot peaks.

Equipped with some of Douglas's guide books and several maps bought from a Bray bookshop, we finally left the seaside town 24 hours after our arrival. Refreshed by rest and a long sleep, I was now ready to start running west.

Suddenly we were free. Ireland was ours. We could move as far or as little as we wanted each day, without telling anyone where we were. The telephone no longer worked, and was buried in the van. We had a freedom of time which we hadn't enjoyed since before Glen Coe.

Nursing our way into a new country and a new style of maps, we opted to meet regularly, as a precaution against losing each other. Hardly four miles out of Bray and I had already doubted my position. With the impressive bright lump of the Great Sugar Loaf to guide me, I headed west on tiny lanes until the crossing of the main N11 route out of Dublin. Constant single file streams of cars were motoring each way in the Saturday afternoon sunshine. Whilst waiting for a gap in the traffic, I noticed a familiar large white camper parked a few hundred yards up the road on the hard shoulder. It was Pauline – confused by the network of tiny lanes leading off the main road. The meeting was coincidental but fortunate. I was running with a 1:63 360 (one inch to one mile) map of Wicklow, whilst Andrew was navigating Pauline with a 1:250 000 chart of East Ireland. The latter was not detailed enough to define the narrow tree-lined lane leading towards the Great Sugar Loaf. After a brief meeting and confirmation of route we parted and set off to cross through the endless lines of cars. Minutes passed by. Pauline was trying to turn right. There seemed no way that either of us could reach the lane on the opposite side of the road. Eventually, I could wait no longer. I stood in the middle of the road with hands in the air. Both sets of traffic came to a halt, Pauline was able to cut through the line of cars travelling north and I was able to cross. There was no honking or jeering, just lots of waves and smiles. It was the last sizable traffic we were to see in the whole transit of Ireland. Now onto quiet lanes, I was accompanied by the rich smells of manure and peat.

Through the villages of Roundwood and Laragh, and after a peaceful night's camp

20   SOUTH EAST IRELAND

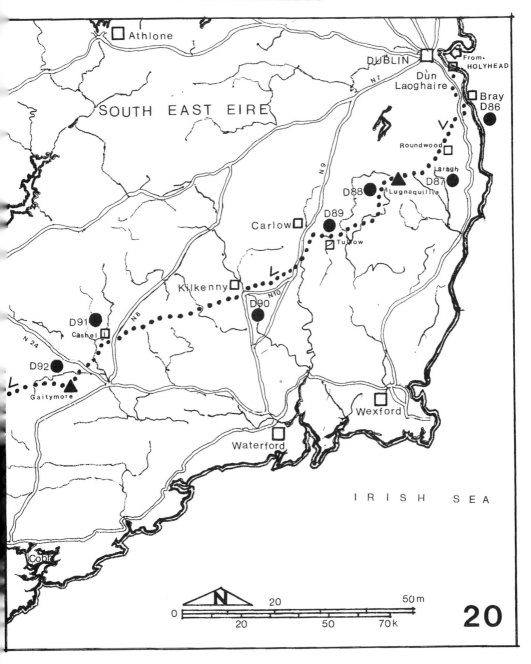

by a high forest, I arrived at the first Irish mountain via the pleasant wooded Glenmalur. Being a Sunday afternoon, there was a handful of hillgoers on the rounded lump of Lugnaquilla (affectionately known as Lug – pronounced softly as Loog). Every person I met gave me a warm welcome to this, the only 3000 foot peak of the Wicklows, or indeed of the whole of the east of Ireland. First there was Mick Monahan and his fiancée at the bottom by Carrawaystick Brook. Their instant warmth, humour and sociability were astonishing. Discovering that my journey was to pass close to his home, Mick lent me maps and gave me an invitation to stay the following night. Halfway up the mountain, whilst crossing the peaty moorland, I met a group of Dublin Scouts who promised and later sent a donation to I.T. Coincidentally, although not with them at the time, their chief scout was Eoghan Llavelle – the sailor that I never met. By the time I reached the summit panorama stone, clouds had closed in. There was no chance of seeing the Snowdon and Cader Idris that the stone's arrows pointed to. Waiting on top was Peadar Dempsey, a Dublin hill runner who joined me for the first four of the 100 miles towards the next mountain of Galtymore in County Tipperary. The half hour's downpour on the western descent of Lug was the last rain of the run.

The remaining ten days to the Atlantic were executed in a fierce heatwave which had me topless, drinking gallons and running scores of miles on sticky melting tarmac. The rich agricultural countryside made off-road running virtually impossible. From junction to junction I met Pauline for refuels of juice and for a check of the maps. On tiny deserted lanes I ran through Hacketstown, past the megalithic stones of Haroldstown Dolmen and through Tullow to Mick Monahan's home south of Carlow.

Pauline's Diary, Monday 16 July

We met Hugh in a small town called Tullow. The children joined the local kids, fishing and playing in the river which was beautifully clear and full of minnows. Sadly the banks were scattered with litter. The Irish seem to be even more oblivious than the English to the eyesore of discarded rubbish, which is remarkably noticeable for a country of only three million people.

Our journey ended at the ancient tower house of Castletown, the family home of the Monahans. As far as the children were concerned the solid granite construction was definitely a castle and therefore our host was christened, 'King Mick'. We were invited into 'the room with the stuffed birds' and presented with an enormous mountain of strawberries, picked from the castle grounds. It was as if we had entered a time warp, watched by the exotic birds in their glass cases and surrounded by gracefully aged furnishings in a room which cannot have changed for more years than my grandmother can remember. The hospitality and genteel conversation of Mick's father, John, and mother, Amy (introduced to our daughter as 'the real Amy') were memorable.

The vast grounds of the estate provided a splendid overnight camp and Mick's guided route through his fields of sugar beet gave an unusual start to the following day's run through to the ancient city of Kilkenny.

Such was the heat that the children took every opportunity to splash each other in rivers, canals and under taps. I stopped at farms to ask for water and occasionally bought coke from corner shops. On the third day of heat, without a mountain, and after another marathon, I was beginning to expire. I was ready to stop for the day but the lane was too narrow for Pauline to park and the only available lay-by was full of gypsy caravans which were surrounded by dogs that chased me up the road faster than I imagined possible. The lack of parking spaces forced me on to the old town of Cashel and a day's total of 31 miles. The effort was rewarded with a superb overnight stop in a large empty car park under the Rock of Cashel – an assortment of ecclesiastical remnants and Celtic crosses standing high above the town, and forming one of Ireland's most important historic sites. Today the 13th century church is undergoing restoration, but the history of the site dates back 1500 years to when the rock was a fortification for Munster Kings.

Pauline

Maybe a conditioned reflex reaction was at work here, for with the heat, reminiscent of continental holidays, developed a holiday mood. A tendency to rise too late, hang around camp too long and delay Hugh's start; posing the unexpected problem of running in the heat during the middle of the day. We degenerated into playing Scrabble and having a wee dram (a present from Bill Richardson with instructions 'not to be opened until Snowdon') in the evenings. The absence of media, pacers and a strict timetable to work to, almost enabled us to forget that Hugh was still on the run and we still had a job to do. This worried Hugh. He didn't want to see his support slacking.

Although Andrew was doing his best with the available maps, navigation was proving interesting. We travelled on very minor roads – single track but plenty wide enough and usually easily graded. The steep sections could be predicted by the 'Unsuitable for Horse Drawn Caravans' signs. The patchwork, uneven surfaces made for slow progress. Towns and villages were signposted in a fairly random fashion and distances were given in kilometres or miles, and it wasn't always clear which was which. Asking the way tended to be unproductive. Our destination, which could only be given in terms of a circle marked on the map, a nameless road junction, a miniscule hamlet or the corner of a forest, was incomprehensible to the average Irish country lane dweller who would usually find it hard to understand why we were not heading for a well-known town or village. Map literacy is not common, and despite a great willingness to help we were usually directed back towards the main roads. At times we had to follow Hugh from junction to junction, spending hours waiting at cramped crossroads in sweltering heat unable to do anything constructive. The children were pretty tolerant really. The size and comfort of the van helped. It was becoming difficult to do anything educational with the children – tempting to give up and declare a holiday – but not yet – not until the end of the run. We collected flowers from the hedgerows, pressed them and painted them. I was beginning to look forward to the real holiday – the end of the run – to be able to escape to one of the many deserted beaches and jump into the sea. The heat was tiring us all. Hugh's ability to keep going still amazed me. He was looking fit, blond and very tanned – an attractive combination!

Much of the Irish countryside was reminiscent of Somerset, but in the Glen of Aherlow, thick tree-lined slopes produced images of Bavaria. After four days on long hot roads, I was ready for a change and for Galtymore, the highest mountain of the Galtees – the rolling range of hills to the south west of Cashel.

21　SOUTH WEST IRELAND

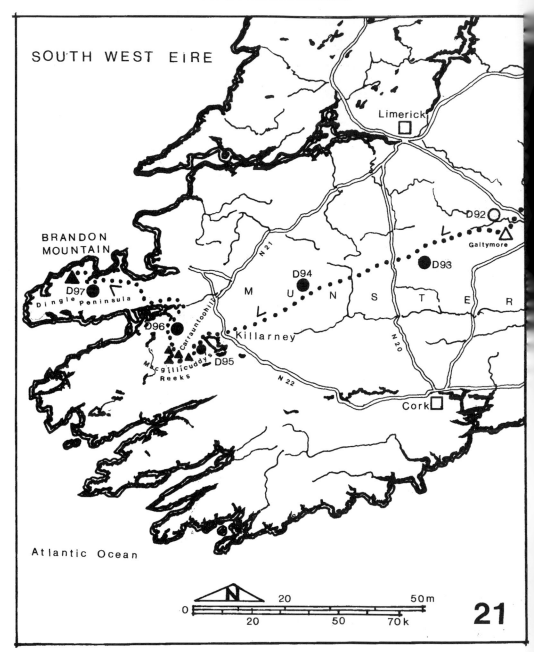

SOUTH WEST EiRE

Limerick

BRANDON
MOUNTAIN

D 92

Galtymore

D97
Dingle Peninsula

D94

M　　U　　N　　S　　T　　E　　R

D93

N 21

D96

Carrauntoohil

Killarney

N 20

Macgillicuddy's
Reeks

D95

N 22

Cork

Atlantic Ocean

N

0　　　　　20　　　　　　　　50 m

20　　　　　50　　　　70 k

21

Pauline's Diary, Thursday 19 July

Leaving Cashel we stumbled upon a large complex of ruins in the midst of the fields, as if unnoticed by modern man. There was no car park – I tucked the van into the road verge and we set off along the footpath over the fields towards the ancient Athassel Abbey. In the absence of a kiosk demanding payment and offering tourist guides, two bullocks guarded the entrance. The children explored with relish whilst I worried for their safety. Spiral staircases led to nowhere, crumbling arches threatened to tumble and vertical drops, too high for comfort, were unprotected by safety rails. Whilst there was no literature to feed the human thirst for information, it was refreshing to enjoy the atmosphere which was strengthened by the lack of the usual packaging. Had this site been in England, it would certainly not have been left in such obscurity.

We finished the day with a round of mini golf at a delightful campsite at the foot of the Galty Mountains – the holiday atmosphere creeping in again!

Friday 20 July

Hugh didn't look too happy as he set off. Could it be something to do with mist and poor maps?

He is beginning to have had enough and will probably welcome a rest when he reaches Brandon. I'm sure that I shall feel the same too!

I left the continental atmosphere of the campsite at Ballynacourty House for the deserted and pathless steep northern slope of Galtymore. The intense heat of the glen was lost in the condensing mist of the tops, and still I was without a view from an Irish mountain. This was my 298th mountain and I was nervous of losing my way. Spoilt by 1:25 000s in Scotland, I was now feeling my way with a 1:126 720. Slowly running west, I passed the eerie summit Celtic cross and ran onwards along 2 miles of isolated grassy ridge to the rounded top of Slievecushnabinnia before dropping, out of the mist, and down to a farm at Ballygeana. The mountain had been a short interlude from the long hot road but a welcome refresher. I was now looking forward to Ireland's most famous group of mountains just three or four days running away. Like Lug and Snowdon, whilst running west from Galtymore in the afternoon, the mist lifted and exposed the rolling slopes behind me, as I traversed more miles of tiny lanes stained brown by years of squashed manure.

I was growing tired of the heat and the road. The first ten miles of each day passed easily, but further fives mounting towards daily totals of thirty and more became an effort. In Britain, I had had the company of friends to take my mind away from fatigue, but now, even my Walkman had failed and I couldn't glide along to the music of Floyd or U2. In the past, long slow guitar strokes had been a recipe for hypnosis and the therapeutic passage of distance and time, but now, my eyes were staring for the horizon and the Kerry mountains of the Macgillycuddy's Reeks.

Weakening in the afternoon heat of County Cork, I collapsed in the back of the van outside the town of Newmarket. I slept for an hour, drank pints of tea and ate a packet of dextrosol in an attempt to see me a few more miles west towards the Reeks. Again we were on lanes without lay-bys and with apparently no overnight stopping spots. Not wanting to go any further, we asked a farmer permission to use his fields. Asking for a corner, he gave us the freedom of acres, told the children to run wherever they wanted and told us we could stay till we needed to leave. Only one more day of road, and I would be in the heart of County Kerry and on the Reeks.

The last county. (P.S.)

It was a Sunday morning. Apparently the whole village of Boherboy was arriving for church. Every kerb space was filled with cars. Seven miles later, scores were emptying out of church at Knocknagree where the streets were again lined with vehicles. I had hoped to have seen mountains by now, but a thick heat-haze obscured the horizon.

Pauline's Diary, Sunday 22 July
We are now parked in Knocknagree, waiting for Hugh. On one side of the large green is a line of about twenty houses, seven of which are bars with names like T. Murphy and C.O' Mahoney, painted all colours – green, blue and pink. Most of them boast very old GUINNESS signs. Do the men come out of church and dive into the nearest bar?

Like the last miles of a marathon, the end seemed to be stretching in front of me. Tired again, and thinking that I was less than ten miles from Killarney, I passed a sign reading, 'Killarney 13 miles'. Dazed by the hazy heat, I drifted on towards the busy tourist town. Killarney was far enough for the day, but not liking the hustle and bustle, and wanting to be closer to the Reeks, I ran a further ten to the end of a lane and a farm and small car park under Ireland's highest peaks. Astonishingly, we were not the only vehicle emblazoned with stickers. The only other car was an Audi estate with four walkers about to embark on 'The Four Peaks Challenge' for 'Children in Need'. There I was, just a few rugged hills, a day's road run and Brandon away from the end of the journey, and here were fellow fundraisers about to set off on a quick trip over Carrauntoohil, Snowdon, Scafell Pike and Ben Nevis.

Pauline's Diary, Sunday 22 July
Killarney and its environs are really busy – we've hit a tourist area. It's very hard on the system when you're not used to it. It was difficult to find a camp spot – we rejected

two awful looking campsites and Andrew has moaned from then on. 'I don't want to just park in a hedge somewhere,' he complained.

Now that we've hit the narrow road heading towards the Reeks – the mountains in the haze and a cool breeze blowing – I feel much more at home. Hugh is tired. He must have run about 40 miles today in the debilitating heat. The kids are fractious to put it mildly. This part of the journey has been harder than I imagined.

It was the fourteenth and last Monday morning of the run, and I was looking forward to my first proper day on the hills since the Carneddau of North Wales. Ahead lay the rugged ridges of the Macgillycuddy's Reeks – a range of four mountains and six tops which speckle the map like the constellation of Taurus. Random spurs and arêtes point in all directions and provide a traverse of 3000 foot peaks which I found superior to Crib-goch of Snowdonia and to the Aonach Eagach of Glen Coe. As a group of hills only surpassed by the Cuillin of Skye, I found myself slowing down to take it all in and at the same time my mind was dancing back to An Teallach and Ben More Assynt. Whilst clambering up the steep slabs of rock on Cruach Mhor, I was reminded of a similar approach on Lochnagar. The difference was on top. On Lochnagar there had been crowds, but here there was no-one, just a large structure of stones with a grotto. Over a thousand feet, almost directly below, lay the rich blue Lough of Cummeenapeasta, and ahead, above steep savage cliffs, lay the mountain of the same name. The route along the arête appeared to be blocked by rock stacks. With some dodging to the left and right, and the occasional hands on rock manoeuvres, a route was found through to Cummeenapeasta at 3191 feet. Disappointingly, the heat-haze reduced visibility to two miles and the broad outline of Carrauntoohil, Ireland's highest mountain, was just a vague silhouette which gradually became clearer as I followed the ridge west over subsidiary bumps. From the summit of Carrauntoohil, two superb ridges branch separately to the north and west. To visit all the Irish Munros of the Reeks in one traverse, one of the ridges must be crossed twice. I contoured under the pyramid of Carrauntoohil and stepped onto the crest leading to Caher – the 300th mountain of the journey. On either side, precipitous chasms drop to loughs which stand in great amphitheatres of rock. Turning to return, I saw the first people that I had seen since leaving the van. The Reeks appeared to be deserted and almost devoid of paths, but there on the Beenkeragh ridge stood two slow-moving walkers that appeared like stick insects on a black and jagged cardboard cut-out.

A distant rumble of thunder gave me a boost of speed and I arrived at the 3414 foot summit of Ireland sweating profusely. Escaping before a threatening storm and in descending cloud, I curved onto the narrow blade of rocks that led half a mile to the 302nd and penultimate mountain of the run. I sat down on the summit of Beenkeragh and watched thick clouds swirl down on the cliffs and chasms of Carrauntoohil. My relaxation was broken by a swarm of midges that soon developed a taste for my blood and sweat. Curiously, these were my only Irish bites, but they soon had me taking a bearing and running away to rough moorland between the lower hills of Skregmore and Skregbeg. Finding my way in these beautiful hills had been a joy with the recently published 1:50 000 map of Kenmare. I felt much more sure of my position than I had on Lug or Galty, but having said that, once on a narrow arête, there isn't much choice about where to go, except on.

Forcing a way through chest-deep bracken I reached the road and van for a late lunch before running five miles to the town of Killorglin, where we spent the night.

Slieve Mish mountains – Dingle Peninsula. (P.S.)

Across Dingle Bay from Killorglin lies Dingle, one of several ragged peninsulas that stretch in to the Atlantic from the counties of Kerry and Cork. At its cliffed tip, the Blasket Islands reach further west than the rest of Europe, except Iceland. Near the end of Dingle, high above Brandon Bay and overlooking the ocean, stands Brandon Mountain, my last 3000 foot peak.

The previous day's threatening storm hadn't materialised. Instead, the humidity and heat had only increased. The day's objective of thirty miles to Brandon Bay seemed a long way, even though this was the last road run of the journey.

It was seven miles to Castlemaine and the foot of the Dingle peninsula, then a further seven on a perfectly straight and uninteresting road. A touring cyclist went by riding a familiar frame. The name Harry Hall from Manchester couldn't escape my attention. I called out, crossed the road and had company on the run for the first time in two hundred miles. John Derbyshire recognised the Intermediate Technology tee shirt and had seen the labelled van earlier in the day. Realising that this was some run or other, he asked me whether I was one of the Crane brothers. I told the man my story. John was also heading for Brandon. Noting my proposed time of noon, he rode off and promised to meet me on the summit the following day.

Leaving the main road on the south side of Dingle, I ran into pleasant and cooler air on a high and tiny lane which flanks the western end of the Slieve Mish Mountains and crosses the peninsula to the more peaceful northern side. Now on the last road to Brandon and with little more than ten miles to run, the feeling of the end was strong and sad. I had passed thousands of children playing in gardens. Rarely had any spoken to me, but on this afternoon, one rode towards me on his trike and asked, 'How far have you run?' It was a familiar question I remember from training on the streets of south Manchester, but not one I had heard in over three months. As if to reinforce the end and the position in this far corner of Europe, cars went by with registrations in various assortments of X, Y and Z. Rounding the end of Brandon Bay I had expected to see Brandon, but thick blackness and haze obscured the hills. It seemed that unless there was a storm I would feel but not see Brandon. Even from our day's end at the quiet village of Cloghane (pronounced 'claw-harn'), there were just hints of the lower slopes which drop down to Brandon Bay from the summit three miles distant.

Before going to bed on the last night before the end of the run, I put the following feelings on tape:

'I can't really understand how I have arrived here. Ben Hope is 500 miles away but over 2000, via all the mountains. I just wonder how I have kept going day after day. Of course there is the determination that has been set in to me over the last few years in preparing, and there is the amazing support that I have had from Pauline, but there is also something else intangible that has just driven me on. I find it hard to understand how I have had energy, good energy on most days. Even today, when the heat was strong at nine in the morning, the idea of another thirty miles wasn't something that I automatically took for granted. The first two sevens went well and then the next fives and sixes just slipped away and I didn't really weaken at all, not even to the end I haven't weakened drastically. Somewhere, there has been some kind of intangible drive.'

Pauline's Diary, Wednesday 25 July

Hugh is off up the last mountain – this time really the last. The top of Brandon is just peeping out of a mantle of cloud. The sky over the sea is hazy. We have found a lovely

Brandon Peak and Brandon Mountain – touching the cloud. (H.S.)

little sandy beach quite close to the pub in Cloghane. It is very quiet. There is no one •
here this time to appreciate the finish – not that we mind. What really counts is the
achievement – not everyone knowing about it.

Still the air was hot and thick, and there was no sign of Brandon. I kissed Pauline and
the children goodbye and departed for the last climb. Leaving the road by the farm at
Faha, there was no doubting the route as signposts directed the way past a walled shrine
and upwards to a footpath following 'the Pilgrims' Route'. Alongside and underneath
the long eastern ridge, the path turned into the vast cwm which I could hear but not see.
The sounds of water falling and sheep bleating came from below and echoed around the
cliffs above. Gradually, as I climbed higher and further into the cwm, the sky began to

The Paternoster Lakes of Brandon. (H.S.)

turn blue above and the mist began to sweep away from the faces of the cliffs. The lower
summit of Brandon Peak pointed above the cloud. I slowed down to a walk and watched
in amazement as in little more than ten minutes the sky completely cleared, revealing a
dramatic corrie and majestic scenery rivalling Skye. Below lay the long line of a dozen
paternoster lakes which stand on a series of descending rock terraces, falling away two
miles to the Owenmore River. Above were boulders, slabs and the precipitous cliffs of
Brandon. Amongst the rocks there were rich patches of green which harboured the
occasional foxglove. There was a tremendous air of tranquillity. I could understand why
the 5th century saint, St Brendan had chosen this summit as his place of meditation.

At the very head of the cwm, the path zig zagged its way up through the slabs and
scree of the corrie wall. All of a sudden, I stepped out above the rocks and onto the green
summit ridge overlooking a hazy Atlantic. Whilst jogging the final few hundred metres
to the top, I could see a small group by the cairn. Somehow they knew I was coming for I

Summit party on Brandon. (H.S.)

was given a tremendous welcome when I touched the final stones and stood by the traditional summit cross.

For St Brendan, the point by 'the Oratory' had been a place from where he had thought and spoken of sailing to a New World. For me it marked the end of a journey and the end of a dream. For a minute, I wasn't capable of talking to the men and children who were watching me by the cross. I was holding the tears back whilst gripping the cross and realising that this, unlike Ben Lomond or Snowdon, really was the end. I came down, came round and shook hands with the well-wishers. John Derbyshire had been by the summit for half an hour and had told the walkers about my imminent arrival. For the young boy from Dingle dressed in Ireland's football strip, it was his first 3000 foot peak. For a while we talked, took photos and shared chocolate. I can only remember the name of one of my summit companions, Tom Fox from the village of Dingle, but we all had a common bond on this remarkable mountain.

They descended west via the Saint's Route whilst John and I returned to the farm at Faha via the eastern cwm. For the last miles of road from Faha to Cloghane, I sat on John's pannier rack, and freewheeled downhill to the pub. Watching the tarmac glide by without moving my legs confirmed that there was no more. Tomorrow I wouldn't have to get up, and go on.

Chapter 20   THROUGH THE EYES OF THE CHILDREN

15 April
Amy: We set off today and people waved goodbye to us. Some of my friends were there.
Joseph: Grandma and Grandad were there. They gave us some Easter Eggs. Mrs Dawson said Daddy should run to Ben Hope.
Andrew: Hopefully tonight we will see a comet which is a moving thing with a tail.

16 April
Andrew: This morning we drove through some blizzards. When the blizzards stopped me and Joseph made a snowman out of an exhaust pipe, some cans, a tooth brush, some grass and a twig. About 1:00pm I finished my last Easter Egg which was a Mars one. We didn't see the comet.

19 April
Joseph: Daddy went for a run up Ben Hope. He started 'Mountains of Britain, Mountains of Help' – the big, amazing trip.
Andrew: I ran two miles with Dad. Then we had a fire that didn't work.

20 April
Andrew: Today I was filmed running along the road. North Scotland had the best weather today and there weren't any midges.
Joseph: I asked Paul and Dave what they were eating. They were eating 'soap' and pasta.

21 April
Andrew: Today North Scotland had the best weather in Britain again.

22 April
Joseph: Today Daddy has gone to Coriemor Bothy and we have gone somewhere different.
Amy: We collected shells by the sea.

23 April
Andrew: We had to get special permission to go up a road which was only 2 metres 87 cm wide, and the van wheels are only 2 metres 67 cm apart.
Joseph: We asked a lady if we should go up the road and we did. She said the man who gives permission lives up there anyway. The man was not there but his wife was, and we told her all about 'Mountains of Britain'. We looked for Dad – just then he came

running down the track. He got two cream eggs and a message on the top of the mountain from Mark and John. We told him about the sea.

24 April
Amy: We have been to school today.

25 April
Amy: I was worried that Daddy might be blown off the mountain.
Joseph: Amy was scared that Daddy might get blown off the hill in the gale, but it wasn't that bad. When he came back (but he wasn't supposed to because he was going to camp two nights), he told us that he had lost his contact lens. Now he can't see with one eye, but he's lucky he had some spare.

26 April
Joseph: Today we did not go anywhere because Daddy did the mountains that he missed yesterday. Roger found a Haggis.
Andrew: In two days' time it is my birthday. We had lots of snow, wind and hail. We made a moss garden.

27 April
Andrew: When we woke up in the morning the place was covered in snow. Dad set off to a bothy. Then we went to the sea.
Joseph: We found some mussel shells. We are going to give them to Daddy when he comes back from the bothy. I want to give Andrew some skis for his birthday (it is his birthday tomorrow) but I might not get them. We went on a walk to see a waterfall. We were so hot we poured water on our heads!
Amy: We made a fire at night at ten past seven. We went for a walk and we collected some Catkins. We made a soup with them.

28 April
Andrew: My Birthday. Off my Mum and Dad I got a micro machine super city. From David Fell I got an Action Force man. From Taid and Nain I got a Post Office account. I got £5 notes from Auntie Linda and Uncle Les and Great Grandma. From Grandma and Grandad I got skate board knee pads and elbow pads.

29 April
Amy: We went mountaineering. We climbed a lot and we saw lots of cairns.
Andrew: Today we went on a walk which was very rocky and steep. It was just as high as Winder (which is one of the Howgills) but it seemed much higher.

30 April
Joseph: Today we went to a deer museum. It showed what antlers look like as the deer grow older. They showed the skulls with bullets in them.
Andrew: . . . we went to a deer museum . . . Amy was frightened.

1 May
Amy: We had an ice cream.
Andrew: We went to see some people weaving some tartan. One type of tartan is called MacAllister, which is the name of a book that we are reading.

2 May
Joseph: Today we went to the river. It was sandy. We made a town out of sand. The water was deep so we swam in it. It was freezing. We went for a walk in the woods. We found lots of interesting things.

3 May
Joseph: We went to a distillery where they make whisky.

4 May
Andrew: Today I ran 2 miles by road with Dad and one of his friends, who is the over 50s fell running champion. When we were driving up a valley along a very rough track, we came to a big puddle that Mum thought we couldn't drive across. Then she looked at the map and said we had gone the wrong way. Then we saw Dad and we turned the van round and set off back, and Dad told us that I had told Mum to take the right turning. Dad had come back because he had thought something bad might of happened.

5 May
Amy: It's sweety day today and we bought some sweeties.

6 May
Andrew: Today we went to a Loch Ness Monster exhibition. Mum thought that it would be touristy and expensive but it wasn't – it was very good.
Joseph: Scientists have seen something queer moving in Loch Ness. It looks like a monster but I don't think it is.

7 May
Amy: We had fish and chips for lunch today.
Andrew: It has been raining almost non stop for three days.

9 May
Andrew: Today we went over a pass to Glenelg. We went to the sea where you can see Skye. It was only 500 metres across to Skye. It was near where Dad is rowing across. We can't take the Glenelg Ferry because someone is trying to sell it.

10 May
Andrew: We saw Dad take the oars and row across to Skye. Then we had to go about 40 kms to the ferry to Skye . . . Tomorrow Dad is going to do what might be the hardest part of the whole trip.
Amy: We made some sand balls on the Island of Skye.

11 May
Amy: Mummy told us not to make sand balls with that snowy stuff.
Andrew: Today Dad got up at 5:00 am and set off to do the Skye Ridge. It is now 8:05 pm and he hasn't come back yet. Keith told us that somebody was carrying his mate's ashes up Sgurr na Stri to scatter them!

12 May
Andrew: Today we walked round a loch and collected lots of crabs. I caught a shrimp. Then we had to go over a pass that was worse than the Ratagan pass. Now we can see Glenelg where Dad is going to row across.

13 May
Joseph: We saw some seals when Dad went across (*to Glenelg*). We drove to the ferry

and went across to get to Kinloch Hourn. We looked for Daddy through the binoculars and we went to meet him.

15 May
Andrew: Today we didn't move anywhere. I don't write much when we don't move because nothing much happens.

16 May
Joseph: I saw a man's head fly off.
Amy: We went to the Little Chef for Andrew's birthday treat.

17 May
Andrew: Dad has now done 109 mountains. Only 187 mountains to go.

18 May
Joseph: We went to Prince Charlie's cave. It was just an overhang where he could hide from his enemies. We drove to a canal where we went across to meet Daddy. We saw a boat go up. When the boats go through they open the locks. Before they open them, they have to wait until the water that comes out of the side gets level with the side. Then the boats can go up into the next part of the Caledonian Canal.

19 May
Joseph: We went to the swimming pool. There was a 'twilly willy' slide.

21 May
Joseph: We went on a walk and did some rock climbing. We found some flowers; Milkwort, Butterwort and Lousewort. I found two friends; the butterfly and Ben (*the Parkins's son*).

23 May
Joseph: We played in the sand and played with the lego, and a camera popped out. He took some pictures and went away.

25 May
Andrew: Today we went to a wildlife park. It had the types of animals that used to live in the Highlands. There were wild horses, Highland Cattle, Soay Sheep, Roe Deer, Mouflon, Red Deer, European Bison, Wild Cats, Martens, Polecats, Hebridean Sheep, Bears, Lynx, Goats, Reindeer, Wolves, Boars, Arctic Foxes, Red Foxes, Badgers and game birds. My favourite animal is a Golden Eagle. Then we went to camp number 38.

26 May
Andrew: Today we went on a walk up to Lurchers Crag. We followed the footpath then a stream. Then we took a short cut straight up some rocks to Lurchers Crag. We had a view of the Lairig Ghru and 50 miles around. Mum has lost her voice so she can't shout!

27 May
Amy: We went to see the Osprey. We looked through the binoculars and saw the nest.

29 May
Andrew: Today we set off to camp number 42. It was 121 kms. Dad only had to do one Munro. On the way up there was lots of life on earth and in heaven, because there were lots of squashed rabbits on the road and pheasants and live rabbits at the side. When we got to camp number 42 Grandma and Grandad came and gave Joseph, Amy and me some sweets and Mummy some 'Roses' chocolates.

30 May
Andrew: Today we went over a bridge which was only meant for vehicles that weigh 2 tons and we weigh 2 tons, but we made it.
Joseph: Today we went in Grandma and Grandad's car. We drove to a 'supper' market; it was the biggest 'supper' market we have been to.

4 June
Amy: We saw the microlight take off. I would like to fly in a microlight.
Joseph: We drove to find a place to fill our water bottles up. I fell in when I was getting a drink! I am now waiting at the station doing my diary. In a minute Dad will come on the train.

5 June
Joseph: Daddy got on a train to where he started so he would not be cheating. We had to drive all the way round to Fort Bill. We went swimming. I went down the slide. I have been down the slide lots of times and I get better each time.

7 June
Amy: My friend Ruth went home today because she had a sore knee. Alan Thomson filmed us driving the van.

8 June
Amy: We saw a video about Glencoe at the visitor centre today. We coloured some Celtic patterns.

9 June
Andrew: On the way down Glen Etive I spotted a big bird. We looked it up in the book and it was a Grey Heron. Then we went up a dirt track. We came to a bridge by a ford. The bridge looked broken and we couldn't go across the ford because it was sandy on the other side. So we left a note saying we were down the road and drove down to the Inveroran Hotel.

10 June
Joseph: We left the 'michy' spot at the Inveroran Hotel. We drove up a narrow road and it said, 'not suitable for big camper vans' so we went up it. We went to a visitor centre. The visitor centre was about animals and nature in Scotland. There were some sculls you could pick up.

11 June
Joseph: We looked for gold in the river.
Amy: I found a flower which we couldn't find in the book.

12 June
Joseph: Today we went on a walk up Schiehallion – that means 'The Fairy Hill of the Caledonians'. We met Daddy on the top. Mummy phoned Grandma and she said she had fallen in the rubbish bin!
Amy: On our campsite there are some ducks, some geese, a fox, highland cattle, spotty deer, red deer, a rabbit and some hens. There is a black and white sheep with a baby lamb. We have also seen a peacock.

14 June
Andrew: I slept in a tent with Daniel Tuson. Daniel woke up then he went back to sleep

again. Then I woke up and went back to sleep again. Then I woke up again and I woke Daniel up. Then Amy woke up. Now it is 7:52 am

Amy: We went to look at some special rocks. We saw some round circles on the rocks.

Joseph: Today we found some unusual flowers called Monkey Flowers. They are Yellow and the petals easily fall off. They come from North America. The leaves are oval shaped. The flower was hairy inside. You can put your finger inside like a mouth opened.

15 June

Joseph: Today we were filmed doing our weather. Then we drove to an old fashioned steamer. We went for a cruise round Loch Awe. They use peat for the fire which heats the water and makes steam to push the steamer along.

Amy: We went inside a ruined castle and saw the prison. Andrew and Mummy went inside it. I didn't because it was very dark and I was a bit frightened.

16 June

Amy: Daddy set off in a boat for Mull today and Andrew went with him.

Joseph: Today we went to a sea life centre. We saw some sharks and some Craw Fish that look like lobsters. We saw some herrings that never stop swimming unless they are dead. We saw some seals being fed. You can tell the difference between grey seals and common seals because grey seals are bigger and have ugly faces. We saw some conger eels that are very long and live in stones. One looked like it was stuck.

17 June

Andrew: We got on a bus which went under the Munro that Dad was going up, to an underground power station which could make enough electricity for a city the size of Edinburgh.

18 June

Joseph: We went to jail and got locked in prison.

20 June

Joseph: Today we swung on a swing and played on the beach by Loch Lomond and we did lots of work. I did some painting, some maths and some writing. Daddy is hoping to finish the Munros on my Birthday.

Amy: I found 'Pop' at the campsite. 'Pop' is a little blue person.

21 June

Joseph: We did some shopping in Killin and we bought some wedding anniversary dinner for Mummy and Daddy.

Amy: I did some running with Daddy on the road.

22 June

Andrew: We met Dad and we walked down to the camper van. They had a tea break. Then Dad and me and Dad's mates ran two and a half miles along a track to a place where we had a drink of Lilt.

Amy: We thought that Taid and Nain would come today but we haven't seen them yet.

23 June

Andrew: . . . Then we set off to camp number 66. On the way we saw Rob Roy's grave. From there I ran down the road a bit. When we got there Taid and Nain were there and they gave me a letter from David Fell, and some sweets and £1.00

25 June
Joseph: My birthday is today. I got a lego model, a game, some crayons from Grandma and Grandad, some book tokens from Taid and Nain and a nice dinner in the Pub. We went half way up Ben Lomond and met Daddy on the top.

27 June
 Amy: We went to Glasgow. There were loads of people in it and loads of traffic. We went for a little walk around. We saw a person with no clothes on. (It was a statue.)

28 June
Andrew: Today we went to Muirkirk and we saw some children in School working!
Joseph: Amy lost her sock down the river and I caught it again and she lost one in the grass and I found it again. It was her favourite spotty sock. Today Daddy saw an owl in the woods.

29 June
Joseph: Today we went to a castle which had a play park by it. It was very good to go to because Mummy said so. Andrew went down a slide. I did not because Mummy said so. Amy went in a little park. I did not because Mummy said so.
Amy: We met Auntie Jane and went for a walk with Auntie Jane and Brooky her dog.

30 June
Andrew: Today we went through Carlisle where we got lost and we had a thunder storm. Then we went to camp number 73 which is a camp site IN ENGLAND!!!
Joseph: Today we had a new teacher – Carol.

1 July
Andrew: Today I was interviewed by Tim Backshall of Radio Cumbria. So was Joseph.

2 July
Joseph: Today we went to the woods and made a wooden den to shelter from the rain. We did some shopping in Keswick. We bought some ice creams and some buns. We bought some bread for Mummy. Mummy went up Skiddaw with Andrew and James (Parratt).
Andrew: . . . When we got to the top we were almost blown over. When we got down we had some iced buns because it was James's birthday.

3 July
Andrew: Today I found a cockchaffer beetle, which is a very funny thing. It has things like antlers and a tail like a fish's head. It has claws that can grip onto sticks.
Joseph: We went on a walk up a cliff. We did some rock climbing to a cave. Mummy was frightened that Andrew might fall down the cliff. I wrote down the flowers. We saw Foxgloves, Saxifrage, English Stonecrop, Heath Bedstraw, Tormentil, Yarrow, Sheep's Sorrel and Thyme.

4 July
Joseph: I am sleeping in Tom (*Clifford*)'s bed tonight.

5 July
Andrew: Today we met the Mayor of Kendal.
Amy: We had tea at Grandma's house. For pudding we had ice creams. I played ball with my cousins.

7 July
Joseph: Today we left Grandma's house and we went to Leila's house. We went to Wales and did some shopping and then we went back into England. We played with Leila's toys. We went to a big grand bridge called the Runcorn Bridge. It was very big.

9 July
Joseph: Today we went up a road that was too hard for us so we went a different way.

10 July
Joseph: Today we set off down that scratchy road to Llanwrst and we did some shopping in a 'supper' market.
Amy: There was an enormous water wheel at the slate museum in Llanberis. We saw two men making a horse shoe. Going up to Pen-y-Pass we were held up by a lot of sheep. Grandma came today.

11 July
Joseph: Today we went up Snowdon and Daddy finished 'Mountains of Britain, Mountains of Help'. Lots of people were there. Grandma and Taid and Nain were there, I went up to the very summIT on top of the trig point, where I gave Daddy some almonds and hazelnuts. Berghaus gave Daddy some Champagne and he sprayed it everywhere. He should have tipped it over his head. We (Grandma, Andrew, Amy and I) went down on the train and we (Andrew, Mummy and I) went up on the Pyg track.
Amy: I had some sweeties and a Coca Cola in the cafe at the top. Loads of people were there. Taid and Nain were there.
Andrew: Today we went up Snowdon and we were filmed on top. Then I got the train down. Then we went to a camp site.

12 July
Amy: I went to
Llanfairpwllgwyngyllgogerychwyrndrobwllllantysiliogogogoch.
I got lost in Kwik Save.
Joseph: In the middle of the night we went to get some chips. We ate them in the queue, then we drove on the boat.

13 July
Amy: I went up the Great Sugar Loaf. From the top I could see the sea and a big town called Dublin.

15 July
Joseph: Today we followed Daddy nearly everywhere. Then he went up a mountain – it was his first mountain in Ireland. We did not do much today.

16 July
Joseph: We went to a river (we wanted to do some fishing but we had no fishing rods, so mummy was so kind she bought three fishing rods) so we did some fishing and also we swam. There were lots of fish though. Today we are at King Mick's Castle. He gave us some strawberries and some potatoes for dinner.

17 July
Joseph: We left King Mick's Castle and we went to a river. We did some fishing. It was a bit too deep for swimming so we swam underneath an outside tap.

18 July
Andrew: Today we went to an old town called Kilkenny. We had a picnic in the castle grounds. Then we bought *Athletics Weekly*, and Dad was in it!
Amy: We tried to find somewhere to plonk the van for the night.

21 July
Andrew: Today we followed Dad all day.
Joseph: We stopped at a crossroads to wait for Dad. At first we thought he was a sheep, then another sheep and then himself.

22 July
Andrew: This morning we set off along the road, stopping now and again to give Dad something to drink and telling him which way to go. Dad went to do a poo. We lost him so we went down the road. Then we went up the road – then we went down the road – then we went up the road – then we went down the road. So we went up the road two times and down the road three times. When we got to a roundabout we didn't know which way Dad had gone so we set off towards the city centre. On the way we met Dad.
Amy: We lost Daddy because he was doing a poo poo.

23 July
Amy: Now there is only one more mountain left for Daddy to climb.

25 July
Andrew: Today Dad set off up Brandon Mountain and we played by Brandon Bay in the sand. We drove back to the pub at 2:45 pm. Dad had been there since 1:30 pm drinking Guinness. We had a little celebration in the pub.

26 July
Joseph: We are on our holidays now.

Postscript

From running a marathon a day, my running mileage dropped to a marathon a week. Running was replaced by writing. The transition took place on the west coast of Ireland. After Brandon Mountain, we spent three days at Cloghane, savouring the Guinness and the folk music. I didn't want to leave. Brandon Bay was a paradise. I returned to Brandon Mountain twice and gradually I gained a perspective of the previous months. We spent a fortnight travelling home via Galway, the Mountains of Connemara and the rough coastline of Antrim. The urge to run was replaced by an urge to write. The story was in our diaries and in our memories, and it had to be written before it faded into the distance. The first words were written by Galway Bay, and the last, six months later,

On the way home. Giant's Causeway. (H.S.)

looking at a white snowy landscape surrounding Sedbergh. One winter's day was spent in a Kendal court facing an accused neighbour, guns, lead shot, forensic scientists, police, solicitors, a barrister and a Yorkshire gunshop owner. Chaos prevailed, and after eight hours the magistrates declared – 'Case Not Proven'. A fortnight later the neighbour upped sticks and left town, never to be seen again.

Whilst on the run, there were two occasions when walkers in the mountains had passed cynical comments such as, 'You've missed the train!' The run had never been a rush – running being just a natural way of moving through mountains. Animals do it! The writing had a sense of urgency that the run never had, and was a task far more time-consuming, and one which required a much greater discipline. Perhaps the hardest task was for Pauline and I to be critical about each other's writing. We were helped by and we are grateful to friend and colleague, Stuart Manger, who read each chapter as it churned off the word processor. Stuart's constructive criticism was invaluable in maintaining our interest and enthusiasm in continuing to write.

Appendices

I   Intermediate Technology

Janet Bell

You get used to it after a while at Intermediate Technology. Complete lunatics often turn up on our doorstep announcing their plans for all sorts of weird and wonderful ventures – from lady poets reciting their way around the Lake District to solo microlite trips round the world.

Many of the proposed flights of fancy never actually materialise, but Hugh had that look in his eye which convinced us all from the word go. Moreover, it never left him (so I am reliably informed), even during the worst days of his marathon/megathon/ultrathon – it's difficult to keep up with the latest terminology for these ever-greater human feats certain individuals of our species insist on challenging themselves with.

It wasn't until I actually met Hugh on his last wet and windy Munro, that the scale of his undertaking really sank in. By then he'd broken the back of the feat, with 277 mountains under his belt and only a handful left to go. As we jumped around on the summit to keep warm, Hugh pointed out his route over the mountains on the horizon. What we could see was just a tantalising taste of the miles and miles of wilderness he'd scrambled over. Despite the miserable weather, I could understand Hugh's sadness in leaving the Scottish Highlands behind. I accompanied him on the first few miles of the road running towards Glasgow – on my bicycle, I hasten to add – and I was left wondering how he would ever manage to put the brakes on.

In the list of quirky and useless facts we put together for the press (which included such notable facts as the number of pairs of running shoes he'd destroyed), we estimated that the 296 peaks Hugh originally planned to climb worked out as the equivalent of 15 Everests. Obscure as it might seem, the Himalayan connection was an important one, because it linked Hugh's exploits here with the greater purpose of his venture. He had chosen to raise money for Intermediate Technology's micro-hydro programme, which does a lot of work in Everest's shadow in the Himalayan foothills of Nepal.

Intermediate Technology (I.T.) was the brainchild of the economist Fritz Schumacher, who coined the phrase 'Small is Beautiful', which is now so widely used that few people are aware of its origin. He identified the need to examine economics 'as if people mattered', and showed how this approach could enable people to take control of their lives and direct their own futures. In the 25 years since it has been established, I.T. has been putting Schumacher's ideas into practice, helping to relieve poverty through the development and application of technologies which are appropriate to the social, cultural, and economic needs of communities.

Nepal is the tenth poorest country in the world, and life is hard for its 13 million population, the majority of whom depend on farming the steep hillsides to support themselves. Many women have to rise at 3 am in order to prepare breakfast for their families, spending hours laboriously dehusking rice by hand and painstakingly grinding corn and millet. For 10 years, Intermediate Technology has been working in collaboration with local organisations on the introduction of very small-scale ('micro') hydro-electric systems to make life less arduous for these rural communities.

Initially, the work focused on harnessing the energy from Nepal's abundant and fast-flowing rivers and streams to be used mechanically to drive machinery, such as rice dehuskers, wheat, millet and maize grinders, and oil expellers. The savings in time are remarkable – what would take four hours to grind by hand can be undertaken in 15 minutes. Released from the daily grind, the women are free to help the men with the farming or use the time to set up income-generating activities.

More recently, work has focused on converting the energy to electricity for light, for heat or to power machines, such as power looms, refrigerators, crop dryers or irrigation pumps. The priority at the moment is to develop low wattage and heat storage cookers,which have the potential to reduce dramatically the fuelwood requirements of families. Deforestation is an extremely serious problem in this small, mountainous kingdom, and since 75% of the wood collected is used for cooking, the search for alternative energy sources is a high priority. More than 300 heat storage cookers are now being tested in the mountain villages. Widespread adoption of the cookers would also reduce the time needed to collect firewood – in the more depleted areas, even a whole day spent collecting fuel will not provide enough for cooking the evening meal.

An important component of I.T.'s work is strengthening communities' capacity to control and direct their futures. It is clearly not enough to provide a quick injection of techno-fix and turn your back. Consequently, the organisation is involved in training programmes, so that the technical aspects of the systems can be maintained locally, and on local production of the components. Fifteen years ago, there was in Nepal one engineering workshop and one manufacturing company capable of servicing the new industry: today there are more than a dozen producing and installing turbines, and the export market is growing.

I.T. works with a number of project partners in Nepal, including the Annapurna Conservation Area Project (ACAP), which espouses a people-centred approach to conservation. Tourists have received a lot of bad press in Nepal because of their contribution to its deforestation and erosion problems. However, ACAP sees trekkers only as a small part of the problem, poverty being the root cause, and acknowledges the importance of tourism to the development of the country, seeing as it generates 25% of the country's Gross Domestic Product (GDP). As part of their joint programme, I.T. and ACAP are planning to introduce micro-hydro systems into some of the lodges on the trekking ciruit, to reduce the negative impact of tourism. In this way, the sort of people with aspirations akin to Hugh's but without his superhuman drive, can enjoy the awe-inspiring beauty and power of nature, while minimising their contribution to its destruction.

Ann Parratt

When Hugh first asked me to be his liaison officer I really had no idea what the job entailed. It proved to be terrific fun and hard work. It was indeed a tremendous privilege to be involved with such a marathon undertaking.

Before Hugh and Pauline left for Scotland we held a few planning meetings, during which most of the ground work was done whilst we supped Hugh's home brew. Here was I, a lady with absolutely no passion for running anywhere at all, being told of the incredible route and timetable Hugh was to follow. My first job was to understand the scale of Hugh's venture so I could pass both information and enthusiasm on to the press, radio, TV, sponsors and supporters. Having been abandoned with piles of correspondence, maps, files, contact numbers and an answer phone, I felt quite envious of the Symonds tribe taking off to the quiet of the mountains.

After the first burst of publicity when Hugh started from Ben Hope, life settled down to about ten phone calls a day. As time went on and it looked as if Hugh was going to beat the record for running the Munros, the phone hotted up considerably. I think my husband David and I managed an uninterrupted evening meal about six times in the three months. Sometimes it was one of Hugh's old friends who had read about him in the national press, or maybe a television company wishing to do a feature if Hugh happened to be near a particularly dangerous or famous peak. Life was never dull.

My job as liaison officer meant that I was in contact with Hugh and Pauline for the duration of the run; they gave me up-to-date information on the camping site for the evening and what peaks had succumbed to Hugh's running feet that day, plus the odd interesting anecdote. I then passed relevant information on to the Intermediate Technology Press Office who in turn faxed interesting stories to the press. If the media wanted updating or a more detailed account then they contacted me directly.

I will always remember the day Hugh's mobile telephone suddenly started to work when he was running the southernmost Munros: the phone rang, I picked it up and heard very heavy breathing!

'Hugh here.' Pant, Pant.

I thought, 'Oops! Hugh?'

Pant, pant, 'Yes, Ann. Hello?' Pant, pant. 'I thought I would ring you . . .' Pant, pant, 'from a mountain as the phone . . .' pant, pant, '. . . has just started to work.' Pant, pant.

'Hugh, you are running with the phone, aren't you?'

On the whole the press, sponsors and film companies were extremely pleasant and helpful people to deal with; Anita Chandler (Janet Bell's predecessor at the I.T. press office) was an invaluable support with her good sound advice on how to cope with the more difficult people.

My final duty as liaison officer came as Hugh and Pauline returned to Sedbergh after a well-earned holiday when a secret celebration party was planned, with family, co-runners and colleagues from Sedbergh School all joining in to congratulate both Hugh and Pauline on such a tremendous achievement.

During the three months of the run we were continually in contact with the following.

The Observer	Radio Scotland
The Times	BBC World Service
The Independent	Radio Cumbria
Outdoor Action Magazine	Radio Moray Firth
Westmorland Gazette	Radio Wales
Press Association	*Bracknell News*
Dumfries Press	Calor Gas
Inverness Courier	Ordnance Survey
Athletics Weekly	Yorkshire Bank
Sunday Correspondent	Berghaus
Aberdeen Evening Express	Rohan
Bracknell Post	Reebok
South China Morning Post	Prolific
STV/ITN	Booths
Border TV	Applefords
BBC Carlisle	Sportswise
BBC Manchester	Refuge Assurance
Radio Good Morning Scotland	Village Bakery
Radio GMR	*Sunday Post*
Radio Sussex	Film Crew – Zanzibar Film Company

II Medical Appendix

By Dr Bev Holt.

As an expedition doctor with experience of high-altitude problems, I was not quite sure why I volunteered my services to Hugh's run, except that this was the first summer for three years that I wasn't off to the Himalayas, and the whole concept was a challenge.

There were really two aspects of the run that needed some sort of medical input. Firstly, there was Hugh's general health to consider, and the provision of basic first aid for himself, his fellow runners and for Pauline and the children. They would be, for much of the time, in isolated and inaccesible areas and the weather certainly for the early stages was guaranteed to be cold, wet, icy, snowy and windy. Even a minor injury or illness could seriously disrupt the very tight timetable.

Secondly, there was the problem of nutrition. Hugh would be exercising at full stretch for approximately 100 days and there was really no good documentation on how the body would react to this. In the Tour de France, the nearest type of thing we could think of, the athletes exercise flat out for a continuous period of three weeks; Hugh's challenge was going to last FOURTEEN weeks. In the end, all I did was to apply experience of high altitude expeditions when mountaineers spend similar lengths of time in a hypoxic (low on oxygen) environment. The result was that we planned a calorie intake of 6000 calories per day, mainly carbohydrate.

At the end of each day, Hugh would be acidotic, i.e. he would have built up excess lactic acid, having metabolised on an anaerobic system. For a fast recovery a good supply of oxygen is essential. Both fat and protein require more oxygen and more time than carbohydrate for digestion, hence the emphasis on the latter. The problem was the bulk of food required, especially as Hugh was not too keen on eating a lot of sugar to make up this carbohydrate intake. The result was that he spent most of his evenings eating potatoes, rice, cereals, biscuits, cakes, etc. But we obviously got it right!

At high altitude and during other prolonged periods of physical endurance, one of the problems is the loss of muscle mass and general deterioration that occurs. There are several reasons for this, but basically the body under stress uses up its own protein (muscle), and this was a real danger for Hugh. In fact, if anything his muscle mass increased, and he ended up by going about 8 lbs (3.5 kg) up in weight from start to finish.

So far as eating en route was concerned, each day he took the usual supply of sandwiches, chocolate, sweets and other goodies that walkers normally carry. In addition he always had an emergency supply of dextrose tablets that he could use if he really felt in need of sustenance. These he used on several occasions and found them a real energy booster. The only vitamin supplement he used was to take occasional doses of Vitamin C. Early on there was no guaranteed supply of fresh fruit and he found the effervescent tablets made a very refreshing drink.

The fluid problem was one we considered essential to his success. When exercising in either cold or hot conditions, when there is a breeze, perspiration evaporates very quickly, and the fluid loss can be very considerable without realising it. The body's essential electrolytes are not uniformly lost in sweat and urine, and very often there is an excessive loss of potassium which unless made up can lead to fatigue and general muscle weakness. To combat this, Hugh had a supply of a balanced electrolyte and glucose additive (Rehidrat supplied by Searle) that he used on a regular basis and found invaluable.

As far as the first aid went, he carried with him a portable first aid pack (the Gregson Pack – a specially designed and commercially available first aid kit) and this in fact was probably the only piece of equipment that actually went with Hugh to every single summit. It was used to treat various minor ailments and its light compact design made it ideal for this purpose. As a back-up, Pauline had a much more comprehensive kit that I had put together. It was kept in the camper and was available to treat both family and also the support runners. Fortunately there were no real medical problems and had anything serious cropped up I was always available via a 24-hour paging system.

So, how did Hugh manage to keep going for nearly a hundred days? Initially I had intended to monitor him carefully at regular intervals to see how his blood and biochemistry were responding, but the stress of this plus the fact that he was obviously going so well soon discouraged both of us. There were certain goals and psychological barriers that had to be attained and overcome but his feeling of wellbeing was probably due to another factor. Many runners have experienced a 'high' from prolonged effort and this is almost certainly due to the production by the body of its own narcotic-like substances known as endorphins. Hugh certainly had a feeling of wellbeing that stayed with him as long as he kept going. We had intended to build in a series of rest days but when he took the first of these he felt so 'down' that he decided to do some running every day, and felt much better for this change of strategy.

There was always the question of how he would feel once he had finished the run, but after adding on the Irish 'three thousanders', he was more than glad to stop subjecting himself to a high daily mileage. He continued to enjoy short training runs immediately after the trip, and has not suffered any obvious 'withdrawal' symptoms.

III Food

We were not aware of any 'wonder' diet which could dramatically affect Hugh's running performance. Special diets, e.g. carbo-loading, used by distance runners to aid performance in particular events were not relevant to an endurance event lasting for almost 100 days and involving prolonged exertion nearly every day. The best approach seemed to be to adopt a normal balanced diet. We all ate the same sorts of things that we usually eat – lots of wholefoods (we always use brown rice, pasta and flour) and fresh fruit and vegetables. The most dramatic departure from the norm for Hugh was in terms of quantity. His meals were three to four times larger than the 'normal' adult helping. He ate to the point of discomfort – a policy which I questioned, but it worked.

Dr Bev Holt recommended an increase in the proportion of carbohydrates in Hugh's diet – a simple matter involving extra pasta, rice or potatoes at the main meal; muesli bars, dried fruit and chocolate on the hill; cakes during tea breaks and Christmas puddings in the evening.

Non-perishable groceries kindly donated by various companies were carefully packed up into three week units and labelled before we left home. Arrangements were made to have these either delivered to us en route or collected from Fort William (Roger's). As shops are thin on the ground in the Highlands, we were spared having to deviate from our route and spend time searching for a suitable store.

We used local village shops where possible, to stock up on fresh supplies – bread, yogurts, milk, fruit and vegetables. For the majority of the time there was no problem although choice was limited. We carried supplies of crispbread and UHT milk (yuk!) to help us through difficult areas. Forays up dead-end roads necessitated stocking up for several days at a time.

Our vast food stores were packed under a double seat. The fridge was essential and large enough for our needs. All the cooking was done on two gas rings. This wasn't an appreciable problem. In fine weather we often cooked outside on a petrol stove. We had decided that the extra cupboard space was more valuable than an oven and grill.

Typical adult meals consisted of pasta with a vegetarian sauce or rice with a bean curry. The children's favourite was baked beans with mashed potato. Once the bothy trips were over, they consumed the rest of the powdered mash with relish! We ate meat about three times a week – chicken, mince, liver. For breakfast we always had muesli. Occasionally we enjoyed a bacon and egg breakfast. We all missed the luxury of toast. The lack of an oven didn't worry me but I would have liked a grill.

Vitamin C tablets, recommended by Dr Holt, were the only vitamin/mineral supplements taken. However, Hugh took the homeopathic substance Arnica, in tablet form. A regime of three weeks on and one week off was followed, taking 3 × 2 tablets a day. Hugh didn't feel any different during the periods on or off Arnica and will never know whether it had any effect in reducing injury/fatigue.

Booths generously supplied the following groceries. The list reflects what we actually used rather than what we were given. The original supply list turned out to be an over-estimate:

Porridge Oats   3kg
Spaghetti   5kg
Soup Mix   2kg
Sugar   3kg
Horlicks Hot Choc   3 × 500g
Branston pickle   3 × 454g
Additive free jam   15 jars
Vecon veg stock   2 × 8oz
Birds custard powder   300g
Tinned tomatoes   45 × 14oz
Tinned fruit   60 × 415g
Ambrosia rice pudding   30 × 822g
Tinned pulses   15 × 415g
Darjeeling tea   6 × 8oz
Cornflour   2 packets
Concentrated juice   3 × ½ litre
Dried fruit   4kg
Nuts (assorted varieties)   about 5kg in all
Crispbread   a few packet only
Brown Wheat Crackers   10 packets (could
have used more)
UHT milk   10 litres
Rice   8kg
Lentils   3kg
Sunflower Oil   3 litres
Instant Coffee   20 × 100g
Hob Nobs (biscuits)   10 × 120g
Sandwich pickle   4 × 310g
Honey   5 × 1lb
Tomato paste   15 tubes
Mayonnaise   3 × 500g
Baked beans   30 × 440g
Tuna   20 × 185g
Sweet corn   10 × 12oz
Tinned bean salads   10 × 415g
Peanut Butter   5 jars
Margarine   10 × 500g

For Bothy trips:
Powdered milk   340g
Instant mash   5 × 120g
Angel Delight   15 packets
Batchelors rice meals   10 packets

Suma Wholefoods donated the following:

Whole Earth Tomato ketchup   12 bottles
Concentrated apple juice   2 × 5l
Pasta Twists   20 × 500g
Mornflake Crunchy cereal   40 × 400g
Crunchy apricot muesli   5 × 3kg
Diced apple   1kg
Organic hedgehog crisps   48 × 27g
Also we used 2 reams of recycled paper.

The Village Bakery in Melmerby, near Penrith
made a very valuable contribution of;
10 × 4 lb Fruit cakes (absolutely delicious)
12 Cumberland Rum Nickys (great on the hill)
24 Christmas puddings (essential for evening
carbo-loading)

Other valuable sponsors were –

Jordans   216 Crunchy Bars
            7kg assorted cereals
Applefords Ltd   288 Cluster Bars
Jacob Suchard Ltd   100 Lila Pause, Yogu
                       Crisps (30g)
                       120 Fruit and nut bars
                       (100g)
Rowntree Mackintosh   48 Yorkie bars
Quiggins   4 × 3 doz mint cakes
Record Pasta   20 × 500g assorted
                  stoneground pasta
Jacqueline Smith   Over 20 delicious
                      homebaked cakes from
                      Sedbergh friend and
                      supporter.

We took from home, herbs, spices, seasoning,
flour, marmalade and ground coffee. En-route
we bought bread, milk, yoghurt, fruit, vegetables, meat and occasionally fish. Our alchohol
intake was negligible. I hid away a bottle of
wine and had the odd glass when times were
rough! Hugh drank a lot of coffee. We have read
that it can be beneficial before taking exercise!

IV   Statistics

The Munros (277 mountains)
(Ben Hope to Ben Lomond – April 19 to June 25)

Distance   : 1368 miles (265 of these were on road).
Height gained   : 427 000 feet.
Time   : 67 days (66 days and 22 hours).

N.B. 1) A day unit being 24 hours. It is possible to exercise on three continuous days but only move for 1 day and 23 hours,

      e.g.   start : Thursday January 1, 13.00 hrs
            finish: Saturday January 3, 12.00 hrs.

N.B. 2) The distance excludes the sea crossings to Mull and Skye. Distances are measured from the map and do not take vertical displacements into account. These would probably add between 5% and 10% to mountain distances.

DISTANCES/DAYS

Miles per day	Number of Days
0 – 5	1
5 – 10	0
10 – 15	7
15 – 20	29
20 – 25	22
25 – 30	8
30 – 35	0
35 – 40	1

Munros per day	Days
0	3
1	11
2	6
3	9
4	12
5	11
6	3
7	6
8	2
9	3
10	1
11	1

Ascent per day (feet)	Number of Days
0 – 3000	3
3000 – 6000	32
6000 – 9000	24
9000 – 12000	8
12000 – 15000	1

Averages: 20.4 miles per day.   4.9 miles per Munro.
6400 feet per day.   1540 feet per Munro.
4.1 Munros per day.   1 hour 54 minutes per Munro.

Average time out per day (including rests, admiration of scenery, photography, filming, etc.): 7 hours 50 minutes.

THE MUNROS AND BEYOND

Mountains of Britain (296 Mountains)
(Ben Hope to Snowdon – April 19 to July 11)

Distance	: 1745 miles
Height gained	: 465 000 feet.
Time	: 83 days (82 days and 23 hours).

Mountains of Britain and Ireland (303 Mountains)
(Ben Hope to Brandon – April 19 to July 25)

Distance	: 2048 miles.
Height gained	: 500 000 feet.
Time	: 97 days (96 days and 23 hours).

Mountains of Ireland (7 Mountains)
(Lugnaquilla to Brandon – July 15 to July 25)

Distance	: 235 miles.
Time	: 10 days (9 days and 23 hours).

DAILY BREAKDOWN OF DISTANCES FROM BEN LOMOND TO BRANDON
(Beyond the Munros)

Miles per day	Number of Days
0 – 10	3
10 – 20	8
20 – 30	13
30 – 40	6

ACCOMMODATION

Number of Nights

Van	87	
Tent	2	(Sourlies + near Dalwhinnie)
Bothy	2	(Coriemor + Shenavall)
Friends	4	(Kendal, Preston (2), Birkenhead)
Boat	2	(Sound of Mull, Irish Sea)
Total	97	

CLEAR SUMMITS

Of the 303 mountains climbed, exactly 200 gave views.
185 of these views were from Munros.

*N.B. Martin Moran enjoyed 172 Munro views during his Winter expedition and
Hamish Brown had 213 views (out of 289 peaks) during his mountain walk.*

WEATHER

*Pauline and the children took readings between 9 and 10 every morning. On 23 of these days it
was raining at the time.*

Shade temperatures

Degrees Centigrade	Days
0 – 5	3
5 – 10	17
10 – 15	57
15 – 20	17
20 – 25	4

Cloud cover

	Days
Clear (less than ⅛ cloud).	18
Overcast (at least ⅞ cloud).	56
Other.	24

Wind

	Days
Calm	29
Slight Breeze	34
Moderate to strong	33
Gale	2

Pressure

Pressure in Millibars	Days	
990 – 1000	2	
1000 – 1010	20	
1010 – 1020	28	
1020 – 1030	30	
1030 – 1040	9	(mainly in Ireland)
No record	9	

N.B. All the above readings were taken at road/van level. Pressures adjusted to sea level.

VAN'S MILEAGE FROM BEN HOPE TO BRANDON

Total distance driven – 3176 miles.

V   Photography

Three cameras were used, the day-to-day choice being made by balancing the merits and disadvantages of each one. A Rollei 35 LED was carried when weight had to be kept to a minimum (e.g. Cuillin Ridge, bothy trips, etc.). This camera produced sharp results even though guesswork was used for distances and exposure (the light meter was broken and has proved impractical to repair). A Nikon L35 AWAF was selected for its robustness and good waterproofing (designed as an underwater camera). Having a built-in flash, it was useful on dull days and for photos inside the van. Being completely automatic, it was very handy for quick shots. When a special effort was made to get a variety of photos, a Nikon FE (SLR camera) was taken with any one or more lenses from the selection of 24mm, 55mm and 135mm Nikkors. This camera was particularly useful to give to accompanying runners when they needed slowing down (total weight at least a kilogram). Matt Dickinson had a 300mm lens which fitted both his Aaton 16mm film camera and the Nikon FE. This long lens was used for stills taken on Ben Macdui. Over a thousand Ektachrome 200 transparencies were taken in the three months. I am grateful to Eric Whitehead of Sedbergh who processed and catalogued these as we posted them to him from far corners of these islands. I am also grateful to Eric for his own photographs, all of which appeared in newspapers. Most other photographs taken during the run were shot by friends who usually carried one of the above cameras. I am also grateful to friend and colleague Jim Fisher, who advised me on photography and inspired me through his own fascinating collection of slides taken from his daring travels to dangerous places around the world.

VI   Clothing

Recent advances in the materials used for clothing enable the runner to stay warm and well protected in the worst of weathers, and yet not be overburdened by the weight of heavy layers. Lightweight protection is crucial in maintaining speed and energy on the hills.

The first layer next to the skin was Berghaus's ACL (Active Comfort Layer). The polyester vest and pants provide comfort and dryness by drawing away the sweat through the soft fibres. On cold days, more than one layer of ACL was worn. The pants were pulled up and down from the ankles to the thighs permitting rapid changes of protection in the temperature variation from summit to valley.

On many days ACL plus a teeshirt was sufficient, but if not, then additional protection was provided by a polarlite sweater. An unexpected benefit of ACL was that it took a long time to build up any smell – hence reducing the need to wash clothes.

Three waterproofs were used throughout the run. They can be classed as high, medium and low quality.

On days of driving rain, a Berghaus Courmayeur smock goretex top was taken. This was light enough to run in but of sufficient quality to keep me dry in the worst of weathers. I regretted not having it on the day of the deluge in the Crianlarich hills. This garment went with me to approximately half the Munros. On warm days of expected showers, a Reebok goretex running top was taken. This worked well on all but the most persistently wet and windy days. On days when no rain was expected, a cheap and nasty crisp packet style nylon top was wrapped round the waist. This was protective against the wind and could keep light half hour showers at bay.

Thin crisp packet type waterproof bottoms were the only ones ever used although high quality ones were kept in the van. I have never minded running with slightly damp legs and prefer that to being weighed down by heavier leggings.

A polarlite balaclava kept the wind and cold off my head and was also a very poor absorber of water, hence reducing the need to keep the hood up.

A silk scarf kept the neck warm and absorbed the drips of rain that get in round the collar. Thin lightweight gloves were satisfactory on most days but I had cold hands in the Fannichs.

Reebok supplied 'Contour' running shoes for the hill and 'Exhilarators' for the road. Four pairs of Contours were sufficient to maintain studs and a good grip over the Munros. The shoes were comfortable and didn't show any signs of shrinking despite being almost permanently wet. The one pair of road shoes maintained their bounce throughout the tarmac sections from Ben Hope to Brandon. Occasionally, a pair of 'Phase IIIs' were used for low level off road running (e.g. in South West Scotland). Berghaus Goretex socks were invaluable during the early weeks of the run. The thin membrane is worn over ordinary socks and helps prevent the penetration of water. They were particularly good at keeping the feet warm whilst running in snow. Two pairs of Goretex socks lasted daily use over the Munros (N.B. half the number of running shoes used). Besides keeping the feet much drier than normal, they prevented the contamination of the socks worn underneath. Fell running through peat hags, tangled heather and mud, normally deteriorates light running socks in a few days. This also reduced the need to wash socks, although the goretex ones became quite smelly after ten days or so and needed a good rinsing in a burn.

Well insulated, easy to wash and dry Rohan clothing formed the basis of the family's clothing, and I found it particularly valuable when sat outside admiring the northern evening skies on frosty nights.

We were fortunate to be given all the clothing used and were always confident that we could comfortably survive and enjoy living an outdoor life.

VII   The Children's Education

When we decided to take our children out of school for a term, in order to take part in the 'Mountains of Britain' venture, we were convinced that they would be enriched by the experience. At the time, only the two oldest children, Andrew (8) and Joseph (6) were attending school. Amy (4) was due to start in September. The school governors readily gave their approval, the only formal consent required.

I made a positive effort to provide an education for the children but from the outset I harboured no illusions as to the potential problems. I reasoned that however disastrous my attempts to teach them, they would still benefit from the experience and learn a great deal as an inevitable by-product of taking part.

I tried to ensure that they kept pace with their classmates in the most important areas. The head teacher (Mrs J. Horton) and the staff at the school (Sedbergh County Primary School) were very encouraging and helpful, in supplying information and materials. These included books from the reading scheme (Ginn) with associated worksheets, books from the mathematics scheme and a variety of extra equipment.

Most of all I tried to optimise the potential of our unique situation and whenever possible base our learning on our experience. A visit to a tartan-weaving factory sparked off a craze for tartan designing. A trip on the Aonach Mór Gondola prompted an interesting discussion on the arrangement of the pulley system. The railway timetable at Tulloch Station provided ample material for calculations involving time and the 24 hour clock. Study of the unpronounceable Gaelic names gave an insight into the language. Often the translations are extremely simple, e.g. Ben Mór – Big Hill, Meall Gorm – Rounded Blue Hill.

Maps were an important feature in our lives. We followed Hugh's route on them, found our way in the van using them and took them on our walks. We looked at the symbols, the scale and the contour detail. Using a wheel Andrew measured the distance covered by Hugh each day. Joseph noted the distance covered by the van. Together we worked out the height climbed by Hugh, often a complicated exercise involving careful study of the contours on the maps. Andrew and Joseph calculated the cumulative totals daily (no calculators allowed).

All three children kept weather records, at a level suited to their ability. We used the Usbourne Spotter's guide *The Weather* for information on cloud types, guidelines on estimating wind speed and general knowledge on the subject. Andrew became competent at using Hugh's altimeter to read the air pressure, adjusting the instrument to account for the altitude of our position.

The children kept a daily diary. As Amy had not yet learnt to write, I helped her by writing out the letters faintly for her to write over.

Completing these daily tasks was often difficult. We tried to note our observations on the weather at a similar time each morning but often the dictates of the run would make this difficult. The children would argue about who should have the wind sock first or which of the two similar but not identical temperature readings was correct! Andrew developed the habit of completing his observations as a matter of routine, but Joseph seemed to tire of this regular task. Keeping a daily diary was an effort for us all but well worth the discipline. The children's interest would go hot and cold on this matter. We often lagged behind on our statistical recordings. Rainy days were times for catching up.

Curiously, Andrew and Joseph had a liking for reminders of school life. They insisted that we had spelling tests every week. I used the mis-spelt words from their diaries as material for these. Joseph was keen to complete his Ginn reading books and worksheets but Andrew would have happily given it a miss.

It was hard to find the time for the children to read to me, but I read to them every night and we discovered some excellent stories based in the Highlands. We all split our sides when reading *The Old Man of Lochnagar* by Prince Charles. Sam Llewellyn's story (*Pig in the Middle*) about a young boy's friendship with a seal was very moving and three fantastic mysteries by Mollie Hunter (*The Haunted Mountain, The Kelpie's Pearls* and *The Enchanted Whistle*) had all of us spellbound.

The various 'Visitor Centres' dotted around the Highlands were excellent resources for information on the history and ecology of the regions. We discovered that there are many different types of conifer, all with differing needles, bark and cones. Even the Loch Ness Monster Exhibition was far more informative than I expected, exploring in detail the life at the bottom of the Loch and the various methods of investigating such deep water. Any point of interest en route was taken advantage of, but we always had to keep an eye on the time as there was invariably an appointment to keep with a runner.

We took a variety of field guides on our walks. Again the 'Usbourne Spotter's Guides' were invaluable as were the little 'Gem' guides. We had books on flowers, fungi, butterflies, trees, rocks, the seashore, birds, pond life and farm animals. The Collins guide to *The Alpine Flowers of Britain and Europe* provided an essential supplement to their guide to *The Wild Flowers of Britain and Northern Europe*. We pressed the common flowers and photographed the less common ones. We tried to identify all that we saw. Identification of the more obscure bog plants using the *Collins Guide to Ferns, Mosses and Lichens*, could be both fascinating and frustrating. Collecting rocks was a favourite pastime and the boot was soon weighed down by our specimens.

There were difficulties and plenty of arguments. As I found it very difficult to adopt the role of teacher, attempts at reading and writing work inside the van were not always successful. It was neither possible nor desirable to keep to any regular timetable. It was usually difficult to find the time to do any formal school work, in the sense of sitting down at a table with books and paper, due to the need to move on and provide for Hugh and the pacers. We were most successful on rainy days and when we were on our own for most of the day. We had a generous share of fine weather, and I couldn't bring myself to interrupt the children playing by rivers or lochs in order to do some 'work'.

Our children gained insights into new and interesting aspects of life. The activities of the film crew always fascinated them. Elements of the planning and organisation of a large fundraising venture must have made an impression through conversations overheard. A vast number of people came into our lives over the four months, encouraging the children to feel at home in the company of new acquaintances. They gained an insight into many different occupations. We all had to learn to be both flexible and patient in trying situations.

Perhaps the most enjoyable aspect of our life on tour was the close contact with the outdoors. Andrew became an expert at putting up a variety of tents and lighting camp fires. Hours were spent pottering in rivers, lochs and forests. Whilst we seldom had time for adventurous hikes, we took every opportunity to go on short walks, collecting and identifying the natural objects around us.

After nearly four months away from Sedbergh, Andrew and Joseph were looking forward to meeting up with their friends at school. Amy couldn't wait to start. I felt that our travelling school had given her a head start. They all settled in to school without any problems and did not seem to have missed out on anything. They had come to know, appreciate and admire the wildest corners of our islands, and above all, they had learnt that a great deal can be achieved with sufficient drive and inspiration, satisfying both a need for personal challenge and a desire to help others.

VIII   Navigation

Finding ways between the mountains and discovering an overall route was an important part of the challenge, and was essential for maintaining day to day interest. I am grateful to the Ordnance Survey for supplying the 67 Pathfinder (1:25 000) maps needed to guide me through the Scottish section of the run.

Maps have always fascinated me but my confidence in navigating through difficult terrain was low until I took to the sport of orienteering in the autumn of 1986. The navigation required for most fell races is minimal, fitness and prior course knowledge being more important than intricate route finding. This is particularly the case in long Lake District races such as Ennerdale, Wasdale and Borrowdale. The exception to this is in events such as the annual Ordnance Survey Mountain Trial, and the Rock and Run and Karrimor two day mountain marathons, where the venues are different every year and the courses are kept secret until the start.

A fifteen minute run and £15 won in a professional (misnomer for races not run under AAA rules) fell race at the Moorcock Show caused me to be banned from amateur athletics in September 1986. The ban prevented me from competing on the fells and my competitive drive turned to 'the Thought Sport'. From seeing stickers pronouncing, 'Fell Runners go up and down a lot' or 'Fell Runners keep it up longer', I was now parking next to cars reading, 'Give me a map and I'm magic' or 'Orienteers have a feel for contours'. Suddenly, I went from a position of being in the top few at fell races to finishing well down the field at orienteering events. The amateur athletics suspension lasted three months, and in that time I learnt more about navigation than I had in the previous ten years of regular fell running. Competing with 1:10 000 and 1:15 000 scale maps exaggerated the need to navigate from ground features. Cheekily placed controls (checkpoints) demand skill in searching for relevant crags, boulders, streams, spurs, depressions, platforms, etc. Gradually I gained a better feel for the map and its relationship with the real terrain. Besides using the compass to give direction, I learnt to check the direction of ridges, watercourses, fences, etc., all helping to fix the location. Coming down from OS maps to the scales used for orienteering, the tendency is to overestimate distances and overshoot controls. A sense of distance is vital in finding a way from loch to lochan or from boulder to burn. By counting strides or watching the time, hundreds of metres or even kilometres can be gauged. However, like using the compass, precision can't be expected and the overall picture and judgement is made through combining all the information. Beyond these skills, perhaps the most important ingredient of navigation is concentration and for that there needs to be motivation. That quality was high throughout my journey over Britain and Ireland. Mistakes made in the mountains can not only be costly in terms of time and energy but in the worst of cases can cost life or limb.

IX Mountain Records in the British Isles

By Martin Stone

The desire to climb increasing numbers of peaks in particular mountain areas of Britain, often against a time deadline, is not just a fad of our current generation. As early as the late 19th Century, intrepid adventurers such as Dr Arthur Wakefield (pupil at Sedbergh School, 1889–1894) and Eustace Thomas were spending up to 24 hours on their feet, tackling ever-longer mountain journeys in the English Lakes and Scotland.

The last 20 years have seen more opportunities for recreation, improved transport and better maps which have made all but the most remote parts of Great Britain accessible to the individual. Lightweight clothing and equipment is now designed specifically for long-distance mountain trips. Improved communication and documentation have brought an awareness of what is possible and exactly how it can be achieved. This allows a far more analytical and clinical approach to setting up record attempts and planning a schedule of times for each summit.

The specific training and preparation undertaken by individuals these days combined with a depth of experience have resulted in some very fine mountain records. This sport of combining long-distance travel over wild tracts of mountain country with many thousands of feet of climbing, all within a strict time limit, is a pursuit unique to the UK. The more extreme ultra distance mountain running performances outlined below are unsurpassed elsewhere in the world.

SCOTTISH MUNROS – SOME NOTEABLE ACHIEVEMENTS

First Continuous Self-Propelled Traverses

Hamish Brown; 4 April – 24 July 1974; completed 1639 miles and 449 000ft of ascent in 112 days mainly on foot but including about 150 miles by bicycle. He used the Skye and Mull ferries as did all Munroists described below who visited the islands. (Described in *Hamish's Mountain Walk*.)

Kath Murgatroyd; 1 May – 11 September 1982; first traverse by a lady and the second continuous one, covering 2250 miles and 460 000ft of ascent in 134 days which included about 1000 miles by bicycle.

Adding The English and Welsh 3000ft Summits

George Keeping; 14 April – 27 August 1984; third continuous traverse and first entirely on foot completing 1784 miles and 464 000ft of ascent within 136 days. He continued south on foot from Ben Chonzie and within 29 days had climbed the English and Welsh 3000 footers.

Mainland Munros – A Fast Traverse

Rick Ansell; 3 May – 10 August 1984; used fell running fitness to complete a fast, unsupported traverse of the mainland Munros entirely on foot, 1270 miles and 407 000ft of ascent within 100 days. This included 8 rest days on which he often hitched to the nearest town for provisions, returning to the same point to continue his walk. He chose not to visit the islands as the ferry crossings would necessitate the use of motor-powered transport.

Adding The Corbetts
Craig Caldwell; February 1985 – March 1986; the 222 Corbetts (Scottish mountains of between 2500 – 3000ft) were climbed in addition to the Munros within 377 days. Craig cycled 4152 miles, walked 3030 miles and climbed 828 000ft. (Described in *Climb Every Mountain*.)

Munros in Winter, Linked By Vehicle – The Only Completion
Martin Moran; 21 December 1984 – 13 March 1985; within 83 of the 100 Winter days he walked and skied 1030 miles and climbed 410 000ft. A motor caravan provided home and transport between the mountain regions. His wife Joy was driver, provisioner, pacer and companion on many Munros. (Described in *The Munros in Winter*.) A number of the runners who supported Martin were to accompany Hugh Symonds some 5 years later.

Martin is also a very good climber and currently holds the Skye Ridge record. On 2 June 1990 he completed all 11 Munros and the 4 major climbing obstacles between Gars Bheinn and Sgurr nan Gillean without support in 3hrs 33mins.

Munros Linked By Vehicle – Fastest Completion
Mark Elsegood; 22 May – 26 July 1988; inspired by Martin Moran's Winter exploits, Mark's fell running background enabled him to make fast daily forays based from a car. Working on a 75 day schedule, he polished off the Munros in 66 days which included 2 days of rest. He covered 1054 miles on foot with 412 000 feet of climbing.

Munros Relay Linked By Vehicle – Only Completion
Team of 7 fell runners; 16 – 28 June 1990; the simple rules for this challenge were that 'the baton' should complete the journey and could only be carried in vehicles on public roads and ferries; at all other times it was carried on foot. Starting on Blaven (Skye) and finishing on Ben Lomond, the team ran day and night. Their time of 12 days 17 hours 8 minutes for a first ever relay attempt sets an interesting challenge for the future.

Scottish 4000ft Munros, English 3000 and Welsh 3000 Peaks
The Scottish 4000s route is 81 miles and 17 000ft ascent from Glen Nevis YH near Fort William to Glen More YH at the foot of the Cairngorms. This 81 mile route links Ben Nevis and the 3 other 4000 ft Lochaber Munros with the 4 Cairngorm 4000 ft Munros, some 50 miles distant. A route first tackled by the Rucksack Club in the 1950s, the record is now 21hrs 39mins by Martin Stone in a solo, unsupported attempt on 4 July 1986. His time from summit to summit was 19hrs 30mins.

The English or Lakeland 3000s as it is often called, is a circular route from Keswick Rugby Club of about 43 miles and 10 000ft ascent which visits the summits of Skiddaw, Scafell, Scafell Pike and Helvellyn. Based on an annual walk organised by the Ramblers' Association, the record is 7hrs 35mins by Billy Bland set in June 1979.

The Welsh 3000s is a classic mountain route in Snowdonia starting on the summit of Snowdon and finishing atop Foel Fras on the Carneddau range. It links the 15 peaks, about 22 miles in distance and 14 000 feet of ascent. First recorded completion was by the Rucksack Club in 1919. Jos Naylor's 15 year record was bettered by 26 minutes on 11 June 1988 by Colin Donnelly in a superb time of 4hrs 19mins 56secs.

BRITISH THREE PEAKS – SNOWDON, SCAFELL PIKE AND BEN NEVIS
The British Three Peaks is from sea level at Caernarfon to sea level Fort William via the highest mountain in each of Wales, England and Scotland. This route has been attempted in a variety of ways, the most 'ethical' of which are described below:

On Foot
Arthur Eddleston; 11 – 17 May 1980; walked approximately 420 miles in 5 days 23hrs 37mins without running a step.

On Foot and by Bike
Stephen Poulton; early 1980s; all the road sections were completed by bike. While running over Snowdon and to the summit of Scafell, Stephen's bicycle was transported to a convenient point where the next road section began. He completed the challenge in 1 day 17hrs 55mins.

On Foot and by Yacht
Queen Anne's Battery; 10 – 12 June 1989; the Three Peaks Yacht Race has been held since 1976. Teams of 5 sail their yachts from Barmouth to Corpach (near Fort William), calling at Caernarfon and Ravenglass. At each port of call 2 members of the crew run to the relevant summit and return on foot to the yacht. The distance sailed from Caernarfon to Fort William is about 340 miles and the running distance about 72 miles with 11 000ft ascent. The catamaran *QAB* completed the Caernarfon to Corpach section in 2 days 4hrs 7mins (including the running).

THE CLASSIC BRITISH 24 HOUR ROUNDS – ENGLAND, SCOTLAND AND WALES

Bob Graham Round; 42 peaks, 60 miles and 27 000ft ascent
In 1932, Bob Graham set a new Lakeland 24 Hour Fell Record which was based on the Moot Hall in Keswick. The route crosses Skiddaw and Blencathra to Threlkeld, turning south along the Helvellyn ridge, west over the Langdales and Bowfell to the Scafells. It takes in the Pillar horseshoe and the Gables to Honister before returning to Keswick via the Newland Fells.

It was 28 years before the round was repeated but since then it has become a classic test of endurance for hundreds of long distance aspirants. Such is its popularity that a club has been formed which meets biannually and presents certificates for successful completions. The men's record is 13hrs 53mins by Billy Bland on 19 June 1982, and the ladies' record 19hrs 11mins by Hélène Diamantides on 12 August 1989.

Charlie Ramsay's Round; 24 Munros, 60 miles and 28 000ft ascent
In June 1964, Philip Tranter made a complete circuit of the Glen Nevis hills, 19 Munros within 24 hours. The route starts and finishes at Glen Nevis YH, takes in Ben Nevis and the Lochaber 4000s, the Grey Corries and the 11 Munros on the Mamores ridge. On 28 May 1990, Mark McDermott set a record of 12hrs 50mins for Tranter's Round running solo, unsupported.

Charlie Ramsay extended that route to the east of Loch Treig in July 1978, adding a further 5 Munros, 25 miles and 8000ft ascent before returning to Glen Nevis YH with a minute to spare. Ramsay's round was not repeated within the 24 hour time limit for another 9 years. It has now been completed by about 10 runners and is Scotland's 24 hour classic. The men's record is 18hrs 23mins by Adrian Belton on 2 August 1989 and the ladies' record 20hrs 24mins by Hélène Diamantides on 15 July 1989.

Paddy Buckley's Round; 47 Peaks, 61 miles and 27,700ft ascent
In the late 1970s, Paddy Buckley devised a round of peaks in Snowdonia to rival the Bob Graham and he based it at Capel Curig. The route climbs Moel Siabod and crosses wild country to the Moelwyns, Cnicht and Aberglaslyn. It follows the beautiful Eifionydd ridge and climbs Yr Aran, Snowdon, Crib-y-ddysgl and Moel Eilio before descending to Llanberis. Then the Elidirs, Glyders, Tryfan and finally the Carneddau before returning to Capel.

Unfortunately both of Paddy's attempts failed and the first fully documented sub-24 hour round was by Martin Stone in July 1985. It has now been completed by about 30 runners. The men's record is 22hrs 5mins by Adrian Belton on 13 August 1988 and the ladies' record 20hrs 8mins by Hélène Diamantides on 3 June 1989.

The Three Rounds In One Outing
Between 13 – 16 July 1990, in a time of 3 days 14hrs 20mins, Mike Hartley completed all three rounds described above. His time includes the two 4 hour car journeys between the rounds during

which he dozed fitfully. His time for Ramsay's Round was 21hrs 14mins, the Bob Graham in 23hrs 48mins and finally an epic struggle in Snowdonia to complete Paddy Buckley's Round in 33 hrs 30mins. The previous year, Mike Hartley had reduced Mike Cudahy's Pennine Way record by more than 4 hours to 2 days 17hrs 20mins.

THE BRITISH 24 HOUR RECORDS – ENGLAND, SCOTLAND AND WALES

Throughout the sixties and seventies the likes of Jos Naylor and Alan Heaton added substantially to Bob Graham's original round. The rule was that any new Lakeland 24 Hour Fell Record should include all the peaks visited on previous attempts. In June 1975 Jos set a record of 72 peaks which was to stand for 13 years, surviving attempts on it by some fine runners. On 18 June 1988, Mark McDermott, a relatively unknown long distance man shattered the immortality of Jos's record by completing 76 peaks based from Braithwaite, 87 miles and 39 000ft ascent within 23hrs 26mins.

When Ramsay's Round received its first repeat in 1987, Martin Stone added a further 2 Munros which lay to the South of Loch Ossian. It was an expensive addition, involving an extra 10 miles and 3000ft ascent. The stakes had been raised to 26 Munros but this record lasted no more than a year. It was Jon Broxap who had originally suggested the extension but he now turned his attention to the hills around Cluanie and Affric. On 25 June 1988, Jon climbed 28 Munros and ran 78 miles which included 33 000ft ascent in 23hrs 20mins. His route from Cluanie took him along the South Cluanie Skyline to the Saddle. He dropped to Glen Shiel and then tackled the Five Sisters of Kintail before heading out to the north of Glen Affric. Later, he re-crossed Affric and finished off with the 5 remaining Munros of the Cluanie Horseshoe.

Paddy Buckley's Round was extended by Adrian Belton on 15 July 1989. He added the 5 remaining 3000ft peaks, Crib-goch and the northern Carneddau, to the original round. The record now stands at 52 peaks, 69 miles and 29,200ft ascent in exactly 22 hours.

X Company/Support

Pacers in the Highlands
I am grateful to the following runners who accompanied me over the Munros, (number of Munros in brackets).

Mike Anderson (1)
Pete Baxter (6)
Dave Bayliss (12)
Adrian Belton (6)
Inken Blunk (5)
Roger Boswell (42)
Eddie Campbell (2)
Phil Clark (39)
Tony Cresswell (41)
Mike Cudahy (6)
Chris Davies (10)
Eddie Dealtry (25)
Hélène Diamantides (6)
Colin Donnelly (1)
Robert Gardner (3)
Bill Gauld (5)
Phil Hughes (8)

Ian Leighton (10)
Martin Moran (9)
Dermot McGonigle (5)
Mike Parkin (18)
Sue Parkin (8)
Dave Peck (7)
Ruth Pickvance (6)
Dave Richardson (20)
Mark Rigby (33)
Davie Rogers (10)
Ian Rooke (7)
Les Stephenson (35)
Martin Stone (7)
Rex Stickland (5)
Frank Thomas (7)
Paul Tuson (48)
Mike Walford (33)
Paul Williams (3)

Pacers – Beyond the Munros
In addition to the above, the following accompanied me south of Glasgow.

Ann Bland	E (England)	Steve Jones	W
Dennis Bland	E	Trefor Jones	W
Bob Boyd	E	Steve Peruzza	E
Andrew Brown	E	Sue Richardson	E
Steve Buswell	E	Bill Ridings	E+W
Andy Clifford	E	Emlyn Roberts	W
Del Davies	W (Wales)	Chloë Thomas	E
Peadar Dempsey	I (Ireland)	Neil Walmsley	E
Vince Devlin	E	Helen Whitehead	E
Bob Douglas	E	Gary Williams	W
Alan Evans	E	Dave Woodhead	E
James Hawksley	E	Guy Woolnough	E

The following also provided invaluable assistance.

Phil Allder – decorating the van with stickers.

Andy Atkinson of Kendal Sports – loan of Phoenix Phreerunner tent and Salewa lightweight axe and crampons.

Martin Baggley – advice with software (mountain lists) and word processing.

Brian Butler and Graham Little – supply of OS maps.

Vivienne Calderbank and Robin Davey – design and creation of the 'Mountains of Britain – Mountains of Help' logo.

Andy and Barbara Clifford – printing of 'Mountains of Britain' sweatshirts, general fundraising and accommodation in Kendal.

David and Kshema Cooper – assistance around Glencoe.

Richard Crane – enthusiasm, experience and motivation.

Julie and Andy Green – accommodation in Birkenhead.

Michael Gregson of Sportswise – supply of Gregson Pack first aid system.

Ian Greig of Calor Scotland – provision of bottled gas for the van.

Keith Helsby (Manager of Yorkshire Bank, Kendal) and Dave Hodgson (Chairman of Fell Runners' Association) – arrangement of loan from Yorkshire Bank.

Stefan Lepkowski – Berghaus liaison.

Fearghas McKay – sailing to Mull.

Gerald Ramsden of Refuge Assurance – printing of sponsor forms.

George Scott of Motorola – loan and free use of portable telephone.

Sir Giles Shaw MP – for letters of support from the Ministers of Overseas Development and the Department of the Environment.

Dave Smith – use of rowing boat for crossing to Skye.

Martin Stone – help in finding a yacht and the assembly of appendix IX.

Dave Wells – on the hill support with tent, tea and cakes.

Peter Yorke – advice and contacts for land access in the Highlands.

XI Bibliography

Hamish's Mountain Walk – Hamish Brown.
Heading for the Scottish Hills – Scottish Mountaineering Trust.
The High Mountains of Britain and Ireland – Irvine Butterfield.
The Island of Skye – Scottish Mountaineering Club District Guide.
The Munros – Scottish Mountaineering Club (Donald Bennet).
The Munros in Winter – Martin Moran.
Munro's Tables – Scottish Mountaineering Club.
Scotland's Mountains – Scottish Mountaineering Club (W. H. Murray).
200 Challenging Walks in Britain and Ireland – Richard Gilbert.

Also, the diaries of Rick Ansell and Mark Elsegood proved very useful in the day to day planning of the route.

Index

Map numbers in brackets.
For location of maps, see map contents on page 11.

RUNNING HIGH

To Mark
   with best wishes.
Remember 277 isn't
that many!
In April 1990, I had
only previously done
a dozen or so.

                    Hugh

16.12.93

RUNNING HIGH

The First Continuous Traverse of the 303
Mountains of Britain and Ireland

HUGH SYMONDS

with comment and diary extracts from Pauline Symonds, Andrew,
Joseph and Amy

Foreword by Chris Bonington

Hugh Symonds

Lochar Publishing • Moffat • Scotland

© Hugh Symonds 1991
Published by Lochar Publishing Ltd
MOFFAT DG10 9ED

British Library Cataloguing in Publication Data

Symonds, Hugh
    Running high : the first continuous traverse of
    the 303 mountains of Great Britain and Ireland.
    I. Title
    914.104858

    ISBN 0–948403–91–8

Typeset in 8.5 on 11pt caxton by The Word Shop, Lancashire
Printed and bound in Great Britain by BPCC Wheatons Ltd, Exeter
Maps drawn by Richard Symonds